How to Map Arguments in Political Science

How to Map Arguments in Political Science

Craig Parsons

OXFORD

UNIVERSITY PRESS

OXFORD
UNIVERSITY PRESS

Great Clarendon Street, Oxford ox2 6DP

Oxford University Press is a department of the University of Oxford.
It furthers the University's objective of excellence in research, scholarship,
and education by publishing worldwide in

Oxford New York

Auckland Cape Town Dar es Salaam Hong Kong Karachi
Kuala Lumpur Madrid Melbourne Mexico City Nairobi
New Delhi Shanghai Taipei Toronto

With offices in

Argentina Austria Brazil Chile Czech Republic France Greece
Guatemala Hungary Italy Japan Poland Portugal Singapore
South Korea Switzerland Thailand Turkey Ukraine Vietnam

Oxford is a registered trade mark of Oxford University Press
in the UK and in certain other countries

Published in the United States
by Oxford University Press Inc., New York

British Library Cataloguing in Publication Data

Data available

Library of Congress Cataloging in Publication Data

Data available

Typeset by SPI Publisher Services, Pondicherry, India
Printed in Great Britain
on acid-free paper by
Biddles Ltd., King's Lynn, Norfolk

ISBN 978-0-19-928667-6
ISBN 978-0-19-928668-3 (Pbk)

1 3 5 7 9 10 8 6 4 2

To my students

Acknowledgements

My doctoral students at Syracuse University and the University of Oregon provided the direct inspiration for this project. Their input and encouragement led me to see that lecture notes from my field seminar in comparative politics might become a book—and that unlike most of the other books I am likely to write, this one might address some fairly widely-perceived needs in our discipline. Later the students in my seminar in qualitative methods helped me broaden and sharpen the framework. I'm extremely grateful to all of them for pushing me to think aloud about these issues.

As the book came together I benefited enormously from comments from many colleagues, including Chris Ansell, Mark Blyth, Jim Caporaso, Peter Hall, Marc Morjé Howard, Nicolas Jabko, Peter Katzenstein, Rogan Kersh, Ned Lebow, Jon Mercer, Ronald Mitchell, Brian Rathbun, Alexander Wendt, and Daniel Ziblatt. The most critical comments (in both senses of 'critical') came from the same person who was most important in improving my first book, *A Certain Idea of Europe*: Andrew Moravcsik. Much like with that earlier volume, Andy provided a wake-up call on this project that made it immeasurably stronger in the late revisions. He may still not find the results persuasive, but I must thank him once again for forcing me to be more careful, comprehensive, and clear.

I could not have finished the book as quickly or as well without generous leave from Syracuse, the research time afforded by the quarter system at Oregon, and the early faith of my OUP editor, Dominic Byatt. And I could do very little at all without the love and support of my wife Kari, and the joy that Tor and Margaux bring to my life.

Craig Parsons

Eugene, Oregon
January 2007

Contents

Part I. Introduction

Introduction   3

1. Boundaries and Divisions in Explanation of Action   21

Part II. Logics

2. Structural Explanation   49

3. Institutional Explanation   66

4. Ideational Explanation   94

5. Psychological Explanation   133

   Conclusion   163

References   174
Index   194

Part I

Introduction

Introduction

As long as the centuries continue to unfold, the number of books will grow continually, and one can predict that a time will come when it will be almost as difficult to learn anything from books as from the direct study of the whole universe.

Diderot, *The Encyclopedia*

This book proposes a typology of explanations of human action. It focuses on explanations of political action—relating to governance, power, and the distribution of resources—but its breakdown applies across the social sciences and history. That is not to say that it covers all scholarship in these disciplines. Some is not explanatory, and some is explanatory but does not directly attempt to explain action. Still, debates about explanations of action form the core of the human sciences. The book's goal is to offer a relatively simple and fundamental map of this core terrain.

The central terms of the typology are very common: structural, institutional, ideational, and psychological logics of explanation. Most breakdowns invoke some similar categories. The novelties lie in my arguments about how we can most usefully define our most common terms, and about the benefits that come from doing so in a certain way. I try to make these logics as distinct as possible, such that they designate the separable elemental bits or segments into which all explanations of action can be broken down. In making them analytically separable, however, I also try to make them abstractly compatible, such that we could imagine a world in which all were operating while we debate how much variants of each contributed to any given action. Four major benefits follow. First, the typology directs our attention to the most basic bits of logic about what causes what. In so doing it helps us set aside some odd historical distinctions and false debates. Second, it is exhaustive with respect to explanations of action. Bounding our options clarifies and focuses our efforts. Third, it defines our core terms in ways that facilitate rather than impede direct competition and combination. Fourth, it leads to revisions

3

of prevailing views on philosophy of science and research design that favor more open, substantive, and rigorous explanatory debates.

I hope the book appeals to two audiences. One is graduate students entering these disciplines (and especially political science). Aspiring academics often feel that they confront a shapeless and near-infinite mass of scholarship. Almost as limitless is the array of different schemes for distinguishing between approaches, theories, or schools of thought. Many breakdowns draw our attention to useful distinctions, but few step back to consider what would be the most helpful, most comprehensive first cut into the imaginable universe of explanatory claims. As a result, their clarifications of certain distinctions or explanatory alternatives often end up obscuring others of equal or greater importance. No typology escapes trade-offs, and later I discuss some of the costs of my scheme. Yet I argue that these costs are smaller, and outweighed more by novel clarifications, than in any other typology of similar scope.

The other target audience is established scholars. Just as a clear and relatively comprehensive typology may help our students find their feet, so it may help us engage more open, meaningful scholarly debates. Most of us survived graduate school by groping our way to some understanding—often idiosyncratic to our doctoral programs of origin—of major terms like 'structure' or 'institutionalism'. These idiosyncratic usages may suffice for thinking on our own, but they become a problem when we try to share our research. We spend a great deal of time and effort, sometimes fruitlessly, explaining to colleagues how we use these major terms and how they relate to the usages of other scholars. This book offers one reference point for our discussions. I have no illusion that it will end debate about any of these terms, but awareness of one clear and complete framework could help us all to communicate a little better.

As I hinted already, the book also has ambitions beyond categorization. It is not intended as an endorsement of any kind of explanation. I mean to clarify, not to proselytize. But the typology leads logically to criticisms of a wide range of scholarship that may be seen as provocative. I try to make these complaints flow from the typology, not my own interests or hunches. Rather than pointing to claims that I suspect are wrong, they underscore those that I find so unclear that they frustrate classification, or that use labels or terms in obscure or misleading ways. For example, we will encounter liberals and Marxists whose confusion over basic logics has muddled how they disagree for almost 200 years; 'rationalist' theorists who trumpet their explicitness but are less explicit than most others about what causes what; 'institutionalists' who do not assign distinct

4

importance to institutions; ideational theorists who both comment on and exempt themselves from explanatory debates; and so on. I hope that these criticisms will encourage scholars to think about their place in the field, and about how to use terms in ways that best contribute to serious debate rather than to the expedient rhetorical advantage of any one argument.

The most aggressive implication of the typology arises at the grandest level of the philosophy of science. One of its key distinctions is between 'general' logics of explanation and what I call 'particular explanations'. General logics can be formulated in law-like regularities, stipulating that any human acts in certain ways under certain conditions (deterministically, or at least probabilistically). Particular logics cannot be formulated in this way. They explain certain actions as the result of earlier contingent developments that we would not expect to turn out the same way even under identical conditions. Particular claims are built on things that did not have to happen the way they did according to some general law, even probabilistically—but because they did, other things followed (deterministically or probabilistically) and those other things can be explained as the consequences. They focus on the causal consequences of resolved contingencies. I argue that prevailing standards for theoretical contribution and 'progress' in the social sciences overemphasize generality, unscientifically rejecting the abstract possibility of particularistic dynamics. A world of human action that was not very general—perhaps where groups of people invented fairly unique institutional or ideational arenas—would not necessarily be one where chaos reigned, causal dynamics did not operate, and nothing could be explained in a fairly rigorous way. We must revise our standards for progress and research design to recognize this point.

The conclusion develops this final argument and offers new criteria for theoretical progress. I keep these observations short, since the main goal of the book is to organize substantive arguments rather than to argue for a certain philosophy of science or a certain tool kit of methods. But I would be missing an opportunity if I did not point out that mapping the universe of arguments has major implications for how we construct any single research design and evaluate theoretical progress. Thus I work my way from an attempt to organize our major terms and logics meaningfully in the simplest possible framework, to criticisms of a wide variety of literatures, to a call to reframe our overarching goals and research practices.

One initial word of warning is important, especially for students. There is tension between showcasing what is confusing in current debates and presenting a framework to clarify them. To do the former—specifying and justifying this project vis-à-vis existing literature—I must expose the reader to the bewildering terrain of contrasting schemes and overlapping terms that I am trying to help us escape. For those who are not already fairly adept at playing with multiple meanings of social science concepts, I recommend jumping over the next section to begin with the 'basic framework' and 'initial illustration' sections below, and then reading the four chapters on the logics before returning to Chapter 1. The chapters are written to stand alone as much as possible, such that students can confront the major concepts piece by piece and then return to grapple with the overarching issues of typologizing. For readers who are already up to their necks in terms and typologies, on the other hand, I must start with why that it is a problem.

The Problem

This project begins from a practical problem. To venture into explanation of action we need some broad sense of our explanatory options, but the basic field of alternatives is very difficult to construct. Scholars disagree about which arguments qualify as explanations. Within these contested boundaries they often offer typologies that only capture some of the options. They often classify the options on the basis of unsystematic divisions with criteria of secondary importance. To top it all, they provide many such breakdowns that use the same major terms for different claims, or different labels for logically similar claims. In this section I mention the key typological issues and some examples of our confusion, without elaborating or clarifying them. Readers beware: the accumulated sense of confusion by the end of the section is unavoidable. It defines the book's tasks.

Contestation on the boundaries of explanation rarely dictates how to map our options within that space, but is obviously important for what our map should cover. At this level the problem in discerning explanatory options is not contestation itself. Disagreement on deep theoretical issues is legitimate and probably irresolvable, and a typologizer can handle it simply by staking out his or her own clear (if contestable) positions. Instead, this part of our problem is just that scholars have tended not to combine boundary-staking efforts with internal maps of explanation. The separation is not surprising: debates on the boundaries of explanation raise a large number of confusing issues that emerged from many distinct historical debates. But it has meant that typologizing efforts tend to deal only erratically or implicitly with the edges of their maps, often trailing off into vague warnings of the 'here be dragons' variety.

The broadest boundary debate is a long-running battle between 'Humean' and non-Humean definitions of explanation and causation. Humeans argue that we never actually see causation at work. We only reach causal inferences (or 'explanations') by establishing cross-case patterns of correlations between conditions or events (Hume [1748] 1975; King, Keohane, and Verba 1994). Other scholars criticize the Humean focus on correlations and define causation and explanation around the tracing of 'within-case' mechanisms by which some conditions produce an event (Harre and Madden 1975; Scriven 1975; Elster 1983; Little 1991; Hedstrom and Swedberg 1998). A semirelated border skirmish concerns 'methodological individualism', or how much valid explanations of human action (whether built around correlations or mechanisms) must pass through or reduce to individuals (Watkins 1957; Lukes 1968; Little 1991: 183–90). Other conflicts arise around the relevance for human action of 'functionalist' explanations on the model of evolutionary biology (Elster 1983; Kincaid 1996). Still others concern variants of Max Weber's famous assertion that the role of meaning and culture in human action calls for methods of 'understanding' (*Verstehen*) or 'constitutive' argument that are distinct from explanation (Weber [1922] 1958; Taylor 1985; Hollis and Smith 1990; Searle 1995; Wendt 1998, 1999).

Although a few scholars of explanatory logic engage many of these debates, to date they have not connected them to efforts to organize the space within the boundaries they propose. Jon Elster, for example, argues that valid explanations of action offer causal mechanisms that at least pass through the intentions of individuals. He suggests that this 'intentional' logic of explanation is different from the more automatic, physical 'causal' logic of the physical sciences and 'functional' explanation in biology (Elster 1983, 1998). But providing a map of variants within valid explanations of action is not Elster's goal. Daniel Little seems closer to this aspiration in providing a rather bewildering list of 'varieties of social explanation': causal, statistical, functional, structural, materialist, rational-choice, and interpretive. He ultimately focuses his attention on boundaries, however, effectively arguing that the valid versions of these common labels reduce to a few ways of fleshing out his 'causal' category (Little 1991).

Conversely, the far greater number of scholars who try to organize some of the internal space of arguments in political science tend to jump past these boundary debates. They start from a map with tattered edges. Most such efforts also fail to offer a satisfying first cut into the options. Their distinctions are almost never useless or wrong, but they tend to be hard to justify as a typological point of departure. Common typologies organize arguments by the phenomena they try to explain, the methods they employ, or the 'level of analysis' they privilege. In charting the subfield of comparative politics for the decadal *State of the Discipline* volume in 2002, for example, David Laitin divides scholarship first by phenomena (democracy, order, forms of capitalism) and then by methods (statistics, narratives, formal theory) (Laitin 2002). These are clearly things we must know to fully map a field—what questions are asked and what methods are used to support answers?—but it leaves out the actual answers to the questions. It also obscures that different methods could lead to the same answer. The same information is missing from the 'level of analysis' breakdown that long prevailed in the subfield of international relations (IR). Realism, the school of thought around which IR was built, saw states as similar actors responding to their position in a 'system level' landscape of geopolitical competition. Against realists arose 'idealist' or 'liberal' arguments that saw states as different over time or space, and argued that these 'unit level' characteristics influenced states' choices. It became standard to divide IR theories first into systemic, unit, and individual-level categories (Singer 1961; Waltz 1964). Over time, however, new arguments like neo-Marxism challenged realism at the systemic level (Wallerstein 1974). Other arguments appeared that saw similar institutional or ideational dynamics operating across the levels (Krasner 1983; Wendt 1987). The levels distinction still pointed to some cleavages, but it was increasingly clear that it did not delineate the primary lines in a complex debate. Like breakdowns by phenomena or methods, levels of analysis simply do not get at the substance of arguments.

Some typologies speak more directly to substantive options, offering a menu of answers or approaches. Often such breakdowns are created to highlight the novelty of one position, though, and serve less well to organize options more broadly. Especially in prominent books, they risk being taken up and used as organizing frameworks even given an author's repeated caveats. One important example is Alex Wendt's *Social Theory of International Politics*. He organizes the system-level IR literature in a matrix of 'holist' versus 'individualist' approaches (relating to positions on methodological individualism, and characterized as ranking high or low on 'the difference that structures make') and 'idealist' versus 'materialist' approaches (high or low on 'the difference that ideas make'). Wendt stresses that the scheme is meant to underscore the distinctiveness of his holist, idealist, system-level approach. But if taken as a map, even of part of the IR field, it contains many ambiguities. Since he argues that much 'holist' work poses 'constitutive' questions that fall outside causal-explanatory scholarship, it is not clear how much the boxes address the same task. Moreover, the two most prominent approaches to IR, neorealism and neoliberalism, appear on the matrix with moving positions and question marks (Wendt 1999: 22–33). The ambiguity of this broader map is mainly our problem, not Wendt's—he did not set out to organize all our explanatory options—but part of our problem is the existence of many such breakdowns.

Unfortunately, the recent typologies that aspire most directly to organize substantive options suffer from odd historical legacies and overlapping categories. Probably the best-known breakdown in comparative politics—and the most systematic attempt at a simple chart of any part of political science in recent years—is a 1997 volume edited by Mark Irving Lichbach and Alan Zuckerman and subtitled *Rationality, Culture, and Structure* (Lichbach and Zuckerman 1997). There is much to be learned from this book, but its major categories are awkward. Structure, however we define it, is something that might explain action: people do something because they inhabit a certain position in structures. People in other positions would do something different. Culture, though it has a troubled relationship to explanation, is also easy to imagine as a cause on a common-sense level: people do something because they hold certain beliefs. People with other beliefs would do something different. Rationality, on the other hand, is not seen by anyone as a cause of anything. It is a process of decision-making that is typically assumed in order to hold constant things that scholars suspect do not matter (culture or psychology). Only once we place rational actors in a context can we see any causes of their actions. If that context includes anything we might call 'structure', then a rationalist category of explanation overlaps with a structural one (as Lichbach and Zuckerman's usage clearly does). This book helps us learn about some historical debates, since it is historical lineages that explain the odd format. But its conceptual lines are crossed.

Another common scheme is to sort arguments by 'interests, institutions, or ideas'. This vocabulary gets at roughly the same divisions that I call structural, institutional, and ideational logic, but the word 'interests' perpetuates some misunderstandings. One just reflects multiple uses of the word. Formally rationalist scholars frequently use 'interests' to mean preferences (Morrow 1994). Interests are the basic goals people seek in building strategies of action. In broader theoretical debates or common-language use, however, 'interests' usually means strategies of action themselves. Interests are the set of choices that will best realize someone's preferences in their current environment, as in phrases like, 'National interests point to war' (e.g. Morgenthau 1954: 5–9). Even if we resolve this confusion by endorsing one definition, any notion of 'interests' as a distinct category of explanatory logic is problematic. Its main drawback is the implication that other categories—institutions and ideas in this common typology—are somehow not about people acting in instrumental pursuit of something they think benefits them. But the main debates between all the claims in this book are about how people define what they think is good for them in some sense (with minor exceptions for the most unconscious ideational or instinctual psychological claims). Some material conditions might encourage what looks like altruistic, other-regarding behavior. Some institutions or ideas might produce what looks like maniacally egoistic instrumental behavior. Thus an 'interests' category both carries a connotation that is simply wrong and leaves ambiguous what is distinctive about its contents. Moreover, one prominent strand of social science explanation—psychology—seems to have no place in this three-way scheme. The alliteration of interests, institutions, and ideas is tempting, but not all poetry brings clarity.

Charles Tilly and Robert Goodin offer another typology to introduce a recent 888-page collection on 'contextual political analysis' (Goodin and Tilly 2006). Their thinking is very rich, but a 'very open-ended spirit' inspires them to broaden and elaborate our theoretical map rather than imposing order on it (Tilly and Goodin 2006: 28). They sketch four ontologies (holism, methodological individualism, phenomenological individualism, and relational realism), four explanatory strategies (law-seeking, propensity accounts, systemic explanations, and mechanism-based accounts), and three mechanisms (environmental, cognitive, and relational). These categories may make sense, but it is hard to know because Tilly and Goodin only touch briefly on distinctions and relationships between them. Some seem to overlap; 'law-seeking strategies' turn out, for example, to 'require mechanisms' (Tilly and Goodin 2006: 14). In just one paragraph they 'begin to detect affinities between ontologies, explanatory strategies, and preferred mechanisms':

Methodological individualists, for example, commonly adopt propensity accounts of social behavior and privilege cognitive mechanisms as they do so. Holists lean toward environmental mechanisms, as relational realists give special attention to relational mechanisms. Those affinities are far from absolute, however. Many a phenomenological individualist, for example, weaves accounts in which environmental mechanisms such as social disintegration generate cognitive mechanisms having relational consequences in their turn. In principle, many permutations of ontology, explanatory strategy, and preferred mechanisms should be feasible.

(Tilly and Goodin 2006: 16)

Rather than developing this bewildering set of relationships, the subsequent chapters add another complication. They are grouped by various things that 'matter': philosophy, psychology, ideas, culture, history, place, population, and technology. Some of these seem to be causal categories to which we might apply the ontologies, explanatory strategies, and mechanisms. Taken individually, the chapters offer many sophisticated insights. As a typological effort, though, the collection is mainly suggestive of the work a useful map needs to do. Tilly and Goodin sketch an intriguing set of categories, but do not spell out underlying boundaries and divisions to give them a comprehensible order.[1]

I could continue with similar criticisms, since almost all scholarship begins by locating itself in some sort of typology.[2] But this brief review of salient examples illustrates the problem and defines my task. I mean to delineate a fairly simple set of distinct basic explanatory claims about action. I will situate these distinct claims within positions on the boundaries of explanations of action, and also argue that they are built on systematic distinctions that highlight our most fundamental debates. The next sections sketch the basic framework I propose and illustrate it briefly with examples. In Chapter 1 I develop my positions on its boundaries, divisions, and costs and benefits. The other chapters showcase why, given multiple legitimate uses of all our major terms, this breakdown is especially clear and useful.

The Basic Framework

Explanatory debates are about what causes what. Debates over causal inference receive more attention in Chapter 1, but that basic point suffices

[1] Tilly and Goodin also seem uncertain that their categories are all logically coherent or theoretically legitimate. They include light criticisms of everything except the relational-realism/mechanism-based/relational mechanism approach that dominates Tilly's work (2006: 10–17).

[2] For other partial and historically based typologies, see Shepsle and Boncheck (1997), which is arbitrarily limited to rationalist scholarship and Hay (2002), which is insightful but largely accepts historically constructed categories that blend debates about causes, methods, and philosophy of science.

to direct our attention to what we would most want to know in a first cut of explanatory options about action. We would want to organize arguments by classes of substantive causes, or the logics in which certain kinds of causes are invoked: what they say makes people do certain things and not others. There are many other things we would want to know about an argument to fully understand it—the phenomena it addresses, the methods it employs, its level of analysis—but they are less important as a first cut than grasping its basic view of what causes what. Such a basic substantive grasp often allows us to extrapolate how an argument would explain a wide range of phenomena or how it might look at various levels of analysis. Understanding the methods that demonstrate a claim is hugely important, but is obviously subordinate to knowing the substance of the claim.

My four logics of explanation, then, are named for the element that does their causal work: structural, institutional, ideational, and psychological. As I define them, structural claims explain what people do as a function of their position *vis-à-vis* exogenously given 'material' structures like geography, a distribution of wealth, or a distribution of physical power.[3] People's actions vary as their position in a given material landscape varies. Institutional claims explain what people do as a function of their position within man-made organizations and rules (and within the 'path-dependent' process implied by man-made constraints: people's choices at time t alter their own constraints at time $t + 1$). Ideational claims explain what people do as a function of the cognitive and/or affective elements that organize their thinking, and see these elements as created by certain historical groups of people. Psychological claims explain what people do as a function of the cognitive, affective, or instinctual elements that organize their thinking, but see these elements as general across humankind, as hard-wired features of 'how humans think' (though there may be multiple psychological dispositions—type A people, type B people, etc.—so not all people are necessarily the same).

In much of the book I argue inductively that these logics capture the range and most fundamental debates of a very wide range of explanatory literatures. But first I argue deductively in Chapter 1 that they follow from a matrix created by two distinctions. The first logical distinction is that

---

[3] The quotes around 'material' stress that such claims may only *treat* constraints as exogenously given and material. For example, Marxists might allow that modes of production may be man-made institutions, but their logic tends to treat them as if they were natural and given like physical geography. See Chapter 2.

structural and institutional claims are logics of *position*, and ideational and psychological claims are logics of *interpretation*.

A logic-of-position claim explains by detailing the landscape around someone to show how an obstacle course of material or man-made constraints and incentives channels her to certain actions. Such claims require micro-foundations in objective rationality. Only if people are reacting regularly and reasonably to external constraints does it make sense to see external constraints as explaining their actions. Conversely, all arguments that assume objective rationality depend on structural or institutional conditions to define certain actions as rational. Thus all 'rationalist' scholarship can be subsumed into my structural or institutional categories.

A logic-of-interpretation claim explains by showing that someone arrives at an action only through one interpretation of what is possible and/or desirable. Ideational claims do so by asserting that particular people have historically situated ways of interpreting things around them. They need not be based in irrationality—perhaps interpretations matter because structures and institutions are objectively ambiguous, allowing people to create 'multiple rationalities' (Lukes and Hollis 1982)—though they can be. Psychological claims assert that people perceive the world around them through hard-wired instincts, affective commitments, and/or cognitive shortcuts. With the exception of rare variants that are just about hard-wired preferences of rational actors, they always imply irrationality.

The other axis is the general–particular divide signaled above. This is a more novel distinction, requiring elaboration in Chapter 1 and throughout the book. The basic idea behind it, though, is that structural and psychological causes are exogenously given (or, we will see, at least *treated* as exogenous over the temporal scope of an explanation) whereas institutional and ideational causes are man-made. To the extent that we trace actions to structural or psychological causes, we argue that people's choices followed from given conditions in the environment or in their brains. To the extent we trace actions to institutional or ideational causes, we argue that people's choices were contingent until they built their own causal dynamics around them.

For man-made institutions or ideas to generate distinct explanatory logics, irreducible to other kinds of causes, we must argue that at some point the selection of certain institutions or ideational elements was contingent—literally inexplicable. Only to the extent that people could just as well have made other institutions or ideas does it make sense to say that it was the presence of *these* institutions or ideas that later made the difference. To the extent the selection of certain institutions or ideas was not contingent at some point—if we have no reason to think that earlier actions could have created other institutions or ideas—they become derivations of preexisting causes rather than introducing their own distinct causal dynamics. Thus institutional and ideational explanatory claims are inherently particularistic, building explanations on the consequences of resolved contingencies.

The same is not true of structural or psychological claims. Like all causal claims they imply similar counterfactuals; the claim that people did something due to material conditions or psychological dispositions implies that different structures or psychology would have led to other actions. But since such claims do not treat structures or psychology as man-made results of earlier action, they need not imply it was ever possible (let alone equally likely) to have other structures or psychology.[4] To argue that people built a patriarchal, fishing-based society due to incentives and constraints in their material surroundings does not imply that the location of bodies of water or the challenges of small-fish capture were contingent. To argue that people went to war under certain conditions because humans are hard-wired to exaggerate threatening intentions of 'out-groups' does not imply that they could have seen things differently. These kinds of claims follow from exogenously-given regularities.

Let me repeat the central observation of this dichotomy, since it is both very abstract and fairly novel (but see Mahoney 2000). To the extent that our arguments build in structural or psychological claims, we portray people's actions as the consequences of some given configuration of an external landscape or their internal makeup. These claims may be probabilistic, not necessarily deterministic, but they are about general regularities that follow from given conditions. To the extent that our explanations build in claims about man-made institutions, ideas, or culture as causes, we are making a particularistic argument that the course of history was open until people embedded themselves in distinct new causal dynamics through their own actions.

Again, these distinctions require more elaboration and some caveats (as suggested most obviously by the dotted vertical line in Figure 1). But before getting to a more elaborate presentation in Chapter 1, two points

---

[4] In other words, the counterfactuals they imply tend to be 'miracle' counterfactuals. It would take a miracle for the causes to have been arranged differently (Fearon 1991; Tetlock and Belkin 1996; Lebow 1997).

	General	Particular

Figure 1 Fundamental matrix of explanations of action

complete a basic summary of the framework. First, the notion that these are 'distinct logics' does not mean that most scholarship falls cleanly into these categories. Instead these are the basic logical segments out of which explanatory arguments can be built. They are different kinds of vectors by which we can picture people being sent in one direction or another—but usually only in combination with other conditions and vectors. The most parsimonious theorists may construct approaches entirely from one category, like Marx's structural theorizing, but even Marx drew on other bits of logic when he turned from abstract theory to explaining historical actions (Marx [1852] 1978). Similarly, while many recent arguments can be identified mainly with one of these categories, this is usually not because they assert strongly that one kind of cause accounts for everything. Rather they tend to pull out what they claim to be segments of separable, demonstrable causal relationships from a multicausal environment. In that spirit of 'problem-driven research' and 'middle-range theory' (to use popular phrases from Peter Katzenstein and Robert Merton, respectively), I am trying to propose basic categories of the 'theoretically understandable bits' that Arthur Stinchcombe promotes as the foundations of good social theory (Katzenstein in Kohli et al. 1995; Merton 1957; Stinchcombe 1978: 14). I do not advocate that we affiliate parsimoniously with one category (though some may choose to do so). Even—or rather especially—those who want to combine logics into complex arguments must break down their claims into comprehensible segments before building them back together.

15

Second, not all explanatory contributions depend on rock-bottom clarity. Often we lack the evidence to arbitrate between logics. We can still make important claims while remaining agnostic over some range of mechanisms and outcomes. In Robert Putnam's well-known work on 'civicness' in Italy, for example, it is not clear whether people exhibit 'civic' behavior for ideational reasons or as rational responses to an unambiguous institutional landscape (Putnam 1993). Arbitrating empirically between such mechanisms is difficult, and both might be operating. Putnam's claims about the effects of social capital can be important even without precise foundations. Relatedly, ambitious scholarship often points to fairly abstract causal dynamics across great scope. Such work tends to gloss over specific causal claims, but arguing at such a level may help us grasp major dynamics. Overly strict insistence that we always start from distinct building blocks could prevent insightful leaps to overarching accounts. An elegant example is Albert Hirschman's claim about the spread of capitalism in *The Passions and the Interests*. He suggests that capitalism took hold in Europe not just as the unintended consequence of Protestant asceticism (Weber's famous thesis), but because some of the aristocratic classes came to believe that capitalism could help strengthen social order (though their expectations turned out to be mostly wrong) (Hirschman 1977: 132). This argument seems to have roots in a mix of what I call structural, institutional, and ideational claims. In the long run, it is fair to ask that such work be able to disaggregate into causal segments. If we wanted to test Hirschman's thesis against evidence and alternative claims, we would need to break it down. Still, there is more than one route to valuable explanations. Every argument needs foundations, but we need not proceed to them only through a precise, bottom-up focus on every little building block.

Some Initial Illustrations

As a last preliminary step, it is helpful to introduce examples of the categories.

For an illustration of what I call structural causal segments, consider Barrington Moore, Jr.'s classic of comparative politics, *Social Origins of Dictatorship and Democracy* (1966). Moore traced the success of democracy or dictatorship in the early twentieth century to differences in the social classes who benefited from the commercialization of agriculture. These differences in turn mainly reflected geography, market opportunities, and other concrete features of each country's landscape. In Britain, for example, topography and the distribution of land favored a shift of some landowners to commercial farming around the sixteenth century. Wool production was especially enticing. It encouraged the 'enclosures' movement, in which landowners fenced in land that had been feudal 'commons'. Commercially-based elites emerged with resources that were largely independent from the Crown. Together with the growth of cities and trade—to which British geography greatly contributed—this gradually shifted power away from an order built on aristocratic privilege and the state. The results were first a Parliamentary victory in the seventeenth-century civil war (a 'bourgeois revolution' for Moore) and eventually dominance of a bourgeoisie with clear interests in free-ranging capitalism and liberal rights. Germany offers one of Moore's contrasting cases. In the Prussian heart of the later German Reich, the landscape featured large estates with labor-intensive grain crops. Landowners responded to growing production and markets not by erecting enclosures but by repressing peasants even more tightly to extract more profit. Expanding trade thus reinforced traditional-elite dominance, allowing them to keep the upper hand even through industrialization. The German bourgeoisie that later emerged was too weak to challenge the landed class. Instead it joined them as 'junior partner' in a conservative coalition. The early twentieth-century regime outcome was a modernizing dictatorship with traditional authority rules. Moore's core claims, then, traced actions to positioning in an obstacle course of resources and competitors. People responded to their position in rational ways, pursuing basic goals of wealth and power. In some ways he allowed that the landscape varied with man-made institutions, like in conventions of feudal rights (1966: 415). But it was mostly an exogenously given—if dynamically evolving—set of material constraints and opportunities.

Next consider an example of institutionalist causal segments from a classic in American politics, Stephen Skowronek's *Building a New American State* (1982). He explained the ill-coordinated, contested condition of late twentieth-century US federal government by tracing it to the institutional inheritance of preindustrial America. The US Constitution created a union with highly decentralized institutions, linked nationally only by courts and political parties. The latter were also highly decentralized, rooted in local political machines. As industrialization accelerated after the Civil War, however, the US confronted a variety of pressures for greater central administrative capacity. Businessmen pushed to broaden state markets into national ones, citizens demanded that regulatory powers keep the same scope as market actors, class conflict extended to a national level, and the country overall faced pressures for a national military. Yet Americans found their responses constrained by earlier institutional choices. Political parties now had vested interests in the local spoils of a decentralized system, and the political elite fought to block the rise of central administration. Although it was structural pressures of industrialization that eventually produced a national administrative state, Skowronek focused on how the unintended consequences of earlier institution-building explained the weak and messy state that resulted. Like Moore, he explained people's choices as a rational function of their position in an obstacle course which they all perceived similarly.[5] But he was most interested in causal segments in which the unintended consequences of man-made organizations and rules altered the shape of the obstacle course, and with it, people's later choices.

For forceful ideational causal segments, we can look to sociologist Frank Dobbin's major work (1994) in political economy, *Forging Industrial Policy*. Against Skowronek, Dobbin argued that as people in France, Britain, and the US confronted industrialization, they perceived and solved its challenges differently due to differing national ideas about legitimate governance. Each country established a distinct political culture prior to industrialization. In France, people came to endorse very centralized political authority. As they dealt with regulatory issues in the emerging industrial age, like safety or financing of railways, they saw inadequate coordination among private actors as the key issue for the state to address. From an early phase of industrialization the state intervened heavily to organize and regulate industrial undertakings. In Britain and the US, political principles privileged the protection of individual rights against concentrated power. They saw potential concentration of industry as the main issue requiring state action. Finer-grained differences in their ideas, however, led to contrasting solutions. Americans focused on federal adjudication of a free market and dealt with concentration through trust-busting. The nineteenth-century British, by contrast, focused on protecting the small businessman and actually encouraged cartelization and other insulation from market competition. Dobbin's point was not that any of these people were irrational, nor did he assert that the material or institutional obstacle course around them was infinitely open to interpretation. But he did try to cut back dramatically the extent to which these

---

[5] See Chapter 3 for more discussion of the role of rationality and objective perception in Skowronek.

nineteenth-century actions could be explained as direct rational responses to clear distributions of resources à la Moore, or to clear institutional obstacle courses à la Skowronek. The causal segments that interested him concerned how adoption of certain ideational elements—culture, norms, ideas, practices—later led people to interpret their environment and 'interests' in certain ways.

Psychological causal segments tend to be rarer and more tentative in political science, for reasons I discuss in Chapter 5. One clear example in IR, though, is Rose McDermott's *Risk-Taking in International Politics* (1998). She aimed to show the explanatory force of 'prospect theory,' which suggests that humans are inherently—and irrationally—inclined to be risk-averse when focused on gains and risk-seeking when focused on losses. When asked in experiments if they prefer a certain gain of $1,000 or a 50-percent chance at $2,500, most people choose the former; when forced to choose a certain loss of $1,000 or a 50-percent chance of a loss of $2,500, most choose the latter. A classically rational thinker would do the reverse. McDermott used this psychological decision rule to help explain President Jimmy Carter's failed rescue attempt in the Iranian hostage crisis of 1979. This is not to say that hard-wired mental processes were her whole story. She argued that it was fairly objective external conditions—falling domestic popularity and a seemingly insoluble international crisis—that led Carter to see himself as 'operating in a domain of losses' and so to be inclined toward high-risk options (McDermott 1998: 47). She allowed that even within this domain of losses, Carter and his advisers held different views on which risky strategy to choose. But the distinctive causal segment that interested her most concerned how regular, hard-wired, nonrational processes of human decision-making oriented Carter toward very risky choices.

This book is not concerned with how much any of these claims are theoretically or empirically convincing. Its framework helps us organize how we *could* explain action, not what we should argue theoretically or what is right empirically. Most of the book is set up to show that these examples represent logically distinct kinds of causal segments whose deepest differences are reflected in my matrix.

Moore's and Skowronek's claims display logics of position. They explain actions as a rational function of where people stand in an obstacle course that is presented as intersubjectively real and unambiguous. But they feature different logics of position, conceiving of the obstacle courses differently. Moore's claims focus on material aspects of the landscape (or, as we shall see in Chapter 2, at least things he and similar scholars *treat* as physical 'material' resources) that are not subject to major manipulation by their human inhabitants. Skowronek's claims focus on man-made organizational parts of the landscape, leading him to emphasize how institution-building choices at one point alter subsequent constraints on action.

Both Skowronek and Dobbin focus on how peoples' actions at one point create a man-made context that later channels them in certain directions. Yet the 'channeling' in Dobbin's core causal segments operates not because actors build a clear organizational obstacle course around themselves, but because they take on certain interpretations of themselves and their environment.

Dobbin and McDermott focus on how the external environment is only connected to certain actions through a certain interpretation of it. But the interpretive connections in McDermott's core causal segments are made not by the historically-situated ideational inventions of particular people, but by a psychological decision-rule that is presented as a hard-wired feature of human cognition.

McDermott and Moore, finally, both build their core causal segments around general conditions that are not derived from or affected by people's actions. But where McDermott is interested in the political consequences of regularities in human thinking, Moore is interested in the political consequences of patterns in material resources.

Hopefully these examples alone make a plausible case for the distinctiveness of these kinds of causal segments and for at least some utility of my matrix in organizing some of our debates. The larger task of the book is to suggest why and in what sense they offer a fundamental and exhaustive map of our explanatory options. Chapter 1 provides the abstract thinking behind that larger set of claims. Again, readers who are new to doctoral-level theoretical debates might want to skip to Chapters 2–5 before confronting the grandest cartographical issues. They should be easier to grasp once these examples are elaborated into broad territories and lines in the sand.

1

Boundaries and Divisions in Explanation of Action

To draw a plausible map of explanations of action—let alone the most useful map—we must explore two complex discussions. The first concerns the map's boundaries. As I sketched in the introduction, not everyone agrees on what counts as an explanation. Nor do all claims in the human sciences that might count as explanatory clearly focus on explaining action. The first major section of this chapter travels through a series of debates on these points, staking out the limits of my map. The debates arise on different edges of the explanatory territory, so some appear as fairly separate issues. I visit the importance of causal mechanisms, the principle of 'methodological individualism', the place of evolutionary theory in the human sciences, the notions of 'understanding' and 'constitutiveness' in ideational scholarship, and lastly revisit the concepts of contingency and particular explanation. Some of these border disputes are indeed unrelated to others, but a tour around them fully traces the boundaries of the typology.

The other discussion concerns divisions within the boundaries. Positions on the edges of the map do not dictate the most useful divisions within it. In fact, we can draw a near-infinite number of plausible lines between explanatory claims. However, many clear and logically correct distinctions are not very useful as a first cut. To take an absurd example, we might divide scholarship by decade of publication. This could be very clear—there would rarely be doubt about how to classify a piece of work—but the typology would tell us nothing about the substance of the debates. The second major section of this chapter suggests why the distinctions in my matrix convey an especially fundamental and comprehensive sense of the debates scholars have engaged. Part of this rationale is deductive, based on logical distinctions in the nature of causes. Part is inductive, based on a search for distinct claims across far-flung literatures. Some of the steps in the deductive claims only come in later chapters, and most of the inductive claims are supported there. But here I summarize my central claim: some logical deductive moves and plausible inductive readings of a great deal of scholarship converge on this matrix as the most useful basic map of our explanatory options.

Boundaries

Explanation and Mechanisms

A boundary-staking effort must begin from a position on the most basic definitional debates on explanation and causality (Keat and Urry 1983; McMullin 1984; Salmon 1998). On the one hand, the Enlightenment philosopher David Hume argues that we cannot observe something causing something else. All we can see are regular conjunctions between conditions or events (Hume [1748] 1975). Many scholars thus suggest that causal-explanatory inferences only follow from general 'cross-case' demonstrations of a correlation that one condition or event always precedes the appearance of another (or at least of a probabilistic version of this relationship) (Hempel 1942; Rubin 1974; Beauchamp and Rosenberg 1981; Holland 1986; King, Keohane, and Verba 1994). On the other hand, critics of the 'neo-Humean' tradition stress that correlation is not causation. Many regular conjunctions reflect third causes rather than causal-explanatory relationships. Barometric pressure drops before a storm, but we do not conclude that movement in our barometer explains the storm. Our acceptance of a relationship as explanatory thus depends on some 'within-case' support of a causal mechanism: a process by which cause brings about effect (Brady and Collier 2004). These scholars argue, contra Hume, that many relationships can be broken down into at least partly-observable processes to see mechanisms at work (Harre and Madden 1975; Scriven 1975; Cartwright 1983; Elster 1983; Little 1991; Hedstrom and Swedberg 1998). General-law advocates retort that only generalizations across comparable cases give us confidence that a causal mechanism necessarily (or probabilistically) produces certain effects (for an extreme view, Beck 2006).

In the face of centuries of entrenched debate, I follow recent work to the middle ground. Since respectable philosophers of causality cannot agree on a single standard model of explanation, we should see the strongest explanations as those that meet more than one of their criteria (Brady and Seawright 2004). In other words, clear explanatory claims rest on both within-case causal mechanisms and cross-case general patterns. That said, I side with Elster and Little in seeing mechanisms as more fundamental. Even strong correlations are not explanations. They may rule out certain relationships, but never offer direct support that something is going on. Causal mechanisms, by contrast, offer explanations, though they depend to some degree on correlations for confidence in their claims. Even where we lack general correlations—given seemingly unique cases, or cross-case patterns so complex that they are impossible to sort out clearly—we can often discard some claims and gain substantial confidence in others by looking at within-case process-tracing evidence (Elster 1998; Collier, Brady and Seawright 2004). In other words, to explain we must always posit and seek evidence for causal mechanisms. We must also show as much as possible that the relationships we present as necessary (or probabilistic) in one case have the same consequences in comparable cases, though the availability of such cases will vary.

A first cut at the boundaries of my typology, then, is to set aside scholarship that does not offer causal mechanisms that link to action. This includes a huge amount of descriptive, typological, methodological, or normative work that is valuable but does not aspire to such mechanisms. It also includes models that may be useful for predictive purposes but do not claim to capture what is really going on causally (Friedman 1953). More critically, this cut leads into a position on the semirelated debates on 'methodological individualism', which concern how much valid explanations must pass through or reduce to individuals.

Methodological Individualism

The most aggressive methodological individualists argue that all observable behavior is ultimately individual behavior, and thus that demonstrable explanations rest entirely on attributes of individuals (Popper 1945; Watkins 1957; also Lukes 1968; Little 1991: 183–90). The most common objection to this view is that the behavior of physical individuals can reflect conditions and dynamics that do not reduce to an individual level. States, markets, social movements, laws, and other typical components of political argument are supra-individual phenomena that can be difficult or impossible to describe as individual properties. Even interactions that seem very raw and material arguably depend on shared understandings

23

and collective intentions. People cannot have a war if one side refuses to fight. The use of money depends on mutual acceptance of the value of certain kinds of specie (Searle 1995; Ruggie 1998; Wendt 1999; for related arguments from an orthodox economist, Arrow 1994). The strongest anti-methodological-individualists go further, arguing either that people simply do not relate to action as individuals—our minds and thinking are literally the product of processes that extend outside our skulls—or that certain macrosocial processes shape overall 'systems' of action at a remove from the traceable actions of any particular individuals (Cohen 1978; Pettit 1993; Kincaid 1996; Wendt 2004).

In opting for a view of explanation centered on causal mechanisms (to be supported, wherever possible, by patterns of correlations) I come to the middle ground of this debate as well. On the one hand, at a common-sense level I think we must accept what Little calls 'trivial' individualism—that only individuals act in a literal sense (Little 1991: 183). If action operates through individuals, then the causal mechanisms we provide to build an explanation of action must ultimately pass through specific physical individuals. On the other hand, there are many abstractly plausible ways to detail causal mechanisms that pass through individuals but involve components that do not reduce to them. We can debate just how much claims about supra-individual dynamics in states, markets, or baseball games can be linked demonstrably to particular actions, but it is not reasonable to exclude such arguments as invalid at the outset.[1] The only claims we can exclude are the most 'holistic' ones that pointedly refuse connections to individual action. As the ideationally-inclined theorist Colin Wight—no strict methodological individualist—observes about states in IR:

In the final analysis, state activity is always the activity of particular individuals acting within particular social contexts. There is an ontological wall here that corporate forms do not cross (or cross only on the backs of individuals). None of this is to deny the reality of a common intention, or collective action, which individuals try to realize in their practices. Nor is this to deny the reality of social structures that enable and constrain common action. Nor does . . . [it] entail that there can be no common and coordinated action that is a bearer of causal powers greater than that possessed by individuals acting individually (Wight 2004: 279).

---

[1] See Little's example of the impossibility of analyzing a baseball game in purely individual terms (1991: 185). For the most sophisticated discussions of supra-individual dynamics that pass through individuals, see literature on collective intentionality and 'supervenience': (Gilbert 1989; Searle 1990; Sawyer 2001; Tollefson 2002). For a defense of nonindividualist Marxism that is mostly (but not entirely) consistent with this literature and my position, see Miller (1978).

As long as arguments make claims about individuals doing something (or could flesh out such claims[2]) without which they assert that we would not know why the individuals did what they did, they enter the book's typology of explanations of action. Supra-individual claims that leap over or reject this kind of connection—like Marxist functionalism driven by the overarching 'needs' of the capitalist system, or some variants of 'structural functionalist' claims about the 'needs' of societies to maintain stability and order—fall outside the typology (Almond 1960; Cohen 1978, 1986). At best the latter remain incomplete and nonexplanatory (Elster 1982, 1983; Little 1991: 91–113). At worst they do not make sense.

Explanations of Action Versus Evolutionary Arguments

To be included in my typology, then, explanations must offer causal mechanisms, and the mechanisms must pass through individuals (but may not reduce to them) to connect to action. Besides legitimate but nonexplanatory claims and illegitimately vague holist claims, the other major strand of social science that falls outside these bounds is evolutionary arguments. I do not mean to suggest that such arguments have no role in the human sciences, but they do not offer mechanisms that connect directly to action. This is because they have a different goal from explanations of action. Rather than trying to account for actions, evolutionary arguments try to explain the survival of certain kinds of actors. Sometimes their claims imply explanations of actions, in which case the implied arguments fall within my typology. But in a direct sense evolutionary arguments ask different questions from the action-focused scholarship at the core of the human sciences. Both kinds of arguments become more comprehensible if we first map this core and then consider how other scholarly questions relate to it.

Let me justify this set-aside at some length, since it is my sole major caveat about the exhaustiveness of my typology for explanatory work in these disciplines, and since evolutionary thinking has become an increasingly large part of social science discussions in recent decades. The basic format of evolutionary logic is that certain features of an environment select certain entities by encouraging the survival of those that are capable of doing certain things and discouraging the survival of the less capable.

---

[2] As Little (1991: 188) develops and my introduction suggests, some arguments might communicate broad causal dynamics elegantly but not fully play out individual-level mechanisms beneath them. In some cases it might add little to go through this tedium, but it is crucial that it be possible.

The Darwinian theory that created this category does not try to explain why any given organism develops the capacities to meet environmental challenges, let alone the more precise actions they undertake to do so. New organisms arise from unpredictable genetic mutations. The claim is just that organisms that survive will be those that can meet salient environmental challenges better than others. In the terms of biologist Brian Goodwin, Darwinian theory does not try to explain 'creative emergence' of organisms or their behaviors (van Pirijs 1981: 52; Goodwin 1994).

Variants of this logic in the human sciences also speak only indirectly to the makeup or actions of any individual or human collectivity. One prominent example is 'neorealist' theory in IR. Its core notion is that the brute realities of an anarchical security competition kill off political units that cannot (or do not) defend themselves. This produces 'isomorphism'—movement toward similar forms—as collectivities converge on the form of states with similar war-fighting capabilities and balance-of-power policies (Waltz 1979: 232). Yet neorealism does not try to explain why any state balances against power or not. Its creator, Kenneth Waltz, stressed that he had no 'theory of foreign policy' about how any given state acted (1979: 121). Sometimes, regrettably, he seemed to slip into the different argument that states rationally respond to balance of power signals—a move analogous to shifting from Darwinian to Lamarckian evolutionary theory, where organisms perceive challenges and adapt themselves. Rather than suggesting that destruction in war is the main force in IR, this shift implies a world where states rarely get killed off (since they rationally shift their behavior to avoid unpromising fights). The latter argument can be perfectly coherent—it employs the combination of rationality and material constraints that defines my structural category—but Waltz himself noted that it is a contradictory argument (Keohane 1986: 172–5; Waltz 1986: 330–5). Nonetheless, Waltz's most prominent statements made neo-realism an evolutionary theory that fits with any manner of explanation of why particular states power-balance or not. It is a claim about long-term selection pressures in the international environment, not about how anybody responds to them.

In the long run—though it is not often clear how long—neorealism's evolutionary logic generates indirect implications for explanations of action. The claim that states who fail to balance get killed off is a strong claim about the environment that faces any given actor. It puts limits on the kinds of culture or institutions we should see in the long term. We should not see enduring societies built on pacificist beliefs or states that enact constitutional rules prohibiting a military. Still, in the short run, this claim allows that states might come up with all sorts of self-destructive (or at least suboptimal) organizations, beliefs, and strategies, just as biological organisms may exhibit dysfunctional mutations. Even if we see neorealist-style isomorphism in the long run, the theory is agnostic about why successful states took the shape and actions they did. Some may have adopted environmentally optimal organization and balancing strategies thanks to exceptionally clever leaders, or a certain institutional inheritance, or certain beliefs, or dumb luck. Neorealism's claims about long-term selection pressures, while not irrelevant to explanations of action, do not directly engage debates about them.

Some evolutionary arguments generate stronger implications for explaining action, like those in evolutionary psychology (Sober and Wilson 1998; Sidanius and Kurzban 2003; Alford and Hibbing 2004). They suggest that in the distant past people evolved hard-wired psychological inclinations that were helpful to survival, just as we evolved an upright stance and dexterous hands. The direct implication is that contemporary actions also reflect these hard-wired inclinations—though inclinations that aided survival on the African savannah may not seem functional today (Tooby and Cosmides 1990). In other words, evolutionary-psychology claims about the past directly generate psychological explanations of action today (like those in my psychological category). Unlike neorealism, which leaves room for many different claims about why certain states survive anarchy, evolutionary psychology connects past selection to current behavior very concretely through inherited genetics. Yet most evolutionary thinking in the human sciences is not similarly grounded in past selection of enduring physiological features. Like neorealism or similar scholarship on market competition, it tends to rely more on continuous selection pressures than 'locked in' past selections.[3] In so doing it remains consistent with a wide range of explanations of action (Axelrod 1986: 1097).

Again, this placement of evolutionary logic outside my typology is not a criticism. Work on environmental selection is interesting and important in the human sciences. In some specializations, like in IR or the sociology of organizations (Hannan and Freeman 1989), it is historically central. But as a first cut into explanatory debates in the social sciences and history, it makes sense to construct a chart of the main kinds of arguments that speak directly to the distinctive core focus of

---

[3] Waltz created neorealism by applying evolutionary theories about the survival of firms in market competition to states and security (1979: 89–91).

these disciplines—explanation of action—and only then to consider the indirect debates these arguments engage with adjacent research questions. Even in areas where evolutionary thinking is prominent, most scholars' overarching enterprise remains the explanation of action. To embark on that enterprise we must first grasp the direct alternatives considered here.

Explanation, Culture, and Ideas

Another major border battle concerns the relationship of culture and ideas to explanation. Much as I suggest that evolutionary work aspires to something other than explaining action, many scholars see ideationally focused scholarship pursuing a distinct agenda. This view traces most famously to Weber, who taught that arguments that invoke meaning engage something other than explanation. Weber posited a difference between an argument's 'adequacy on a causal level'—its explanatory force—and the kind of understanding, or 'adequacy on the level of meaning', to which ideational scholarship aspires (Weber [1922] 1958). He thought we could capture causality in action (being confident that under certain conditions, certain people would do certain things) without understanding the significance of what people were doing as they saw it. Later scholars expanded on Weber to put ideational work in its own inter- pretive or 'hermeneutic' category, setting it off from the causal dynam- ics that nonideational explanations of action ostensibly share with the natural sciences (Taylor 1985; Hollis and Smith 1990; Wendt 1999). This move is tied to the notion that much ideational scholarship asks 'how' or 'what' questions in a 'constitutive' mode, creating a division of labor, with the 'why' questions posed by explanatory work (Searle 1995; Wendt 1998). Culture and ideas define certain realities and imbue them with meaning in inseparably constitutive ways; explanatory scholarship plays out the more mechanistic causal workings within that context. We need constitutive scholarship, for example, to see how the norm of sovereignty constitutes the state. This is not a separable, temporally sequential, causal- explanatory relationship. The very minute that people accepted norms of sovereignty they looked around and saw states. Explanatory approaches can analyze dynamics within that socially constructed reality.

In my view, however, the Weberian distinction is built on poorly chosen definitions. Unlike evolutionary thinking, ideational scholarship does not ask distinct questions that place it outside explanations of action. Breaking with Weber may seem heretical to many readers and requires elaboration in later chapters. But two main points support my position that nothing fundamental sets ideational or 'meaning-based' scholarship in a distinct realm of inquiry. First, all the arguments in this book interpret how people saw and thought about their actions. Weber's definition of explanation as arguments that eschew such claims was premised on purely correlative views of explanation that I and many of today's scholars reject. If we take even a partial causal-mechanisms view of explanation, as I have, then no coherent explanation of human action bypasses mental processes. That ideational and psychological claims pass through mental processes is obvious. No less clear, as rational-choice theorist John Ferejohn remarks, is that any explanatory claim that invokes objective rationality 'obviously has an embedded interpretive perspective' (2002: 227).[4] Only if rationalist work operates purely in a correlative or predictive mode—not claiming to capture what is going on causally—might it avoid interpretation of mental processes. Explanatory work based on rationality (in my structural and institutionalist categories) must offer at least some interpretive, rhetorical evidence that people thought in roughly rational ways. The correct line between arguments that make claims about 'understanding' and others, then, is not between ideational scholarship and other work in the human sciences. It sets off any coherent explanation of human action from arguments about other things (with the fairly small exception of instinctual psychological claims).[5]

Second, constitutive dynamics do not conjure up a weird mode of relations distinct from the sequential, causal creation of the present from the past that characterizes the rest of our universe. Constitutive thinkers are correct to underscore that 'how' and 'what' questions are fundamental. But they are fundamental precisely because they are not ultimately independent from 'why' explanatory questions. As Wendt notes, definitional and descriptive questions underlie all explanation, whether it concerns culture, nonideational social science, or natural science (1998). We must define and describe to have anything to explain, and in so doing we

---

[4] Ferejohn seems not to accept this point in other work (2004), where he contrasts 'external' causal explanations in mainstream social science to 'internal' and ultimately nonexplanatory work in an ideational vein. He portrays the latter as taking the actor's point of view to arrive at reasons for action—normative justifications—rather than causes. Then he argues, however, that rational-choice work contains both 'external' and 'internal' components. Again, my view is that all coherent explanations of action have 'internal' components, with the fairly small exception of instinctual psychological claims.

[5] Relatedly, none of the causes in this book are more physical or mechanistic than others (except in the small category of instinctual psychological claims). It is common to remark that cultural norms make possible or legitimise certain actions, but do not actually push anyone to anything. But neither does economic competition, a threat of war, or even the approach of a rolling boulder or an attractive member of the opposite sex.

impute some debatable properties to the world. Ideational theorists suspect that the people we observe do the same thing, constructing aspects of their own worlds in defining, describing, and explaining it. Thus the project of ideationally inclined constitutive thinkers is an important one: they pose 'how' and 'what' questions that might lead us to unearth some socially constructed deep background conditions to certain actions, and also (at the level of observers) to some of our scholarship. These thinkers are wrong, though, to the extent that they imply that this project somehow uncovers components of action that cannot be built into explanations of action.

Constitutive relationships are themselves explicable. The state and norms of sovereignty may coexist inseparably, but at some point some mechanism brought about the first state-sovereignty system. In principle we should be able to explain how this happened. As I develop below in elaborating on particular explanation, scholars have shied away from doing so because the mechanisms behind constitutive relationships necessarily incorporate creative or accidental leaps across contingency. If the norm of sovereignty were fully explicable from pre-existing conditions, this derivative, inevitable by-product of something else would not deserve the heady label 'constitutive'. But once we recognize the logical possibility of particular explanation, we see that constitutiveness does not imply some mystery beyond combinations of causal mechanisms and contingencies. Placing constitutive claims within explanatory arguments simply requires a two-stage, diachronic demonstration. In a present, static stage, they claim that certain actions make no sense without—are inseparable from—certain meanings. For this claim to be significant beyond basic description, though, it must imply in a past, dynamic, causal sense that these actions would not occur had it not been for some historical mechanism by which these meanings (as opposed to other possible meanings) were put in place. Again, and as I discuss more below, this mechanism necessarily involves contingency.

On the other side of explanatory equations, constitutive norms can explain. This revisionist assertion requires several moves in Chapter 4, but the key point is that if norms may be inseparable from categories of action, they are separable from any concrete action (which is ultimately what we want to explain). To borrow a Wendt example, people might not be able to imagine selling a slave without certain norms of race, ownership, and exchange. These norms are indeed constitutive of this kind of action; if we ask, 'How is it possible for a man to sell a slave?' as Wendt does, the possibility looks inseparable from the norms that define it. But if we ask about a concrete action—why *some* man *did* sell *his* slave at some point—then separation opens up between the norms and their effects. Presumably norms of slavery were in place the day before the sale. We can gather evidence of these norms in a variety of earlier patterns of life. We can gather separate, temporally-subsequent evidence of the concrete act in question. Then we can have a debate about how much we need the former—relative to other demonstrable conditions that could have led to this action—to explain the latter.

Chapter 4 builds on these points, but this summary sets my basic boundary position. Neither meaning nor constitutiveness challenges the inclusion of ideational claims as explanations of action. There is no coherent option of nonideational explanatory mechanisms for human action that forego interpretation of meanings and mental processes. Ideational scholarship does not imply a world made up of anything other than causal mechanisms and contingencies. It is more the basis of ideational claims in contingency—their 'particularity'—that conflicts with conventional notions of explanation. As a final step around the boundaries of the map, then, let me turn to a more direct defense of the notion of particular explanation.

Particular Explanation

'Particular explanation' is an oxymoron in conventional terms. Humeans define explanation as the relating of general, systematic patterns. Even advocates of causal mechanisms recognize that claims about general regularities are a necessary part of any causal argument. They may insist first on logic and evidence of how an outcome came about, but to make a strong explanation they too require that the same conditions should always produce the same mechanism and the same outcome. Even a claim about unique things like 'the unprecedented notions of citizenship invented in the French Revolution led French people to act in certain ways' requires that if we ever saw other people with similar notions of citizenship, the same cause–effect dynamics should apply.

This is also true for the classically explanatory components of what I propose to call a particular explanation. The segments of logic in which they assert that one thing followed from another are no different from standard general explanations. What makes them a distinct kind of argument is how they combine such segments of classic causal mechanisms with segments about contingency. General explanations can certainly incorporate contingency, especially in probabilistic variants, but they portray it as random variation alongside a range of variation that is systematic and explicable. Particular explanations, by contrast, offer a segmented logic through time. First, a range of variation is contingent. Outcomes are unpredictable going forward and inexplicable looking back across that range. Once something underdetermined happens, causal consequences are engaged across the same range of variation. After this point, dynamics become explicable and perhaps predictable. The overall claim across the segmented story, however, is that we would not expect the same outcome to result even given identical starting conditions. If we could run the process again as an experiment, the initial contingency could just as well be resolved in some other way, engaging different causal consequences in the second stage. Such arguments are 'particular' in the sense that their account of one situation does not imply that similar cases will turn out the same way. They focus on the causal consequences of things that do not arise in regular explicable patterns.

Some might object that I stretch 'explanation' too far to include such arguments. Contingency, after all, seems to be the enemy of explanation. In my view, however, when we seek 'explanations', we genuinely want to know why something came about—not just whether and how it relates to general regularities. One logical possibility is that the process that produced it leapt over some contingency. Some segments of mechanisms may be unpredictable no matter how much information we have, like flipping a coin, and for those segments our best 'explanation' takes the form, 'Across these possible outcomes it was contingent'. Unless we reject the possibility of real contingency in the universe, it seems odd to denigrate a potentially accurate claim involving some range of contingency as 'not an explanation'. (This is not to say that supporting an accurate claim about contingency is easy, but I argue in Chapter 3 that it is the mirror image of demonstrating a claim about causality, which is not easy either.) Some readers might still prefer another term for this sort of argument, retaining a more strictly deterministic usage of 'explanation'. That reasonable semantic objection does not challenge the substantive point. One logical set of processes that might fully capture all we could know about how something came about would be built around the causal consequences of resolved contingencies.

In the human sciences, another reason to accept this term—or at least something similar to label this logically valid form of argument—is that a great deal of historically important scholarship effectively employs it. As I suggested above, all explanations involving institutions and ideational elements take this shape. Admittedly, this is far from obvious at first glance. In the abstract there may not seem to be any logical relationship between particularistic logic and any kind of cause. Complexity theory outside the social sciences, for example, essentially applies combinations of contingency and causality to many kinds of phenomena (e.g. Nicolis and Prigogene 1989). Similarly, it may seem that the four categories of causes I have sketched could relate in any way to contingency. Structural-material or psychological conditions might be arranged into particularistic dynamics. Institutions and ideational elements, if we accept them as causes at all, would seem to be able to produce general regularities.

The first of these two objections is correct, and leads to the dotted-line caveat in my otherwise-clean matrix in the introduction. We might imagine an avalanche zone, for example, where conditions are ripe to wipe out a village. If a bird lands in the right spot—or some other contingent event occurs—the avalanche takes place. A series of causal dynamics are engaged, and major structural consequences follow for the villagers. If nothing touches off the avalanche, a different set of material developments ensue, and rational villagers end up undertaking different actions in response.[6] Psychologically, we could imagine someone who suffers head trauma in a freak (contingent) accident, altering their hard-wired inclinations and changing the causal dynamics affecting their behavior. The caveat, then, is that the structural and psychological categories shade into the particular side of the matrix (as suggested by the grey zones and dotted line in Figure 1). In terms of historical arguments in the human sciences, arguments in this zone are fairly rare.[7] But they are a logical possibility that makes my matrix a bit messier.

If structural and psychological claims are not fully confined to general explanation, however, institutional and ideational claims are inherently particularistic. This is not for reasons of scope or a logical capacity to generate expectations about causal regularities. It is perfectly imaginable that institutional or ideational claims could cover everyone on Earth, if certain institutions or ideational elements spread across the whole population (e.g. Meyer et al. 1997). We could make a broad claim about regularities that all people who inhabit parliamentary institutions are channeled toward certain actions, or that all people who believe labor is a commodity tend toward certain actions, and these would be just as much about broad regularities as a general argument that all people who live in a material landscape of deserts are channeled toward certain actions.

---

[6] Thanks to Andrew Moravcsik for this point.

[7] See Chapter 2 for examples on the historical consequences of the Black Death in fourteenth-century Europe.

Once again, the distinctiveness of particular explanations does not lie in the nature of their segments of causal logic. Any causal claim at all invokes a regular expectation that reproduction of the same conditions would produce the same result. Their difference from general explanations concerns how causal segments are placed in relationship to claims about contingency. Within the basic notions of man-made institutions or ideational elements as causes there is a connotation of past contingency. It makes claims about these human creations as autonomous causes logically different from general arguments about structure or psychology as autonomous causes.

Institutions and ideational elements, if they are anything distinct at all, are products of human action before they are causes. One of the main points of calling something an institution or an 'idea' or 'culture' is to underscore that it is a man-made creation. In order for these results of earlier actions to become a distinct cause of later ones, at some point it must have been possible—and even equally likely—for the same people to have other institutions or ideas. In other words, over some range of options the emergence (or conceivably endurance) of certain institutions or ideational elements must have been contingent and inexplicable. Only if this is true does it make sense to say that it was the presence of *these* institutions or ideational elements, as a distinct and fundamental cause in the story, that made the causal difference (across that range of options). If preexisting factors dictated the constellation of institutions or ideas, then institutions or ideational elements might enter the argument as lagged derivatives of other things, but we would not have a distinct logic of institutional or ideational explanation. To put it differently, if we want to claim something basic and distinct about the nature of causes at work in some situation, we must do more than make the kinds of claims about regularities suggested in the previous paragraph. For claims that institutions or ideational elements generated effects or regularities to be meaningfully distinct from other causal claims—getting at different ways in which the world could be put together, not just addressing apparent regularities at the tail end of causal chains—we must argue that some new causal process began with the establishment of certain institutions or ideational elements. Since institutions and ideational elements are the results of earlier actions, the kind of causal break that would let them start new causal processes requires a claim about a range of contingency in the earlier actions.

Let me repeat that the general–particular distinction is not about the geographic or temporal scope of an argument. We might say that capitalism is a 'world system' that affects all human beings, but we could offer either general or particular accounts of its emergence and spread. Nor is the distinction about the degree of determinism. General arguments can be phrased probabilistically and might assign low probabilities to any outcome, incorporating much contingency. But they do not build contingency into their causal process the way particular arguments do, constructing a causal claim on the underdetermined resolution of contingencies. It is tempting to move from this observation to the notion that the general–particular distinction is just about how we frame our questions and time periods relative to contingencies out in the world— not about some fundamental difference in explanatory logics. We might simply see general claims as those that look at stable periods or dynamics, where fairly fixed conditions play out into some combination of systematic outcomes and random noise. Particular claims might just be those that focus on accidents, 'critical junctures' or 'unsettled periods'. This is not entirely wrong. It is logically possible to combine these modes of argument in analytically segmented ways, and the clearest and most nuanced arguments may well use general and particular claims to bound each other. Yet debates between general and particular claims are not simply about a division of labor in research interests. Since these logics connect to certain kinds of causes, their debate is substantive as well. Even if we declared interest only in the dynamics of a highly stable period or arena, claims that 'institutions' or 'ideas' *caused* observed regularities would imply a particular logic built on contingencies at an earlier time— since otherwise it would not be clear how much we were claiming the causes were distinctly institutional or ideational. Again, claims about structural or psychological causes would not carry this implication. The deepest explanatory debates are ultimately about the nature of causes, not just about observable regularities, and a fundamental cleavage in our explanatory options is between general and particular logics.

I have now dealt with the most salient debates on the bounds of the map. I insisted that explanations feature causal mechanisms, setting aside a great deal of descriptive, predictive, and other potentially valuable but not explanatory work. I required that the mechanisms pass through physical individuals at some point, excluding vague holist claims but not many arguments in which individual action reflects supra-individual dynamics. I carved out a special space for evolutionary scholarship, which is historically central to many social science debates but does not directly explain action. I contested the view that ideational scholarship deserves a similar opt-out clause, arguing that all explanations of action invoke meanings and that 'constitutive' relationships do not imply a realm free of causation. Lastly, I called for including arguments that combine sequences of contingency and causality in ways that do not fit with conventional general explanation, and argued that claims about man-made institutions or ideational elements as autonomous causes necessarily take this format.

Divisions

As I noted earlier, positions on the bounds of our map do not tell us how to organize it internally. Within these bounds we could still create an infinite number of different explanations of action, and draw nearly as many valid distinctions between them. I suggested in the introduction that our first cut should concern basic kinds of causes or causal logic, but that still leaves us far short of organizing principles. Explanations employ many different things as causes, and connect them to action with a huge variety of logics. Why claim that positional–interpretive and general–particular distinctions offer a fundamental and exhaustive sense of our basic options?

This is less of a grandiose ontological assertion than it sounds. Its foundations are relative and pragmatic. The reasons why a typology built on these distinctions is especially helpful lie in how it improves on other available breakdowns, and in how clearly and completely it captures the range of arguments we currently have before us. I cannot offer a deductive framework that moves from simple axioms about human existence to a fully described set of imaginable logical dynamics. I cannot prove the negative that there are no kinds of causes of action that escape or range across my scheme. I strongly doubt that it could ever be possible to deduce a full and finite landscape of causal claims we could make about action. The best we can do is draw some deductive lines through the landscape and then make inductive claims about how well they capture the range of existing scholarship.

Simply grounding a broad breakdown of causal claims in systematic distinctions is a major improvement on available typologies. While some focused frameworks chart a small range of arguments in logical dichotomies or matrices, like Wendt's (1999), those with broadly comprehensive ambitions take a more historical format. 'Structure, culture, rationality' and 'interests, institutions, ideas' are ultimately laundry lists of different things that scholars have focused on historically, not interrelated and systematic definitions of distinct explanatory spaces.[8] This is why their categories overlap conceptually. Such lists also seem boundless, since they do not directly suggest why we might not someday tack on other approaches.

My two dichotomies, by contrast, define competing arguments in interrelated ways and divide the explanatory terrain independently from inductive reference to historical literatures. Let me restate them quickly. First, a clear segment of an explanation of action can locate its moving parts either in the environment, portrayed as existing in an objective state separate from the actors, or 'in the actors' in some sense.[9] We can explain why people do things either by pointing to direct consequences of their position in an environment or by pointing to their internal drives and interpretation of the environment. As I stressed in the introduction, this choice is only unavoidable at the 'basic causal segment' level. Full explanations often combine segments that fall to either side of this distinction. They might argue, for example, that salient intersubjectively present (or 'objective') features of the environment set some broad limits on the action of boundedly rational people and that interpretive elements led them to more specific choices. To connect action to causes in comprehensible ways, though, even compound arguments must be disaggregated into cleanly positional or interpretive claims. Of course, such specific claims will often be beyond our grasp. We practically never enjoy the methods and evidence to disentangle interpretation from the objective world neatly and confidently. Still, we will only make clear explanatory claims to the extent that we do.

Second, causes we connect to action can either be general, stipulating regular consequences that follow in deterministic or probabilistic ways from given conditions, or they can be particular, engaging causal force after leaping over a range of contingency. While this distinction is more novel than the position-interpretation divide—some hint of which appears in almost every major breakdown in the social sciences—it may be easier to see how it is unavoidable at the level of basic causal segments. At each step in our argument, either we note a range of outcomes across which we can neither explain nor predict, or we do not. As with the first dichotomy, there is no insuperable logical barrier to combining

---

[8] Most introductory breakdowns are even more like laundry lists. Marsh and Stoker (2002), for example, offer chapters—many very good!—on behavioralism, rational choice, institutionalism, feminism, interpretive theory, Marxism, and normative theory.

[9] The quotation marks and plural 'actors' allow that interpretive elements need not be fully internalized by individuals, somehow being carried at a supra-individual level.

particularistic dynamics with general ones in an overall argument. We might argue that some actions are essentially impossible in some situations (or people are compelled toward some range of options) for general reasons, while choices within that range reflect the consequences of resolved contingencies. We only make clear explanatory claims, however, to the extent that each segment in our explanation commits to a view on this distinction.

Hopefully these deductive moves come across as plausibly important cuts into our terrain of explanation, but they alone cannot make a strong case for the utility of the framework. As a first cut, typologies built on conceptual dichotomies are surely preferable to historical lists. They get at what we could argue rather than just at what some people argued. But since I do not claim that the full substance of arguments can be deduced from these distinctions—just that these are two choices, among others, we must make about causal claims—it is not deductively obvious why these dichotomies have more organizing power than others. Ultimately our view of their mapping power depends on more inductive claims about how well extant scholarship falls out along these lines. The same is true with respect to the exhaustiveness of the resultant map. In a trivial sense, any breakdown grounded in reasonable dichotomies is exhaustive. As long as it is persuasive that arguments really must choose between features *a* or *b*, then 'arguments take form *a* or *b*' covers all arguments. But again, since we could draw so many reasonable dichotomies, seeing some as usefully exhaustive ultimately depends on how convincingly they sort out the terms we use and illuminate the real arguments we encounter. The proof is not in the recipe but in the pudding.

For a taste of the pudding, let me summarize the chapters. Rather than working outward from the boxes in my matrix, each chapter asks how to capture a distinct but still widely applicable definition for some of our most commonly used labels for arguments: structural, institutional, ideational, and psychological. I argue that this more inductive operation carries us back into my deductive matrix. The result is the grandest— and from my point of view, the most debatable—claim of the book. My moves on the boundaries of explanation are somewhat revisionist, one of my internal dichotomies is partly novel, and the philosophy of science views elaborated in the conclusion challenge the orthodoxy. But all these arguments are founded mainly on abstract logical steps. The cumulative point of the chapters, on the other hand, is a broad inductive, historical claim about what the human sciences—to the extent that they have made sense over the past few centuries—have ultimately been debating. If we try to extract nonoverlapping varieties of explanation from a very wide range of historical literatures, we find that the deepest debates fall out along positional–interpretive and general–particular lines. The full argument of the book is that some reasonable deductive moves and plausible inductive interpretations of a great deal of literature converge on this matrix as the basic framework for debates about explaining action.

Chapter 2 notes that scholars have invoked the powerful words 'structure' and 'structural' to communicate practically all kinds of argument. I suggest we use 'structural' to designate any claim that explains actions as an individually-rational function of position in a 'material' landscape. By 'material' landscape I mean any sort of obstacle course that is treated analytically as an intersubjectively present, given environment. Some of the most prominent theoretical schools in the social sciences are largely constituted from segments of this kind of logic. The most salient three are Marxism, economic liberalism, and realism (but not neorealism). These approaches have major differences, but their debates concern the configuration and dynamics of the given landscape, not the basic logic of action. They all point to the same fundamental kind of cause of action but vary on how that kind of cause is arranged in the world.

The labels 'institutional' or 'institutionalist' are also claimed by a wide variety of social scientists. To give these terms a distinct meaning, I argue in Chapter 3 that we should narrow them to those logics in which institutions are clearly asserted to exist in some definite form—meaning they are intersubjectively present, not subject to interpretation—and in which the institutions enjoy some clear range of causal autonomy from other intersubjectively present factors (meaning structure). Institutionalist claims are those that explain action by pointing to someone's position in a man-made but intersubjectively present obstacle course. Their man-made quality creates a logic of 'path dependence', in which earlier choices shape later ones in unintended ways. It requires foundations in contingency, as discussed above. Claims within the category may disagree about the historical contingency and subsequent causal consequences of any particular institutional arrangement, but they share a distinct logic of action.

As we have seen, 'ideational explanation' is often seen as a contradiction in terms. Chapter 4 argues in more detail that the philosophical, methodological, and historical reasons for contrasting ideational argument to explanation are misplaced. Once these objections to the category per se are set aside, defining its basic explanatory logic is not very difficult. Ideational claims explain actions by tracing them to some constellation of practices, symbols, norms, grammars, models, beliefs, and/or identities through which certain people interpret their world. Since these ideational elements are man-made, like institutions, they too can only ground a distinct and irreducible causal logic in a particularistic format, as the consequence of earlier contingent actions. Many variations on the nature and dynamics of ideational elements can lead to substantial theoretical and empirical debates within the category, but again they share a distinct view of the basic nature of causes of action.

Chapter 5 is less revisionist than the others, defining psychological explanation in a way that fits with widespread usage. Claims that employ psychological logic explain action in terms of the causal effects of hard-wired mental processes that depart from a simple rational model. In most cases this means claims about irrational decision-making due to biases, misperceptions, instincts or affects. In rare cases it can also mean arguments that explain preferences prior to rational decision-making. Once again we find a wide range of very different claims about psychological makeup, but they all begin from the same distinctive kind of cause.

I already issued one caveat about how neatly these extrapolations of our common labels match up to my deductive matrix. Structural and psychological claims can take a particularistic format, though such arguments are rare. The claim that these categories capture and exhaust our fundamental options also depends on accepting a priority on dividing arguments by the basic nature of causes or causal logic. In some contexts we might want to divide arguments by other first-cut criteria. A developing-country policymaker, for example, might care a great deal about debates between economic-liberal structural claims and Marxist structural claims about how international markets relate to development. She might care less about debates between economic-liberal structuralists who see a 'neoliberal' world of markets as objective and natural and ideational claims that also accept a powerful neoliberal context but argue that it is socially constructed. But for teaching and theorizing about explanatory debates, the rock-bottom distinctions concern arguments that feature different kinds of causes.

At that level I submit that these are our alternatives. People arrive at certain actions due to some combination of causal forces from their structural-material surroundings, their man-made organizational context, their socially constructed ideational elements, or their physiologically hard-wired mental dispositions and motivations. Neither in logical speculation nor in inductive readings of scholarship can I find coherent segments of explanatory claims that fall outside these categories. Perhaps someone else will do so, drawing an additional basic distinction that further differentiates our causal options. Such a move could complicate this framework, and I cannot rule it out. It would only supplement, not replace, the lines drawn here.

Costs and Benefits

Major choices in theorizing, like in everything else, involve trade-offs. Drawing certain lines through our theoretical options clarifies some claims but makes the communication (and perhaps even conception) of others more difficult. In my view this framework has room for any coherent explanatory claim about action, but its distinctions do deprive us of some terms or phrases that could be elegant and helpful to formulate some arguments.

Each chapter raises some such problems. Probably the strongest objections will concern 'structure'. The notion of socially constructed norms as deep 'structure' is especially central to a great deal of ideational scholarship. Institutionalists also stress the structuring role of organizations and rules, and one of the original 'structuralisms' was the semipsychological analysis of Claude Lévi-Strauss (1966). My narrowed definition of institutionalism steals the term not only from some 'rationalist institutionalist' scholars (whose logic is often structural by my definition) but also from most 'sociological institutionalists' (whose logic is usually ideational by my definition). The latter move may seem especially unjust, since it was culturally inclined sociologists who first made 'institution' into a serious analytic term. The choice of 'ideational' to cover the full category of claims about ideas, culture, and so on—even the individual level of idiosyncratic personal beliefs—might be seen as obscuring arguments in which 'culture' is defined as an intersubjective group phenomenon. A definition of psychological claims as contradicting or preceding rationality, while consonant with common usage, might discourage those who wish to investigate the mental processes of outwardly rational decision-making. If we consider these complaints separately, as objections to stylistic restrictions on how to communicate one kind of claim, they are justified. Scholars generally have reasons for using terms as they do. My distinctions will force some claims to be wordier, and this can only be seen as a cost. Still, as I have argued above, we simply cannot allow ourselves to choose major terms as a function of convenience and elegance for any one argument. These terms only take on clear meanings when defined relative to each other and to a map of the universe of possible arguments. Ultimately some stylistic adjustments are a small price to pay for a clarified arena of debate.

Beyond semantic turf wars, some may suspect that the greatest costs of this framework reflect the general danger of seeking sharp distinctions in a complex world. Establishing greater separation between logics could make them harder to combine, blocking more nuanced positions. Exaggerated separation might even rule out direct competition, erasing common terrain over which they could do battle. A glance at recent commentaries on compatibility and competition in political science encourages this fear. One common theme is that approaches are already so different that they cannot engage. Some rational choice scholars seem to imply that they hold the only model of argument worth considering (Kiser and Hechter 1991; Bates 1997). Some postmodern theorists reject the possibility of recognizing some causal arguments as better than others (among others, Ashley 1987; Walker 1993). The less aggressive but similarly divisive Weberian view stresses separate-but-equal realms of explanation and understanding. A related (if opposing) theme is that we should focus on synthesis and 'middle ground' approaches, since overdrawn distinctions lead to arguments that talk past each other. In an important symposium on theory in comparative politics, Peter Katzenstein, Peter Evans, James Scott, and Theda Skocpol call for a 'middle way' within the 'messy eclectic center' that favors 'blurring of distinctions' and emulation of 'the hybrid vigor of the plant and animal breeding world' (Kohli et al. 1995).

These warnings are important. Scholars often engage dialogues of the deaf. Yet both themes run into common-sense objections if stated very strongly. Taking a step back from rarified meta-theory, it seems odd to imagine that claims based on different kinds of causes would be incompatible or exist in separate realms. Surely the most intuitive point of departure is that there are some fairly unambiguous given environmental conditions out there (the Rhine flows north, the Mississippi flows south), some fairly unambiguous institutional features (US presidents are selected by an electoral college), at least some demonstrable ideational elements with some autonomous force (the Pope and the Cardinals believe contraception is wrong), and something like human rationality bounded by some irrational psychological dispositions (as anyone who has spent time as a human being can appreciate). All have imaginable causal consequences in the abstract, though we will argue about what they are. All are to some degree in competition. They may run parallel in overdetermined situations, but broadly, the more one causes an outcome, the less the others did. If we cannot make different causes speak to each other competitively and work together in combination, this seems much more likely to reflect poor theorizing than the real existence of weirdly separate realms of action. Moreover, even if brilliant future theorists managed to reduce most action convincingly to one causal category, this would not be because only one kind of causal claim qualified as scientific and plausible in the abstract. It would be because the theorists persuaded many others, to some pragmatic standard of intersubjective truth with a small 't', that their approach was empirically right and the abstractly plausible alternatives were wrong.[10]

Advocates of eclecticism may welcome the previous paragraph, but they too must be careful not to overstate their case. There is no solid middle ground without poles, no useful eclecticism without distinct things to mix. Even Marxist advocates of dialectics, cultural proponents of mutual constitution, or sophisticated students of other endogenous relationships must recognize that synthetic claims are only as clear and coherent as their constituent parts. To make a comprehensible mutual-causality argument necessarily entails 'bracketing' of some sort, where we first show the distinct effect of one side of the relationship on the other (while setting aside the reverse causality in conceptual 'brackets') and then do the same thing in the other direction (Giddens 1979: 80–1; Wendt 1999: 34). We cannot leap past distinct building blocks of argument to a mélange that somehow emits a nuanced enlightenment directly. A dialectic or endogenous relationship without bracketable components is not a sophisticated combination. It is a hash.

Even eclectic theorists need sharp distinctions, then, and if we draw the distinctions usefully they should direct our attention to separable but not incompatible features of our world. The upshot is that what may first look like a potential cost of my framework turns out to be one of its largest benefits. Rather than impeding direct competition or compatibility, these distinctions greatly increase our ability to engage and combine different claims. This benefit of the typology stands out most clearly if we consider the commonly-perceived divide between rational-structural arguments and ideational ones. Their gap stretches across the diagonal of my matrix, combining issues of interpretation and meaning with questions about

---

[10] I think this very hard to imagine, but it seems unscientific to declare it impossible a priori.

the relationship between explanation and generalization. It is commonly seen as the most troubling split in the social sciences and history. The framework bridges it in two main steps.

One is to avoid the word 'interest' and to set aside the red herrings often associated with 'rationalism'. As I suggested in the introduction, the notion that certain theories are about 'interests' and others are not is misleading. With only partial exceptions for the most unconscious ideational or psychological logics, all arguments center on how people arrive at the view that certain actions are in their 'interest'. Similarly, it makes little sense to see 'rational choice' or 'rationalism' as an explanatory approach to action. Rationality dictates nothing about action in the absence of external constraints and opportunities. Chapter 2 cites many prominent 'rationalist' scholars who note that their explanations focus above all on how the landscapes around people are configured. The arguments that are usually seen as interest-based and rationalist are much better summarized with the language of *position*. Their distinctive format is that people arrive at certain actions by extrapolation from a certain unambiguous position in an intersubjectively present environment. Such arguments depend on regular rational decision-making to translate position unproblematically into interests and action. Taken together, these fairly simple rephrasings turn longstanding debates between positional arguments and others (and between different positional arguments) into variations on a concrete empirical question that facilitates engagement. How much do patterns of action trace logically to demonstrable positioning in some sort of objective obstacle course (whether material or man-made)?[11]

[11] This move relates to my lack of attention to 'relational' approaches in sociology. Some theorists posit a basic difference between 'substantialist' and 'relational' theorizing (Dewey and Bentley 1949; Emirbayer 1997). The former ostensibly pictures a world of discrete entities which carry their own attributes and motives. The latter pictures a world in which actors and action only exist and make sense through relationships. I find the relational literature very insightful, but not this definition of it. It constructs the 'substantialist' category only by accepting the misleading self-characterization of much 'interest'-based and rationalist scholarship. As we will see in Chapters 2 and 3, even if much work on 'interests' claims to stress the internal rational choices of atomized individuals with certain attributes and resources, its actual explanatory logic focuses on the relational positions of individuals in markets, security competitions, or other structural or institutional patterns. The debate Emirbayer describes actually plays out across the general-particular divide, between claims built around exogenously-given versus man-made causes. 'Relational' theorizing like in Burt (1992), White (1992), Padgett and Ansell (1993), or Bearman (1993) offers unusually explicit analysis of configurations of networks of man-made relationships. Their key distinction is not a relational approach but rather an emphasis on endogeneity between network patterns and people's identity, interests, and action. In my terms they employ combinations of institutional and ideational logics. Their actors construct and reconstruct themselves and their action in man-made networks. 'Substantialist' work presents actors and their environment as more exogenously given and less interactive. To see the latter as explaining action without

The other step meets this move halfway, carrying us out of the Weberian isolation of culture. It involves first cutting away some weak reasons for separating constitutive and causal scholarship and then recognizing the foundations of ideational claims in contingency and particular explanation. These moves are a bit more complex than the rephrasing of 'interest'-based claims as positional, and receive important elaboration later in the book. But in broad terms, they connect all of our basic causal logics to the same explanatory tasks in the same broad ontological universe. The logics remain contradictory on any given point, making it our crucial task to debate how much each one operates. In order to make one of these claims, though, we need not assume that the others are always and everywhere wrong.

In fact, just as the categories' definitions are interrelated, so their demonstrations are interdependent. The next four chapters each consider some basic methodological issues about supporting each kind of claim, and stress that a clear claim within each category depends logically on making clear claims about at least some of the others. Only in the rare case of a fully monocausal argument—asserting strongly that other kinds of causes do not matter at all—can a causal assertion be clear without such interrelated 'how much' arguments. Otherwise any explanatory argument necessarily combines different causal segments, using them to bound each other. Structural claims only become clear and persuasive if they specify how much other factors created 'wiggle room' within structural givens. Institutionalist claims only become clear and persuasive once they detail and support claims about a range of structural contingency that institutions resolve (and note any interpretive wiggle room). Ideational claims only become clear and persuasive once they detail and support claims about a range of imaginable interpretive variation, presumably within a structural and institutional landscape, and perhaps subject to psychological regularities, from which certain ideational elements selected one path. Psychological claims tend to reverse the analytical order, detailing and supporting claims about hard-wired dispositions and then showing how other factors connected them to certain actions. Distinctiveness, competition, and abstract compatibility between the logics are all unavoidable components of any clear claim at all.

There is much more to be said about theoretical and methodological moves that can knit these causal logics together into convincing empirical

reference to positioning in supra-individual patterns is to mistake rhetorical emphasis on individualism and rationality for a logic of explanation (see Chapters 2 and 3; also Arrow 1994).

arguments. At the broad level of this framework, though, the crucial point is that we should be able to pull off such combinations coherently. We tend to have different hunches about which causal categories are most important, but ultimately, we are all trying to reconstruct the world of action with the same basic tool box.

Conclusion

To close the introductory section, let me be clear about what I see as the book's main contribution, as opposed to secondary points which may have value but without which the larger undertaking still stands. I claim that if we define the four kinds of causal segments as I suggest, all coherent and specific explanations of action can be broken down into these categories. I claim there is no equally systematic and clear breakdown that captures as much of the substance of our main explanatory debates. In the conclusion I also assert that this typology leads unavoidably to the view that social scientists must set aside generality as a defining criterion for scientific contribution and progress.

The secondary points concern the location of any particular literature or work within the typology and my criticisms of unclear vocabularies or arguments. Surely some will object that I have read some important figure or literature in an unusual or incomplete way. As long as I have successfully communicated the framework, however, I will be happy to admit that these finer points may be debatable—especially if such debates encourage us all to read carefully with a sharp eye for the core logic of explanatory arguments. I have written this book first and foremost to learn how to do this myself. Hopefully my effort will make it easier for others.

Part II
Logics

2

Structural Explanation

'Structure' is arguably the core concept of the social sciences, especially when vaguely defined. In its broadest usage, scholars invoke the 'structure-agency debate', which concerns how much people are free 'agents' who choose their fates and how much their choices are dictated by larger forces (Giddens 1979; Wendt 1987; Dessler 1989). At this level 'structure' refers quite literally to *all* the things we use to explain particular actions. Agency is that element of idiosyncratic free will that we can neither predict nor explain; understanding structure is the whole task of those interested in explaining action. This also reflects how we use the verb *to structure*: 'to construct, form, or organize' in any way. Structure is everything that gives shape to human action.

This chapter proposes a more specific definition, however, referring solely to the 'material' landscape (though the quotation marks hint that this move is not free of problems). I justify this definition in detail below, but as with the book overall, my deepest motivation is simply to save the term from complete ambiguity. 'Structure' is of little use if it refers to the substance of any explanation of any action (Waltz 1979: 73). Still, narrowing its meaning has two drawbacks. My stricter usage has a stylistic cost in depriving us of phrases like 'institutional structure' or 'cultural structure' which might seem useful and elegant in some contexts. More importantly, given the common-language meaning of *to structure*, drawing a line between structure and institutions, ideational elements, or psychology risks implying that the latter are not so important in constructing or organizing action. Whatever I leave in the 'structure' category may sound more fundamental. While this is precisely the gist of many well-known arguments assembled mainly from structural segments—that institutions, ideational elements, and psychology are at most secondary factors in politics—it is certainly not what this overall framework is meant to suggest. We can advance institutional, ideational, or psychological claims about organizing causes of action without employing the word 'structure', and this is what I ask us to do in the name of clear logics of explanation.

Defining Structural Explanation

Since every social scientist would like to claim to be studying the fundamental things that construct, form, or organize human behavior, at some point practically every scholarly tradition has laid claim to 'structuralism'. Sitting in a Left Bank café in Paris in the late 1960s, one might have overheard several intellectuals calling themselves structuralists who shared practically no points of agreement. They could have included old-style Marxists, who saw behavior organized by a material reality; quasi-Marxists like Althusser or Poulantzas, who emphasized the organizing power of culture, ideology, and institutions; cultural sociologists like Foucault, who preached a different view rooted in culture and ideology (and whom admittedly would later settle on the label 'poststructuralists'); and anthropologists and linguists in the vein of Lévi-Strauss, who saw society as organized by deep psychological laws (Lévi-Strauss 1966; Althusser 1972; Foucault 1972; Poulantzas 1973). A little time in cafés in Cambridge and Berkeley would have added several other variants.

A first reasonable step to reduce this Babel is to limit 'structure' to those kinds of claims that do not have other obvious terms for their main causes. Scholars who ultimately see actions flowing from man-made organizations and rules (institutions), cultural beliefs or norms, or psychological regularities can make their claims in other ways. Of our Left Bank friends, that leaves only traditional Marxists in need of the term. For Marx (or at least for the most straightforward reading of Marx's vast and complex scholarship), 'structure' meant a largely physical reality consisting of a distribution of resources and technology:

In the social production which men carry on they enter into definite relations that are indispensable and independent of their will; these relations of production correspond to a definite stage of development of their material powers of production. The sum total of these relations of production constitutes the economic structure of society—the real foundation on which rise legal and political superstructures and to which correspond definite forms of social consciousness. The mode of production in material life determines the general character of the social, political, and spiritual processes of life. It is not the consciousness of men that determines their existence, but on the contrary, their social existence that determines their consciousness.

(Marx [1859] 1978)

Here Marx portrays people reacting directly to an 'economic structure' that is as much a given as physical geography. People may elaborate complex 'relations' and 'legal and political superstructures', but the way these are set up is 'indispensable' (i.e. there is only one obvious way to react to the underlying economic structure, meaning no room for idiosyncratic institutional arrangements) and 'independent of their will' (i.e. neither culture nor psychology should matter either). In other words, Marx suggests an analysis in which all aspects of human life—even 'spiritual'—coalesce in direct reaction to an objective, physical, 'material' landscape. Since I see no reasonably elegant alternative to 'structure' to capture what Marx is talking about[1]—and since, as we will see, this usage is common to a wide range of scholarship—I suggest we assign the term this strict meaning.

For students of Marx who protest that his work is more complex than vulgar materialism, I reiterate that my goal is to isolate a basic kind of causal segment. Marx and many scholars who rely mainly on structural explanatory segments certainly adorn their claims with all sorts of caveats and nuances. Only if we extract the core logic of their central claims, however, can we begin to understand and evaluate the complications these authors build around them, or to contrast their arguments to other logics. In my usage, then, a structural explanatory claim pictures people reacting in regular, direct ways to their 'material' surroundings. Such logic explains variation in action by showing that people are positioned differently in the 'material' landscape (or, over time, by pointing to exogenous changes in the 'material' landscape which orient people toward new actions).

To complete the first step in defining structural explanation, we need to remove the quotation marks from 'material'. They are there because even if a structural claim *treats* the elements it uses to explain action as physical, exogenously given landscapes that exist 'independent of the will' of humans, alternative claims might portray some of the same elements as man-made institutional or ideational constructs (and structural

---

[1] Marxist and similar arguments are often called 'materialist', and this nicely captures their thinking. But it creates stylistic problems. It does not make sense in English to say that 'material' causes actions in materialist explanation, whereas it does make sense to say 'structure' causes actions in structural explanation—allowing a rhetorical parallel to the other logics (where institutions cause actions in institutional explanation, and so on).

thinkers too may allow, as caveats or nuances, that this might be the case). Marx's underlying 'economic structure of society' is built on all sorts of principles that might not be the only and obvious ways that people could have reacted to their basic physical and technological environment: certain kinds of property rights, political authority, elaborate principles of exchange, and so on (Brenner 1977). Even when they admit that their core explanatory elements might actually include 'material' things (in quotes, potentially containing man-made ideational or institutional elements), structural claims as I define them treat those elements over the scope of their explanations as material things (without quotes, as natural or physical givens). In a clean causal segment of structural explanation, people choose their actions as a direct function of what is taken to be a concrete, exogenously given environment.

Structural Claims and Rationalism

Two other steps carry us to a narrowed definition of structural explanation. First, we need more of a mechanism that makes action into a 'direct function' of a concrete external environment. Second, we must consider how such thinking relates to other apparently overlapping kinds of claims that do not call themselves structural. Both steps lead into the same discussion. A great deal of scholarship focuses on the mechanisms of choice by which people select actions to fit their given external environment. It is frequently labeled 'rationalist', however, and is often seen as quite different from anything that could be called 'structural'. I argue here that rational choice is a necessary component of structural explanation, and that most 'rationalist' claims can be subsumed under my structural label. (Chapter 3 argues for subsuming the remainder of 'rationalism' into institutionalist claims.)

Consider first the self-presentation of the scholarship that commonly calls itself 'rationalist' (as in Lichbach and Zuckerman 1997). Its claim to this label is no mystery, since its most explicit point of departure is an assumption of rationality. To assume rationality means to assume that people know their own preferences over outcomes, tend to be aware of their capabilities relative to their goals and relative to other people, and so choose the actions that will best realize their preferences given their resources, constraints, and the likely actions of others. In other words, rationalist thinking begins from the assumption that all people (or at least all the people whose actions it seeks to explain) share the same, invariant decision-making process. What certain people do is then a function of two things that *can* vary across actors in these approaches: individuals' preferences and the environmental conditions they face (the distribution of resources and constraints). Much of the most highly regarded rationalist work focuses on an especially elaborate aspect of environmental conditions: strategic interaction between people. Game theory analyzes how rational individuals choose their strategies while taking into account the likely strategies of other rational actors. Whether they employ formal game-theoretic models or not, rationalists then tend to explain ultimate outcomes—the actions people choose—as 'equilibria' that reflect all individuals' most rational strategies. Thus the 'keys' to rationalism are 'the assumption of rationality, the forms of constraint, the nature of the strategic interaction, and the search for an equilibrium solution' (Levi 1997: 23).

Given some of the apparent implications of an explicit assumption of rationality, it is also unsurprising that this work has often been seen as different from anything that could be called structural. Taking much of their vocabulary from economics, rationalists picture people as relatively 'free' agents with the ability to make a wide range of choices. This is why identifying their most rational strategies (and strategic interaction) is so important. Many critics of rationalism decry it as an 'undersocialized' view of human action that exaggerates how much individuals can be treated as atomized, self-contained, autonomous actors (Granovetter 1985). This seems to contrast structuralism of all varieties, which emphasizes how people are shaped and guided (sometimes in a very deterministic way) by their environment. In one famous quip, 'Economics [and rationalism elsewhere] is all about how people make choices; sociology [implicitly structuralism] is all about how they don't have any choices to make' (Duesenberry 1960: 233). This basic view is repeated in the Lichbach and Zuckerman volume: rationalism focuses on the free choices of preference-maximizing individuals, while structuralism concentrates on the larger relations in which all actors are embedded (Katznelson 1997).

If we try to categorize arguments according to the logic by which they explain actions, however, this distinction falls apart. Most rationalists use exactly the logic defined above as structural. Again, if we assume objective rationality, particular actions become a function of two things: individuals' different preferences, or varying environmental conditions (since rationality itself—like anything that one assumes to be true of everyone at all times—cannot explain any particular action). In practice, rationalist work across the social sciences focuses its efforts on the latter cause of variation. This is because rationalists tend to follow economists in holding that people's preferences are either inexplicable (and so can be taken as given) or do not actually vary much with respect to certain arenas or behaviors (and so, for example, a study of any economically related action can reasonably assume universal preferences for wealth-maximization). This leaves variation in environmental conditions as the sole focus of most rationalist analysis—the only source of variation that is not being assumed or taken as given. As Margaret Levi summarizes of all rationalism, 'The real action in the model does not...come from the internal considerations of the actor but from the constraints on her behavior' (Levi 1997: 25). For game theorist George Tsebelis, 'The rational-choice approach focuses its attention on the *constraints* imposed on rational actors...' (Tsebelis 1990: 40, his emphasis; see also Powell 1991).

When we add that most rationalists focus on environmental conditions that they treat as objective, material aspects of physical reality, we fall solidly into my category of structural claims. (Again, Chapter 3 notes that some rationalist claims focus on organizational conditions and so invoke institutional logic.) People choose their actions as a direct function of things that are at least treated as material resources and constraints. To take one famous example, Robert Bates investigates why rational African leaders select economic policies that harm most of their farmers (Bates 1981). He argues that it is rational for them to do so in African conditions of coalition-building and political competition. A variety of market interventions generate resources that can be used to pay off supporters and maintain coercive control. Not all the environmental conditions he invokes are entirely material; some minor points bring in what seem to be institutionalist causal segments.[2] But the core story portrays leaders responding to a fairly raw landscape of resources and coercive power. Most of the variation in man-made institutions across the countries is itself explained as responding rationally to underlying material patterns in crops, industrial activity, and social groups (1981: 120–8).

In a few other well-known examples, Ronald Rogowski points to the relative scarcity or abundance of labor and capital to explain why rational actors form certain political coalitions; Samuel Popkin emphasizes the economic challenges and investment opportunities of village markets to explain political mobilization by rational peasants; and John Mearsheimer

---

[2] For example, Bates sees some variations across countries depending on whether they inherited 'marketing boards' for agricultural products from their colonial predecessors (1981: 122).

traces states' behavior to their position in a global distribution of coercive capabilities (Popkin 1979; Rogowski 1989; Mearsheimer 1990). In each of these works, the core explanatory claims play out how certain actions trace to position vis-à-vis salient material structures. The rest of the equation is taken as constant (rationality), given or assumed (preferences), or as caveats allowing for other kinds of causes that receive little direct attention. Even most elaborate game-theoretic analyses ultimately employ the same logic. People may choose their strategies as a sophisticated function of others' strategies, but the games that people play are explained as derived from their material environment. The environment dictates a certain range of conceivable strategies for each actor, and then game theorists show us that a unique (or small) set of actual choices follows rationally from this 'game'. Actions are still being explained as a direct function of structure, but game theory adds a powerful apparatus to see how that function plays out in interaction (Morrow 1994; Bates et al. 1998).

Structure and rationality are thus sides of the same coin. If we assume rationality and do not focus on variation in preferences, only variation in structure (or institutions) can explain variation in action. Rational pursuit of certain preferences does not dictate any action until we analyze the structural obstacle-course actors inhabit. Conversely, making a strong explanatory claim about material structure implies an assumption of rationality. Though Marx wrote long before the notion of rationality was formalized (and though he played confusingly with vague holist thinking), his arguments only make sense if he also pictured regular, self-interested individuals responding directly to material constraints. If people were not universally rational, they would presumably react in varied ways to the same structural context.[3] As Tsebelis suggests, even if Marx's own writings left individual decision-making in a 'black box', his arguments can be translated into a rationalist vocabulary (Tsebelis 1990: 21; also Roemer 1982, Miller 1978). In terms of what explains particular actions, then, whether rationality is explicit or implicit is not terribly important (though today's rationalists certainly deserve credit for being explicit about their assumptions). The most crucial thing distinguishing all these claims from others is that variation in material structure does their explanatory work.

---

[3] Students of Marx may object that he wrote of situations where people did not respond rationally to structure, as in his thesis of 'false consciousness' (when certain workers do not perceive their interests). Again, my goal is to isolate a core logic, not to acknowledge caveats and nuances.

This relabeling of rationalism is not a criticism. It is a semantic shift intended to facilitate a simpler ordering of the field. In one respect, however, it does conflict with the presentation of some rationalist work. I noted above that both advocates and critics of rationalism often portray it as positing relatively free individuals with a broad margin of maneuver for strategizing. Ostensibly unlike more deterministic approaches, it is 'all about how people make choices'. But the rhetorical claim that one's explanation is about 'rational choice' does not mean that it incorporates agency and freedom. Indeed, the presumption of most rationalist explanation—that external conditions leave only *one* rational choice—is just as deterministic as Marx's statement that structure dictates behavior 'independent of the will'. To the extent that the structural conditions leave more than one rational option—room for meaningful 'choice'— that choice cannot, of course, be explained by structural-rationalist logic (Elster 1986). This is certainly not to say that all structural-rationalist claims are wholly deterministic. It is perfectly feasible and common to argue that structural conditions narrow down a rational actor's options but leave substantial room for agency or other causal elements. Still, if a certain structural-rationalist argument does in fact incorporate more agency, freedom, or 'choice' than a Marxist or other rigidly structural one, it is because the former is a looser, less deterministic, and therefore less powerful version of the same logic.

This last statement segues to the next step. Giving structuralist logic a core definition and subsuming most of rationalism into it establishes its boundaries, at least as well as can be done before getting into the other chapters. The next step is to fill in the boundaries: what kinds of structural claims are out there?

Variants of Structural Explanation

When scholars who emphasize this kind of causal segment disagree substantively, it is about what kinds of structure matter most, whether structure has its own internal dynamics (and what they are), and/or how tightly people are constrained by structure. As suggested above, the last kind of debate is usually best described simply in terms of strong and weak structural claims. Two Marxists might agree on the major patterns of economic structure in the world, but disagree on how fully under-lying structures dictate 'legal and political superstructures'. A strongly structural Marxist sees even the fine points of political institutions as set by available economic resources or technology, while a weakly structural Marxist allows that individual creativity or chance (or some other distinct causal claims) may have filled in elements within the broader lines of rational reactions to structural positioning.

Simple strong-weak terms only *usually* capture the degree of determinism of structural claims because there is also the possibility of particularistic structural claims. It can be perfectly coherent to organize structural logic in a particularistic format, though this is fairly rare. Probably the best-known instances involve natural disasters. The Black Death in fourteenth-century Europe, for example, is often seen as a crucial cause of social and political change in subsequent centuries. Europe's population fell by about a third from 1347 to 1351. This created a labor shortage, leading wages to quintuple in some places, and also concentrated wealth more in the middle and upper classes. A large literature argues that this altered material context—the product of a very contingent development—led to a wide range of reactions that drove economic, social and political change (Gottfried 1983; Herlihy 1997; Huppert 1998). Despite the contingent starting point, we cannot just describe this as a 'weak' structural argument. Some such claims are very deterministic about what happened once the plague had spread. We need the general-particular divide set out in the introductory chapters to capture the distinctiveness of this kind of structural claim.

But the more important historical differences between structural claims concern how they picture structure. What many scholars see as a fundamental divide between rationalism and structuralism, for example, in fact largely reflects a debate between liberal structuralism and Marxist structuralism. These schools of thought are both built almost entirely from causal segments in which rational people react to material constraints and incentives, but they posit different structural landscapes. Both for Marxists and for liberals in the tradition of Adam Smith, the problem of *scarcity* sets the most fundamental constraints and incentives in our lives (Janos 1986). Most action then reflects rational attempts to maximize preferences for wealth (which allows us to overcome scarcity). But these schools offer different analyses of the nature and dynamics of wealth generation— the basic character of 'economic structure'—and so different views of the constraints and incentives that people face. Liberal structuralists see wealth generation as a positive-sum game. Economic exchange (whether of goods, labor, or capital) profits both trading parties by definition (otherwise, suggest liberals, someone would refuse to exchange). Exchange itself effectively creates more wealth. The more individuals can exchange freely—creating broad and deep 'free markets'—the more opportunities all have to gain. More exchange also generates competition between producers of similar products, forcing them to develop their individual productivity and creativity. This enhances the products on offer to all others and increases the general wealth. Thus the strong version of liberal-structural thinking asserts that the basic material structure of human life on Earth signals huge incentives to the expansion of free markets (and, in many variants, to the rise of the 'superstructural' things that many liberals think go with markets, like democracy; as more people get wealthier, they insist quite rationally on equal political participation and rights).[4] Rational people everywhere will eventually follow these incentives to free-market democracy, with some variation given their place in the distribution of economic resources.

Marxists, on the other hand, see wealth generation more as a zero-sum game because they describe economic structures differently. New wealth is created through labor, but some actors possess coercive capabilities (usually through control of means of violence) that allow them to skew the terms of exchange for the products laborers make. Laborers generate all wealth, but the actors who control the 'means of production' (and terms of exchange) take the major cut of the benefits.[5] This basic conflict divides societies into two groups, or 'classes'. In each era of history, the development of new technology and a gradual escalation of conflict between the classes eventually produce a violent revolution, in which coercive capabilities and control of the means of production are reassigned. Thus the strongest version of Marxist thinking asserts that the basic material structure of life on Earth leads rational individuals forward through a step-wise 'dialectic' of class conflict, encouraging them to form and re-form into collective actors based on economic position. Political institutions and other superstructures change with this underlying progression, such that all societies proceed through stages culminating in capitalism and finally socialism—with some variation given local aspects of the distribution of economic resources.

It is easy to understand how debates between these schools came to be seen as pitting a logic of atomized, autonomous, free individuals against a deterministic, collectivist logic of structural relations. The kind

---

[4] Classic 'modernization theory' provides the strongest examples (though with many caveats and ambiguities, see Lerner 1958; Lipset 1959; Rostow 1960).

[5] This is not a fully 'zero-sum' situation in the sense that the amount of wealth in a society is fixed; new technology makes laborers more productive. But at any level of technology that can create a certain amount of wealth, a zero-sum game plays out between laborers and those who control the means of production.

of structural landscape liberals posit keeps rational individuals distinct. People are encouraged to specialize and to develop their own talents in competition with others. The kind of structural landscape Marxists posit drives rational individuals together to collective action. Whatever a laborer's individual talents, her dominant condition is that she and other workers are exploited by the upper class. However much employers may compete for wealth, their dominant condition is a shared interest in keeping up the exploitation. This makes it a small step to conclude that liberal theories take individuals as their 'units', whereas Marxist theories reduce only to classes. Normative agendas encouraged this misleading distinction in the cold war context of the 1950s and 1960s, upholding liberal scholarship as the intellectual defense of individual rights against 'collectivist' Marxist thinking. It was further strengthened by methodological fights around the 'behavioral revolution', which was led by liberals who asserted that direct study of physical individuals was 'scientific' but attention to non-visible 'structure' was not (Farr 1995). Yet to isolate where these schools logically diverge, and where their arguments stand in relation to other scholarship, it is crucial to understand that they are variants on the same causal logic. Marxists (or at least Marxists who make sense) focus on classes not because they somehow dismiss individuals as units for action, but because their view of structure leads individuals to coalesce into classes. Marxists and liberals disagree not about *how to explain action* but about certain features of the environment people inhabit (Roemer 1982: 513).

This point about how structural claims vary on views of structure is just as important to understanding the category as its boundaries. It includes a very wide range of scholarship. In the abstract, there is no limit to the number of ways that we might describe the salient material structures that organize action. Marxists see one kind of material obstacle course that sorts individuals toward certain actions, liberals see a different one, and scholars might be able to come up with many other relatively plausible, coherent ways to describe major structural patterns. We could accept Marx's analysis of economic exchange and class organization but somehow dispute the dynamics of a dialectic of revolution, for example, generating a different overall analysis of structure. We could admit some elements of coercion into a liberal world of mutually beneficial exchange and arrive at a different theory. Or we might assert that the salient patterns of structure in our world are distinct from either Marxist or liberal thinking.

The best-developed example of the latter is realism. Realist thinking ranks the problem of *security* as more fundamental than the scarcity that preoccupies Marxists and liberals. Most action then reflects rational attempts to maximize the kinds of power that allow control of the means of violence. The major constraints that define actors' rational strategies consist of the distribution of resources that relate to physical power— most obviously military or police forces and material, but also underlying components like geographic positioning, demographics or technology. For example, the historian Otto von Hintze famously explained the rise of different kinds of states in Europe as a function of geographic positioning, which dictated the level of security threats:

The different systems of government and administration found among the large European states can be traced back in the main to two types, one of which can be called the English and the other the continental.... [The main difference between them] consists in the fact that on the continent military absolutism with a bureaucratic administration emerges, while in England...the older line of development continues...and leads to what we usually term parliamentarism and self-government. What then is the cause of this pronounced institutional differentiation?...The reason lies above all in the fact that on the continent compelling political imperatives held sway which led to the development of militarism, absolutism, and bureaucracy, whereas such pressures were not present in England.... It was above all geographic position that had its effects.

(von Hintze 1970; also Ertman 1997)

For von Hintze, the island location of the English left them relatively isolated from the kinds of threats from other groups that prevailed on the continent. Continental groups reacted rationally to their high-threat environment, building militaristic absolutist states. The English reacted rationally to their low-threat environment, enjoying a more decentralized, trade-oriented society.

The scholarship that builds in this kind of causal claim is vast. A variant of realist thinking created the split that separated comparative politics from IR as subfields. Hobbes and others reasoned that the creation of the state (Hobbes' 'Leviathan') essentially solved security problems within its borders by centralizing control over the means of violence (Hobbes [1660] 1968). This meant that realism had little to say about domestic politics, which operated on hierarchical principles, rules and law. Interaction between states, however, occurred in 'anarchy' of a 'war of all against all' making security concerns fundamental. This logic simultaneously justified IR as a distinct field of study and made realism its dominant school of thought. Nonetheless, some variants of realist thinking remained alive in comparative politics, especially in the literature on state formation, state breakdown, revolt, and revolution. Scholars like Charles Tilly (1990), Theda Skocpol (1979), and Thomas Ertman (1997) invoke this strand of structural thought (though they all combine such claims with institutionalist segments). They see rational actors whose structural context is as much (or more) about a competitive struggle for security as it is about the pursuit of wealth.

Much like Marxism with its 'class actors', realism has long been attacked for suggesting that states can be treated as unitary actors. Again it is an error to see this position as an unjustified assumption, even if many realists present it this way. The notion that states can be treated as unitary actors flows from substantive and potentially demonstrable claims about the nature of salient structures. The patterns of structure hypothesized by realists create such pervasive threats to rational individuals that people clump tightly together at the level of organization that is best able to provide security—creating the large war-fighting machines of modern states. The context of external threat is hypothesized to swamp other internal disagreements, making it reasonable to treat states as unitary actors. Of course this view leaves many things unexplained. Just as liberals have a hard time with collective action (Olson 1965; Hardin 1982) and Marxists have a hard time with a lack of collective class action (or with the wrong kind of collective action, like nationalism), realists have a hard time squaring their view of structure with intra-national debate or the endurance of small, weak states. Still, critics of realism should combat it on the empirical grounds of perceived threats (or of the links of such threats to state-level cohesion) rather than just suggesting that the unitary state is a silly assumption to make in general. Saying that realists just assume unitary states or that Marxists just assume class actors sets up a straw man competitor, overlooking the testable structural claims both theories posit behind their views of collective action.

In principle, then, structural logic includes a near-infinite number of claims and theories. All posit rational people channeled through material structures, but each describes different patterns and dynamics of structure. In practice, the Marxist, liberal, and realist variants account for the vast majority of fairly 'pure' structural scholarship. On the other hand, variation within the structural category has expanded in recent years with the growth of rationalism. This is because many self-labeled rationalists, while employing what I define as structural logic, have a different goal from more traditional structuralists. The basic project of Marx or Smith or Hobbes (or of contemporary structural thinkers they inspire, like Adam Przeworski (1985) or Ronald Rogowski (1989) or John Mearsheimer

(1990)) is to argue that a *certain* set of salient material structures sets the main framework for much of human action. The basic project of many rationalists today, by contrast, is to show that a great many behaviors are explicable as rational reactions to *some* sort of constraints. Rather than using rationality to focus attention on a certain pattern of structure, they look for whatever structures would make observed choices rational. This means that some rationalists roam fairly freely among the infinite ways in which one might describe structure, highlighting the pattern (or syncretic combination of patterns) that appear to fit observed behavior in a given case. This agenda has also led many rationalists to forage outside of structural claims and into institutionalist ones, as they have found that many patterns of constraint appear to be man-made (Tsebelis 1990; Shepsle and Weingast 1995; Bates et al. 1998).

In their more extreme versions, these moves have provoked criticism. If rationality and preferences are given or assumed, too flexible a treatment of constraints risks voiding the analysis of any substance. Rationalism that is not grounded in specific structures or institutions becomes little more than a vocabulary, plus the assumption that ideational elements and psychology do not matter. As I develop more in Chapter 3, the ironic result is that some of today's 'formal' game-theoretic rationalists are among the least explicit theorists of all in terms of clear claims about how the world works (Elster 2000). On the other hand, this spreading rationalist agenda has also made the assumption of rationality—and so usually, if sometimes implicitly, some kind of structural logic—an expanding feature of the social science landscape. A great deal of scholarship today is built around causal claims that explain people's actions as rational reactions to exogenously given structures in their environment.

Supporting Structural Claims

This book speaks mainly to substantive explanatory options, not the methods by which we demonstrate them. Still, a basic logical sketch of any argument is incomplete without some attention to what it looks like in practice. At the simplest level, demonstrating a structural claim requires four steps. The obvious starting point is evidence of some sort of pattern of structural constraints or incentives: that actors perceived the existence of some concrete landscape. The second step is evidence that patterns of behavior matched position vis-à-vis patterns of structure: that people in similar positions acted similarly, that significant differences in behavior reflected differences in position, and that changes in behavior over time are traced to identifiable changes in structure (or in someone's position within structure). The third step provides the crucial mechanism: logical claims about how the combination of certain preferences with a given structural position dictated observed behavior as the most rational course of action. For a strong structural claim, this means showing that given an actor's preconceived goals, the structural obstacle course left only one best path of action (or that people in a looser structural obstacle course arrive at individually best strategies as a function of each other's options, as showcased in game-theoretic analysis). Lastly, structural claims require at least some evidence of the right kind of decision-making process: that actors sought information about their environment, studied alternative courses of action, and tried to choose the best means for conscious ends.

This last step calls for some evidence of objective rationality. Given that all structural claims confront alternative explanations that dispute the extent of objective rationality, a structural claim must offer evidence of rational processes based on certain preferences to show that its version of events is more accurate than alternatives. An important caveat follows, however, since few scholars argue that full demonstrations of rationality are possible about real-world actions (Fiorina 1995; Levi 1997; but see Tsebelis 1990: 31–9). Documenting rationality demands a huge amount of information: evidence of an actor's relevant preferences, that these preferences and related beliefs contained no internal contradictions, that the actor took all relevant preferences into account, that she gathered the optimal amount of information to inform her choices, that she formed the most rational beliefs given her information, and that the action she chose was the best way to satisfy her preferences given her beliefs and all available options (Elster 1986: 12–16). Most scholars who invoke structural causes adopt a pragmatic solution. Even if a tight empirical demonstration of rationality is impossible, some basic evidence of rational-looking decision-making is acceptable as a conceptual bridge in a causal claim given strong evidence of the other steps in structural logic. At some point we must simply rest our case to have offered evidence of basically rational mental processes, even though this assertion will always be contestable in a strict sense. Since we will see that all logics must make similar pragmatic moves in their evidence of decision-making, however, structural claims are not unusually vulnerable on this score. Institutionalists face the same problem of rationality, and ideational and psychological logics of interpretation must also deal with our limited ability to get into people's heads.

Conclusion

This chapter has made four main points. First, though practically all social scientists lay claim to the powerful word 'structure', only 'materialist' arguments need it to capture their core claims elegantly. Moreover, structural-materialist explanation is so widespread that it deserves its own major category. Its core logic explains people's choices as a direct function of their position in a 'material' landscape—an obstacle course that is at least treated as if it were composed of intersubjectively present physical constraints and resources. These constraints and resources are presented as exogenously given. They may be dynamic, but they are not manipulable by people over the temporal scope of the argument.

Second, explaining action as a direct function of exogenous constraints implies that neither ideational elements nor psychology have major effects on choice, implying the assumption of intersubjectively rational rules for individual decision-making. This means that structure and rationality are complements in explanation. Most of the scholarship described as 'rationalist' can be subsumed under structural logic. We will see that rationalist claims that are not structural are institutional.[6]

Third, there is still huge variation among structural claims. They characterize the patterns and dynamics of structure in many ways. Most scholarship that is built mainly around structural causal segments has emerged from three schools of thought with distinct views of salient structures— Marxism, economic liberalism, and realism—but in principle there is no limit to the number of plausible structural logics.

Fourth, while structural claims depend on rational decision-making processes that are not empirically demonstrable in a strict sense, most scholars will accept a structural argument as well-supported against alternatives given good evidence of structural patterns, evidence that behavior traces to those patterns, logical claims linking the two as tightly as possible, and some evidence of broadly rational-looking decision-making.

---

[6] Some ideational arguments are what I call 'a-rational', arguing that people are rational but confront such an objectively ambiguous world that they can rationally rely on a wide range of interpretations. A small number of psychological arguments are also 'a-rational' (see Chapters 4 and 5).

One reasonable narrowing of the term 'structure', together with an inductive identification of the shared core logic behind some major historical schools of thought, thus takes us into the first cell of my master matrix. Much of the oldest and most highly regarded thinking in the human sciences explains action by tracing people's rational reactions to positioning in an exogenously given obstacle course.

3

Institutional Explanation

Almost as many political scientists claim the title *institutionalist* as the word *structure*. In common social science parlance, an institution is any enduring pattern of behavior among a group of people. Sometimes these patterns take on formal organizational shape, manifesting themselves in buildings, resources, and groups of people who act collectively according to certain rules. In this vein we commonly refer to states, militaries, universities, or other formal organizations as institutions. Sometimes the patterns do not produce formal organizations, such that their only manifestation beyond the behavior is in rules. Thus scholars often describe explicit commitments like laws, treaties, or standards as part of the institutional landscape. Sometimes these rules or commitments are not even explicit, residing only in informal norms or expectations like the handshake. The notion of institution usually incorporates all these phenomena, stretching from concrete organizational actors to intangible traditions or conventions.

More important for this chapter than defining *institution* is to identify what kind of causal claim we can most usefully call institutional*ist*. Not all arguments about institutions are institutionalist arguments. A structurally inclined theorist might use *institution* to designate a set of rules or organizations—say, the Swedish welfare state—but then argue that people maintain this pattern of behavior because they are positioned in certain ways vis-à-vis material structures. Thus a Marxist might claim that Sweden's welfare state reflects a standoff in class conflict, with the bourgeoisie deferring proletarian revolution through side-payments. A strong ideational argument might claim that people maintain certain institutions because they share certain beliefs. Perhaps Swedish cultural attitudes orient them to views of social solidarity that sustain a generous welfare regime. It seems unhelpful to call these claims *institutionalist*, since institutions enter them only as dependent variables, or as by-products of causal processes that are structural or ideational. We should reserve the institutionalist label for claims in which institutions cause something—in which the configuration of formal or informal organizations, rules, or norms around someone causes her to act in certain ways.

Especially since the explosion of the 'new institutionalisms' in political science, economics, and sociology in the 1980s, there is no shortage of such claims (March and Olsen 1989; Hall and Taylor 1996). Three main schools put institutions at the core of their worldview. 'Rationalist institutionalism' shares the rationality assumption of structural logic, but emphasizes man-made institutional constraints in addition to structuralism's material landscape (Williamson 1975; Moe 1984; Shepsle 1986, 1989; Weingast and Marshall 1988; Eggertsson 1990; North 1990; Martin 1992; Oye 1993; Weingast 2002). In principle they see rational individuals channeled to certain choices by a man-made obstacle course of organizations, rules, and flows of information that alters actors' cost-benefit calculations. 'Sociological institutionalists', by contrast, see institutions affecting action through a dynamic of legitimacy or appropriateness (Fligstein 1990; Powell and DiMaggio 1991; Dobbin 1994; Scott and Meyer 1994; Katzenstein 1996). People behave in patterned ways in line with organizational models, rules, and informal norms because they 'take for granted' the legitimacy of these patterns (and assume the illegitimacy of alternatives, or never even imagine them). 'Historical institutionalism' is usually described as standing between these two, combining mechanisms of constraint and legitimacy (Skocpol 1979; Skowronek 1982; Zysman 1983; Hall 1986; Steinmo, Thelen, and Longstreth 1992; Hattam 1993; Steinmo 1993).

On their own terms, all these schools have good reasons for calling themselves institutionalists. Like my treatment of structure, however, this chapter argues that a more restricted use of the label maximizes its usefulness by linking it to a distinct causal logic. A distinctively institutionalist claim, I suggest, argues that the setting-up of certain intersubjectively present institutions channels people unintentionally in certain directions at some later point. Due to their inheritance of a certain institutional obstacle course, actors confront unambiguous constraints that orient them to certain behavior. This differs from structural claims in two fundamental ways. First, it explains action as a reaction to positioning vis-à-vis man-made organizations, rules, or conventions, not vis-à-vis nonmanipulable, given material structures. Second, an implication of focusing on man-made constraints is that people can affect their own constraints to some degree (at least at certain historical junctures). Thus institutionalist explanatory segments incorporate feedback between action and constraints within the temporal scope of their causal claims. This is commonly known as 'path dependence' (among many uses of the phrase: Mahoney and Schensul 2006). The choice of institutions at one point has the unintended consequence of steering subsequent actions along a particular historical path.

Defining institutionalism in this way keeps a large number of important claims in the category, but also excludes much self-labeled 'institutionalist' scholarship that invokes noninstitutional causes. It is widely recognized, for example, that the mechanisms of sociological institutionalism are ideational. Though it may seem an injustice to distance sociologists from the vocabulary of institutions they invented, I will argue for placing that literature in Chapter 4.[1] A bit more complex is my assertion that some rationalist institutionalists do not assign institutions distinct causal importance. When some of these scholars write that a pattern of action is 'institutionalized', they just mean that enduring structural constraints keep rational actors behaving in that pattern. Other rationalist institutionalists adopt the first part of institutionalist logic (explaining actors' choices as a function of position in man-made institutions) but do not invoke the distinct causal mechanism of the second (feedback, unintended consequences, and path dependence). I argue that this is best described not as institutionalist explanation but as a looser kind of structural explanation—following the same kind of logic as structural claims that *treat* a wide range of factors as if they were material, exogenous, nonmanipulable features of the landscape. By showing that sociological institutionalism centers on ideational logic and that some of rationalist institutionalism is either an elaborate or a loose version of structural explanation, I pare down 'institutionalism' to a distinct and widespread logic of argument for which no other elegant term exists.

The main claim of this chapter, then, is that we should limit *institutionalist* to claims that (like structural claims) invoke objective rationality but (unlike structural claims) emphasize man-made constraints *and* path dependence. Some self-labeled institutionalists will dislike this restriction, but I ask that they consider the case below. Once again, it reflects an attempt to clarify causal claims, not to criticize them (except where they are unclear about what causes what—and we encounter a few such cases

---

[1] But note that 'sociological institutionalism' is a certain literature within sociology and political science; there are sociologists who are rationalist or historical institutionalists and remain within the category as I define it.

here). If we want to help our students and our own communication by providing the most pithy, consistent, and comprehensive typology of argument, we must consider the best use of terms for the field as a whole. As with structure, we must give institutionalism a more precise meaning.

Defining Institutional Explanation

The challenge of defining the distinct logic of institutional explanation is different from the challenge of defining structural claims. Whereas scholars use *structure* in a wide range of incompatible ways—and so defining structural explanation consists largely of arguing for one definition of structure—there is relatively little debate about what is an institution. Instead the contradictions arise between the different mechanisms or logics within which scholars invoke institutions. They largely agree on what they are studying but disagree about how it relates to action. Defining institutional explanation consists mostly of considering why only some of the claims that invoke institutions do so in what can usefully be called an institutional*ist* way.

Definitions of *institution* across the social sciences vary in emphasis but are mostly compatible with each other and with the opening paragraph above. The economist Douglass North (who won a Nobel Prize for his contributions to institutionalist economics) defines institutions simply as 'any form of constraint that human beings devise to shape human interaction', or as 'regularities in repetitive interactions... customs and rules that provide a set of incentives and disincentives for individuals' (North 1986, 1990: 4). IR theorist Stephen Krasner defines institutional 'regimes' as 'sets of implicit or explicit principles, norms, rules, and decision-making procedures around which actors' expectations converge in a given area...' (Krasner 1983: 2). Comparative political economist Peter Hall—a leading historical institutionalist—defines institutions as 'the formal rules, compliance procedures, and standard operating practices that structure the relationship between individuals in various units of the polity and economy' (Hall 1986: 19). Even sociological institutionalists tend to be comfortable with similar definitions. In the book that brought sociological institutionalism to the attention of most political scientists, Walter Powell and Paul DiMaggio cite a definition from political scientist Oran Young—'recognized practices consisting of easily identifiable roles, coupled with collections of rules or conventions governing relations among the occupants of those roles' and note that it is 'consonant with much recent work in sociology' (Young 1986; Powell and DiMaggio 1991: 8).

Practically all students of institutions agree, then, on what phenomena they are studying. Yet they have different views of how these phenomena relate to action: where institutions come from, why individuals act within institutionalized patterns of behavior at any given moment, and why institutions endure. Much of this chapter will look at their different approaches in greater detail. Before doing so, however, let me make a case for a tighter definition of *institutionalism* simply by taking a few logical steps from the widely agreed basic definition of institution.

To synthesize the definitions given above, institutions are formal or informal rules, conventions or practices, together with the organizational manifestations these patterns of group behavior sometimes take on. To arrive most logically at a discrete kind of institutionalist explanation, we should focus on what it would mean for this sort of phenomena to cause action in the most direct and distinct way possible. Since rules, conventions, and practices are properties of groups, it is instructive to think about a new individual entering a group within which certain institutions are established. In what kind of claim would the institutions themselves be given the most direct, unmediated causal role in explaining this person's subsequent actions?

For the claim to derive as much of its explanatory power as possible from the shape of the institutions, we must think of our new individual as making regular, predictable decisions based on intersubjectively real external conditions. If we do not, then the new individual's ideational or psychological interpretation of the institutional arrangements he or she is entering might claim some of the causal influence on his or her behavior. Unless we assume very regular decision-making across humans, we might expect for example, that introducing a Chinese woman from 1,000 BC and a twenty-first-century Scandinavian man into this institutional context would lead to different actions for reasons that do not derive from the institutions. In other words, to craft a claim where institutions do as much causal work as possible, we must assume objective rationality. Otherwise our institutionalist claim gets entangled with ideational or psychological logics.

Thus it is most reasonable to see institutional logic as sharing the rationalist micro-foundations of structural causal segments. As my scenario of an individual entering an institutionalized arena suggests, institutionalist claims share with structural ones the basic goal of explaining action by pointing to the shape of an unambiguous external context that exists independently from any individual.[2] We have seen that structural logic relies on rationality to hold preferences and decision-making constant, such that variation in action can be explained as a direct function of structural positioning. The same assumptions allow us to assign the clearest causal force to a position within institutional constraints and incentives. From this perspective, the fundamental difference between structural and institutional logics is that they invoke a model of objective rationality to focus our attention on different kinds of constraints: exogenous, non-manipulable constraints on the one hand, and man-made conventions, rules, and organizations on the other.

But this difference is a big one. It leads to very distinct views of causality. If objective rationality assumptions allow us to distinguish institutionalist claims from ideational or psychological ones—making possible a claim in which institutions themselves shape action, rather than interpretations or misperceptions of them—the key move in distinguishing institutionalist claims from structural ones is to show that man-made constraints are genuinely different and autonomous from the material landscape. The necessary point of departure for this move is a claim about either indeterminacy or unpredictability (or both) in the structural context.

To create the possibility of variation caused directly by man-made institutions, we must begin by arguing either or both of two things. To build an institutionalist claim on structural indeterminacy, we would begin by arguing that loose structural conditions leave rational people without clear signals about how to act over a range of possibilities. Within these indeterminate conditions they choose to create one set of institutions, though others would have been just as reasonable. Then this choice later limits them to certain actions within the previously available range of options. For example, a multinational firm finds that the costs and benefits of setting up production in Indonesia or China are roughly equal. It chooses Indonesia for minor reasons (the CEO had her honeymoon in Indonesia and thinks fondly of it), and enters the Indonesian arena. The firm educates managers in Indonesian languages and culture. Relationships are developed with suppliers and shippers, and management becomes expert in Indonesian politics. Soon the firm's relationship to Indonesia is institutionalized in a set of commitments, accumulated expertise, and a particular organization of resources. The firm sees well-developed institutional resources in Indonesia and high

---

[2] This is not to say that a convention or rule exists independently of the people who accept it, but if the rule or convention is clearly and similarly understood across a group then we could swap out any individual for an outsider and the latter would perceive it similarly.

transitional costs for shifting to China, and so directs all later investment in Asia to Indonesia. Amid fairly loose structural conditions, rational people have built a path of institutional constraints and incentives around their action.[3]

To build an institutionalist claim on structural unpredictability, we would first argue that structural conditions dictated a pattern of action as rational at one point. When structural conditions then change in unpredicted ways, however, people find that man-made institutions dissuade them from adjusting to altered structural incentives. In this scenario the multinational firm initially calculates that Indonesia is the more profitable location and invests there. Then a volcanic eruption severely damages key subcontractors and markets and contributes to political instability. Now China would be the better place to produce in structural terms, but the established organizational resources in Indonesia and the high cost of a move—learning how to work in China, building new relationships there, etc.—keep the firm in Indonesia anyway. A man-made institutional path trumps changing structural conditions in the choices of rational people.

In either scenario (or in one that combines them[4]) it is man-made institutions, neatly distinct from structural conditions, that cause the firm's later choices for Indonesia over China. The abstract logic is that early contingent choices create a pattern of relationships (and perhaps some physical location of concrete resources) that feed back unintentionally to alter constraints and incentives for later decisions. This is how I use the phrase 'path dependence': once someone takes a step down one path, he engenders commitments, expectations, and 'sunk costs'[5] that encourage further steps in similar directions (Krasner 1984; David 1985; Arthur 1988;

---

[3] Institutionalists have increasingly emphasized incentives in addition to constraints, portraying institutions as resources that facilitate certain actions as much as walls that box them in. Thus we might see our firm as having cultivated resources in Indonesia that it is reluctant to relinquish (Streeck and Thelen 2005).

[4] The firm is initially indifferent between Indonesia and China but invests in the former; the volcanic eruption makes China more attractive; but still the costs of reorganization keep the firm in Indonesia.

[5] Note that 'sunk costs' is a phrase taken from economists, and that they use it differently from political scientists. Political scientists use 'sunk costs' to mean 'unavoidable costs of reorganization', as in Paul Pierson's discussion of policy feedback: 'Policies may encourage individuals to develop particular skills, make certain kinds of investments, purchase certain kinds of goods, or devote time and money to certain kinds of organizations. All these decisions generate sunk costs. That is to say, they create commitments' (Pierson 1993: 609). The implication is that rational individuals would factor in these 'sunk costs' in deciding what to do down the line. Economists, by contrast, invented the phrase to designate capital that is already spent and not recoverable, with the implication that a rational individual would *ignore* these costs (they are already 'sunk') in future decisions.

North 1990; Collier and Collier 1991). Other paths were equally available and attractive prior to the first step but are later foreclosed. Arthur Stinchcombe called this a logic of 'historical causes', as opposed to the 'constant cause' logic of structural explanation (Stinchcombe 1968). It is a deeply different way of thinking about action from structural claims, which trace action directly to the current configuration of structure. This does not mean that structuralism is static, of course. There may be dynamics of change within structures themselves. But structural claims treat these dynamics as exogenous and nonmanipulable by the actors. The institutionalist focus on man-made constraints and resources generates a profoundly different mechanism, in which past choices interact with the environment to form the context for future choices.

For path dependence to operate, the impact of institutions on subsequent action must be unintended. If people set up certain institutions in order to 'tie their hands' down the line—consciously creating rules and organizations because this will bring them benefits even if it constrains them somewhat—then we cannot say that the institutions themselves cause them to keep these commitments later on. They decided they wanted to act within the institutional pattern before the institutions existed. Each day thereafter they presumably make the same calculation: that conditions outside of the institutions make continued respect of the institutions desirable overall. Their institutions might look constraining in undesired ways, since they might have had to make some compromises with others to get the institutional features they see as beneficial, but it would still be the external-to-institutions cost–benefit analysis that is doing the actual 'constraining' and 'incentivizing', not the institutions. To make a clear claim in which the institutions themselves become the source of pressure on people's choices, we need to separate the institutions' effects from an external-to-institutions cost-benefit analysis. This means disconnecting institutions' effects from prior-to-institutions foresight, either by arguing that conditions prior to the institutions were ambiguous, or that prior conditions changed unpredictably and people found themselves stuck in 'sticky' (hard to change) institutions. Either way, a claim is only institutionalist to the extent that it sees institutional effects as unintended.[6]

---

[6] Institutionalist arguments need not insist that the effects were unintended by everyone. Imagine, for example, that the Swedish Social Democrats set up the welfare state with considerable foresight, because they knew it would benefit them in various ways. Many middle-class voters initially opposed this, but later on came to see that they too benefited from a wide range of welfare-state programs. Thus they shifted to voting for the Social Democrats and made them the most powerful party in Sweden for fifty years. We need unintended

Three other important observations follow from this basic definition. First, since path dependence is integral to its causal logic, an institutionalist claim cannot be demonstrated by a historical snapshot. It requires a narrative that extends over time. We can only see how the creation of certain institutions matters if we follow their effects on later action (Pierson 2004). Second, the stronger the initial claims about structural indeterminacy or unpredictability, the wider the effects that institutionalist logic can claim. Strong institutionalist claims are especially likely to begin in periods of upheaval, when previous patterns of action are disrupted and options appear fairly open. Peoples' choices at these 'critical junctures' (or 'unsettled periods', 'epochal moments', 'context-making' eras, 'institution-building moments', 'constitutional moments', or times of 'historic commitments': Dahl 1986; Swidler 1986; Unger 1987; Ackerman 1991; Collier and Collier 1991; Berk 1994; Fligstein and Mara-Drita 1996) may select one path from a wide range of possibilities. Third, as I suggested in the introduction, claims about man-made institutions that emerge from indeterminate or unpredictable environments make for inherently particularistic explanations. They suggest that at some point, extra-institutional conditions did not propel people to construct or maintain a certain kind of institutions across some range of options. But after a leap across contingency that set up one institutional arrangement, this man-made obstacle course generated new causal pressures or incentives around subsequent action.

These points receive more attention below. For now I return to the major task of defining what is and is not an institutionalist claim. A few logical steps have connected common definitions of *institution* to the main lines of a definition of *institutionalist* claims. Next I ask how this definition fits the self-labeled 'institutionalisms'. Only a subset of these literatures employs this distinct logic.

'Sociological Institutionalism': Ideational Claims about Institutions

Of the three 'new institutionalisms', sociological institutionalism is easiest to put in its own logical category. It is an ideational approach about institutions, not an institutionalist logic as defined above. This is no secret,

path dependence to explain the middle-class behavior (since if they had been reacting with rational foresight to unambiguous structural conditions they would have supported the Social Democrats from the beginning) but not that of the party leaders.

and any confusion on this point endures only because of the multiple usages of 'institutionalist' that I am trying to discourage. As Powell and DiMaggio note in the magisterial introduction to their 1991 volume, this literature emerged from scholars who were 'intrigued by the effects of culture, ritual, ceremony, and higher-level structures [meaning ideational 'structures'] on organizations'. Their school 'stresses the role of culture in shaping organizational reality', and suggests that 'taken-for-granted scripts, rules, and classifications are the stuff of which institutions are made' (Powell and DiMaggio 1991: 12–15). Sociological institutionalists do not claim that all enduring patterns of behavior reflect taken-for-granted cultural scripts—they typically allow that other things are going on as well—but the institutions that interest them are those that 'take on a rulelike status in social thought and action' (Douglas 1986: 46–8; Powell and DiMaggio 1991: 9). Their actors inhabit a prison without bars or locks, being channeled to particular actions by shared perceptions of appropriate or conceivable options rather than by a tangible obstacle course.

Sociological institutionalists have a good historical and logical rationale for seeing ideational scripts as the core of what we might call institutionalist thinking. Historically, it was sociologists in the tradition of Émile Durkheim who made 'institution' into a key analytical term in the social sciences (as opposed to just a dry object of legalistic study), and they usually used it to mean norms or rules of behavior that were internalized or 'infused with value' by members of a group. Logically, one might argue that patterns of collective behavior that are *not* somehow embedded in culture or ideas—rules or practices that people just adhere to out of convenience on some level—are not really 'institutionalized' in the deepest sense. Mere change in what is convenient can lead people to abandon previous patterns. Thus in partial contradiction to my claim that scholars share a definition of institution, Powell and DiMaggio note:

whereas economists and public-choice theorists often treat *institution* and *convention* as synonyms, sociologists and organization theorists restrict the former term to those conventions that, far from being perceived as mere conveniences, 'take on a rulelike status in social thought and action'.

(Powell and DiMaggio 1991: 9)

Still, this point can be rephrased to be consistent with my claim. Sociological institutionalists focus on the subset of institutions (defined broadly) that affect action by becoming cognitively 'rulelike' aspects of how people interpret the world. People maintain such patterns not because it is just less costly to do so, as in my Indonesian examples above, but because they have difficulty imagining other behaviors, or because they see other behaviors as illegitimate.

Thus the causal force of sociological institutionalism clearly operates through the ideational logic charted in Chapter 4. As unjust as it seems to deprive these sociologists of a term they coined, sociological institutionalist claims will lose none of their force in using an ideational label more consistently. Claims in which institutions affect action through actors' beliefs or norms of legitimacy should be called an ideational claim *about* institutions rather than a sociological institutional*ist* claim. This frees up 'institutionalist' for the distinct logic in which institutions directly shape action by unintentionally altering the costs and benefits of conscious choice over time.

(Some) 'Rationalist Institutionalism': Elaborate and/or Loose Structural Logics

I have argued so far for a rationalist definition of institutionalism. It pictures people responding rationally to man-made constraints within partly indeterminate and/or unpredictable material structures. In my terms, then, 'rationalist institutionalism' is redundant. Unfortunately it does not follow that my definition fits the scholars who call themselves rationalist institutionalists. Many employ logic that is better characterized as structural, in either of two ways.

One variant of noninstitutionalist logic is the kind of claim that founded this school of thought. Consider the following passage from a recent book by some of the most prominent rationalist institutionalists:

Institutions, we argue, induce choices that are regularized because they are made in equilibrium. In equilibrium, no actor would unilaterally choose to alter his or her behavior, given the options, the payoffs, and expectations regarding the choices of others; nor would that actor have reason to revise or alter his or her expectations. Should exogenous factors remain the same, we would expect behavior to remain unaltered. Behavior becomes stable and patterned, or alternatively institutionalized, not because it is imposed, but because it is elicited.

(Bates et al. 1998: 8)

Here a pattern of action reflects 'exogenous factors': constraints and incentives that exist independently from the institution. These factors dictate broad strategic orientations to each actor, and a game-theoretic analysis of strategic interaction further defines each actor's best strategy as a function of the others'. As the phrase 'should exogenous factors remain the same' makes clear, at any given moment it is the constant pressure of extra-institutional factors and strategic interaction that leads actors to their strategies. They are not maintaining a pattern because prior choices led them to commit resources in ways that are now hard to alter (the path-dependent logic of the Indonesian examples). They stay at an equilibrium as long as current exogenous pressures make it their best choice. Instead of displaying the stickiness of past commitments, this situation will apparently move fluidly to a different 'equilibrium' should exogenous factors change. What looks like an 'institutionalized' pattern is just a spontaneous reaction to constraints that exist independently from institutions.

A glance at how this thinking emerged helps clarify its logical foundations. Today's rationalist institutionalist school originated concurrently from two areas: studies of the American Congress and economics. In both areas, certain structural theories suggested that the world should be highly unstable and uncooperative. In the Congress, theorists of 'voting paradoxes' showed that if all members were rational, votes might well switch back and forth between different majorities without any enduring decisions (Arrow 1951; Riker 1980; Nurmi 1999). William Riker summarized: 'What we have learned is simply this: disequilibrium, or the potential that the status quo be upset, is the characteristic feature of politics' (Riker 1980: 443). Similarly, economists observed that problems of incomplete information and opportunism—risks of getting cheated—created 'transaction costs' that seemed pervasive and should deter rational people from trading much (Williamson 1975; North 1990). In the real world, however, it was clear that Congress and other majoritarian bodies made enduring decisions all the time, and that a great deal of transacting went on. This led theorists like North, Riker, and Kenneth Shepsle to reason that something must be structuring collective action to keep rational people at certain 'equilibria'. They developed the view that by agreeing on certain institutional rules and procedures (rules for agenda-setting, adjudication of disputes, requirements for provision of information, etc.), people made their interactions more predictable, overcame transaction costs, and gained the collective capacity to strike enduring deals.

This thinking seemed to showcase institutions that matter. The whole point was ostensibly that the creation of institutions led decision-making to more enduring and cooperative outcomes than were otherwise likely. In Shepsle's summary, 'A configuration of institutions—a framework of rules, procedures, and arrangements—prescribes and constrains the set of choosing agents, the manner in which their preferences may be revealed, the alternatives over which preferences may be expressed, the order in which such expressions occur, and generally the way in which business is conducted' (Shepsle 1986: 52).

Yet this core point was obscured by the view these scholars took of how institutions were created and maintained. They argued that institutions arose and endured precisely because they responded to actors' preexisting interests in more enduring outcomes (and typically in fairly specific enduring outcomes). Proposals to create or modify an institution were 'assessed over many policy choices and evaluated over the duration it [was] expected to survive', and rational people figured out that certain rules would best enable them to reach certain stable outcomes (Shepsle 1986: 74). This theory of institutional creation undercut the subsequent causal impact of the institutions, since it blocked the inherently unintended dynamic of path dependence. Again, if institutions arise and endure because they meet the participants' preexisting interests, then we do not need the institutions to explain why people undertake the 'institutionalized' pattern of action. If for some reason the institutions disappeared—if, say, all the Congressional rulebooks were lost in a fire— the same patterns would presumably soon re-emerge as a function of the same exogenous interests. Conversely, if changes to exogenous conditions altered actors' preferences today—if war or economic downturn shifted the policies politicians wanted—nothing would prevent them from altering the institutions to arrive at different outcomes. Such people are not defining their strategies in response to a man-made institutional obstacle course. Nor does the creation of institutions affect their action in a meaningful sense. They are defining their strategies in response to an obstacle course that exists independently from the institutions, and generating institutions as a by-product. Rather than institutionalist logic, this is an elaborate structural logic about institutions. Shepsle's use of the phrase 'structure-induced equilibrium' for this logic was more appropriate than he intended (Shepsle 1979).

This reasoning is common to most rationalist institutionalists. Most also introduce some more genuinely institutionalist logic alongside it, however. As Powell and DiMaggio write,

Most [rationalist institutionalists] assume that actors construct institutions that achieve the outcomes they desire, rarely asking where preferences come from or considering feedback mechanisms between interests and institutions. To be sure, actors' options are limited by sunk costs in existing arrangements, and their strategies may even yield unintended effects. But the thrust of these approaches is to view institutional arrangements as adaptive solutions to problems of opportunism, imperfect or asymmetric information, and costly monitoring.

(1991: 9)

The 'to be sure' phrase notes that these authors often include the dynamics of my Indonesian examples. If structures change such that institutions no longer reflect an 'equilibrium' (i.e. no longer effectively lessen transaction costs and generate stable, desirable outcomes), it may be costly to get all the participants together again to change the institutions. In other words, there may be transaction costs to institutional change, and so institutions may be somewhat constraining and nonadaptive to structural conditions. Except under conditions of dramatic exogenous change or where renegotiation is unusually easy, then, people will tinker with institutions instead of crafting new ones de novo—respecting at least some constraints from their institutional heritage. Many of these authors also emphasize some degree of uncertainty, and so allow that institutions can have unforeseen consequences. Unforeseen exogenous developments may make institutions ill-fitted to current problems, but they may be retained anyway because of 'sunk costs'. Unforeseen consequences may also arise at a deeper level in daily practices. As North (1990) develops, institutions can organize the flow of information and so the perception of future problems. People with bounded rationality—rational decision-making but a limited capacity for gathering and processing information—may be carried along a particular path by their previous institutional choices.

The good news, then, is that there is some institutionalist logic in rationalist institutionalism. But this is true only to the extent that this work emphasizes uncertainty, unforeseen developments, and the nonadaptive nature of institutions. Rationalist institutionalists who strongly emphasize rational foresight and adaptive institutions have a very ambiguous relationship with institutionalist explanation. Even some who refer to the transaction costs of institutional change do not end up ascribing clear causal force to institutions. If we treat people as very rational (accurately perceiving transaction costs or voting paradoxes and building precise institutions to solve long-term problems) then presumably they also foresee the future transaction costs of institutional modifications. If such people enter into new institutions knowing they will be difficult to alter—if, say, they know that institutional negotiations can only feasibly be held every ten years—this is because their preexisting rational interests make it a good deal. But if this is the case, then at every moment during those ten years, they are going along with the institutional rules not because they are somehow bound into them, but because they calculated going in that the benefits of having such institutions over that period would exceed the costs. Only to the extent that unforeseen developments arise— if conditions change and they want to modify the institutions before the ten years are up, but cannot—does this approach assign any clear causal force to the institutions. Only then do path-dependent consequences of the institutions trump an extra-institutional calculation of costs and benefits.

Thus the structural logic of 'structure-induced equilibrium' is one way in which self-labeled rationalist institutionalists step away from a distinct institutionalist logic. Once again this is a point about categorization, not a substantive criticism. An elaborate structural logic about institutions may well capture important political dynamics, but it is confusing to call it institutionalist explanation.

The second way that some rationalist institutionalists fall outside my institutionalist category is still messier to categorize. At first glance it looks like a sort of 'half-way institutionalism'. On closer inspection it is best seen as a loose version of structural logic.

These arguments portray actors reading their initial interests at least partly off organizations and rules—rational people *are* being channeled to certain actions through a man-made obstacle course—but do not invoke dynamics of feedback and path dependence. This scholarship tends to be game-theoretic, and effectively omits path-dependent dynamics for the reason discussed above: it assumes very rational actors with strong fore-sight, rarely including unintended consequences, such that any creation or modification of institutions is a derivation of initial or exogenously changing conditions rather than the development of distinct new con-straints. They take an institutional landscape as their starting point but do not make institutionalist claims about it.

Prominent examples in political science arise in the work of Robert Bates, Margaret Levi, or Barry Weingast (authors of the *Analytic Narratives* cited earlier), or that of George Tsebelis (Bates 1981, 1989; Levi 1988; Tsebelis 1990; Weingast 1997; Bates et al. 1998). In all of this literature the actors tend to seek material outcomes—generally more wealth or security—but their position in an institutional landscape is crucial to how they formulate their initial interests. Much of Bates' and Levi's work focuses on rulers whose institutional positions lead them to perceive interests in maximizing state tax revenue or political support. Especially

prominent in the wide-ranging work of Weingast and Tsebelis are legislators or administrators whose institutional positions lead them to favor
certain electoral strategies, coalitions, or new institution-building. Tsebelis
is especially explicit about taking the institutional landscape as his point
of departure:

The rational-choice approach focuses its attention on the *constraints* imposed on
rational actors—the institutions of a society. That the rational-choice approach is
unconcerned with individuals or actors and focuses its attention on political and
social institutions seems paradoxical. The reason for this paradox is simple: individual action is assumed to be optimal adaptation to an institutional environment,
and the interaction between individuals is assumed to be an optimal response to
each other. Therefore, the prevailing institutions (the rules of the game) determine
the behavior of the actors, which in turn produces political or social outcomes.

(Tsebelis 1990: 40, his emphasis)

This passage is odd given that so much rational-choice work highlights
material rather than institutional constraints, but it displays well that
there is rationalist theory that takes institutions seriously as a point of
departure. Such a view seems to be borne out in these scholars' substantive
arguments. Bates relies on institutional actors (the executive and two
houses of Congress) to analyze US support for the International Coffee
Organization (ICO), and asserts that the institutional rules of the ICO
'shape[d] the conduct of actors...' (Bates 1998). Levi's discussion of rules
for military conscription is built around institutionally defined actors like
the army, state policymakers, and legislators, and explains the nineteenth-
century disappearance of paid 'commutation' (where the rich bought
exemptions from military conscription) partly as a result of increasing
state institutional capacity to monitor conscription (Levi 1998). Tsebelis
and Geoffrey Garrett approach integration in the European Union (EU) by
focusing on interactions between the European Commission, European
Parliament, and national governments, and argue that recent modifications to the EU institutions have substantially altered governments'
abilities to influence concrete policy outcomes. They conclude, 'It is only
by analyzing the effects of institutional rules on the interactions among
these institutions that one can understand the policies that are produced
every day in the EU and hence the nature of the integration process itself'
(Garrett and Tsebelis 1996).

The paradox of this scholarship is that it combines this institutional
starting-point with an especially strong emphasis on rationality, foresight,
and fluidly adaptive institutions. This means that it jettisons (or at best

81

renders ambiguous) causal segments of institutionalist explanation. In contrast to related scholars like North or even Shepsle, Tsebelis and the contributors to *Analytic Narratives* pay almost no attention to uncertainty or unintended consequences (Tsebelis 1990: 18–47; Elster 2000). Bates, Levi, or Tsebelis take preexisting institutions as important parts of the landscape that define actors and their initial interests, but only in their point of departure. Beyond this exogenously given obstacle course, they portray action as proceeding with such complete rational foresight that institutional dynamics of path dependence and feedback are never engaged. New institutions arise, change, or fall in relatively fluid adaptation to conditions external to the institutions. In Bates' ICO study, for example, exogenous changes eventually alter US strategies and the ICO collapses almost immediately. The construction and operation of the ICO does not affect the bottom line of the story. It arises as a by-product of the initial configuration of actors' strategies, and disappears when that configuration changes. Overall, the argument is one of 'structure-induced equilibrium', with the modification that preexisting institutions are taken as a major part of the original conditions. Weingast (2002) echoes this characterization, presenting rationalist institutionalism as focusing either on adaptive reactions to extra-institutional problems or on institutions as exogenous structures.

Since this kind of argument incorporates half of my definition of institutionalist logic (man-made constraints) but not the other half (path dependence), a label like 'half-way institutionalism' might seem appropriate. Why then do I suggest it should be seen as loose structural explanation? The answer recalls an argument from Chapter 2. There I noted that many structuralists *treat* the constraints they highlight as material and exogenous to human action, even though the natural, given quality of these constraints may be open to debate. Marx may not have believed entirely that property relations emanated fully from underlying material reality, but he almost always treated them as if they did. In his core logic, these elements became just as independent from human choice as the physical geography of mountains and oceans. Even though Tsebelis, Bates, or Levi see institutions as more important features of the landscape, they make the same move. They treat the institutions in the initial landscape as exogenously given structures. Any change to the institutions occurs for exogenous reasons. The institutions that are part of the actual action—created or modified by the actors within the period analyzed—only appear as flexible, adaptive by-products of extra-institutional strategic deals.

What distinguishes these scholars from more obviously structural thinkers, then, is not that they add in claims in which institutions play a distinct causal role, but that they broaden the scope of exogenously given 'structures' to include not just material or possibly material patterns but also a wide variety of man-made institutions. Despite the purely institutional language of the Tsebelis passage above, all these scholars mix in more standard material factors as part of their landscapes. Bates' coffee-market regulators are under pressure from hard-core business interests and security concerns, Levi's conscripts are worried about death and money, and Tsebelis's EU protagonists are concerned about material aspects of policy outcomes. In effect they draw very freely on a broad array of structures or institutions to set up initial conditions, and then make structural claims (and in particular 'structure-induced equilibrium' claims) within them. Once we characterize them this way, their place in my typology finally becomes clear. They are a very loose version of structural logic, allowing an unusually wide range of things to be treated as a 'structure', and making no general claims about the salience of particular 'structures' across time and space.

This brings me back to a further point from Chapter 2. There I mentioned that some of the more recent rationalist theorists do not invoke rationality to focus our attention on the causal impact of a certain kind of structural landscape (as did traditional structural theorists like Marxists or realists). Rather, their explicit goal is to show more broadly that most action can be explained as a rational response to *some* set of constraints. These self-labeled rationalist institutionalists are the clearest examples. Rather than using rationality as a tool to display the power of a substantive view of the world, they just aim to show that rationality is a useful tool in a wide range of situations. They disconnect the powerful tool of rationality from foundations in a view of salient constraints, allowing them to draw on a very wide menu of structural or institutional factors to interpret action as rational.[7]

This is not necessarily an illegitimate move. Few political scientists today commit to a strong general theory like that of Marx or other traditional structural thinkers. The 'historical institutionalists' we will see in the next section, for example, also draw on a wide range of structural, institutional, and even ideational factors to explain any given action. In principle nothing prevents loose structuralists from moving from their

---

[7] Some of these loose structuralist scholars also expand their view of things that can be treated as 'structures' so far as to include ideational elements like emotions and ideas as fixed 'constraints' on rational actors (Friedman 1996; Shapiro 1998; Blyth 2003).

framework to robust explanatory claims that they demonstrate as summarized at the end of Chapter 2: searching for structural or institutional conditions that might make observed actions rational, documenting these conditions, elaborating the rationale for why they dictated certain actions, and offering some evidence of largely rational decision-making processes (and also providing evidence to undercut alternative explanations). But in practice, these scholars have confronted serious criticism about the weakness of their empirical work, both in supporting their own claims and in taking alternative explanations seriously. According to scholars as different as Ian Shapiro (a prominent critic of rational choice work) and Jon Elster (a major theorist of rational action), this kind of formal rationalism without substantive theory often produces ad hoc, poorly researched arguments (Green and Shapiro 1994; Shapiro 1998; Elster 2000). Bates, Levi, Tsebelis, and others tend to speculate that certain conditions might have made observed actions rational, offer some evidence that this speculation is not obviously wrong, and leave it at that. Their critics suggest that they mistake game-theoretical methods for a substantive view of the world, and so do not take seriously enough the task of empirical demonstration against competing claims. I suspect this is related to the misperception that 'rationalism' is a substantive approach to explanation. As we saw in Chapter 2, that view requires an odd inattention to the structural or institutional conditions that do all the explanatory work in rationalist claims (even though Levi and Tsebelis point out this logic in passages I have cited).

But I will leave more substantive critiques to others. This section argued that we must look closely to find distinctively institutionalist logic in rationalist institutionalism. Some scholars who use this label belong solidly in the structural category. Another subset are very loose theorists who effectively expand structural logic to include institutions. Lest this be seen as an attack on rationalist institutionalism overall, let me repeat that the chapter's main point is the opposite: I argue that a variant of rationalist scholarship should define institutionalist logic overall. The logic in which institutions exert the most distinct causal effects is one in which rational people respond to an institutional landscape, and are carried along by the dynamics of path dependence that man-made constraints and incentives imply. By no means is this logic crippled by any of the issues raised above. The problem of foresight is only a problem for arguments that insist on foresight. There is no reason why we cannot assume rationality and also picture a relatively unpredictable and/or indeterminate world in which rational people have incomplete foresight.

In such a world, institutions could have unforeseen consequences all the time, and path dependence could be pervasive.

Historical Institutionalism: Institutionalism and More

So far I have staked out the terrain for institutionalist logic by cutting away literature on its ideational and structural flanks. Most overviews of 'institutionalisms' place the other major school, 'historical institutionalism', in a middle position between their rationalist and sociological compatriots. Readers may thus expect my middle-ground definition to correspond largely to this school. This is not entirely wrong, as historical-institutionalist scholars like Theda Skocpol, Stephen Skowronek, or Sven Steinmo offer some of the cleanest examples of institutionalist logic. More generally, historical institutionalism as a school is more consistent than any other in building its claims around institutional logic as I have defined it. But some historical institutionalists also lay claim to the middle ground in a way that clashes with my calls for clarity. They hold a middle position partly by using the widest definition of institutionalism, drawing eclectically—and often ambiguously—on both institutionalist and noninstitutionalist claims. There is nothing wrong with combining theoretical logics, of course, and this eclecticism is often portrayed as their strength. But as historical institutionalist Peter Hall writes:

[E]clecticism has its costs: historical institutionalism has devoted less attention than the other schools to developing a sophisticated understanding of exactly how institutions affect behavior, and some of its works are less careful than they should be about specifying the precise causal chain through which the institutions they identify as important are affecting the behavior they are meant to explain.

(Hall and Taylor 1996: 950)

I will argue that historical institutionalism is best seen as a relatively diverse group of scholars, of which some offer fairly distinct institutionalist claims and others mix institutionalist and ideational logics. In my view—biased, I should note, by my own intellectual proximity to this work—the latter group often offer especially intriguing accounts of the impact of institutions. I suspect that organizational channeling does often interact with beliefs or norms of desirability, feasibility, and appropriateness. But I expect that both champions and critics of this literature will agree that it would contribute more if its compound logic were more explicit.

85

Historical institutionalism emerged in the late 1970s and early 1980s from a series of studies in historical sociology and political economy. Though they worked on a variety of empirical issues, they coalesced as a school around a basic point: organizations are partly autonomous from the structural landscape and constrain or empower certain kinds of action. Skocpol's *States and Social Revolutions* (1979), for example, argued that social revolutions occur when two things happen: ruling classes break normally close ties with state organizations (weakening a country's top-down repressive apparatus) and lower classes obtain the organizational means to revolt (allowing a bottom-up challenge). On the one hand, Skocpol framed these stories within structural claims. She placed a realist emphasis on geopolitical constraints, with pressures from war-fighting driving the state to demand more resources from ruling classes and so embittering their relationship. She also borrowed a basic model of class conflict from Marx. On the other hand, whether or not geopolitical pressure and class conflict escalated into revolution turned on the organizations that countries inherited from the past. Some states were better able than others to extract resources from ruling classes and neutralize their objections; some organizational patterns in village life facilitated collective mobilization while others blocked it. No one created these institutions to have these effects, but their unintended consequences later steered countries into or away from upheaval.

To take another prominent example, Skowronek (1982) argued that the institutional inheritance of preindustrial America was to blame for the weak, disjointed condition of federal government in the twentieth century. The US Constitution created a union with highly decentralized institutions, linked at the national level only by courts and political parties. The latter were themselves highly decentralized, rooted in local political machines. As industrialization accelerated after the Civil War, however, the USA confronted a variety of structural pressures for greater central administrative capacity. Businessmen pushed to broaden state markets into national ones, citizens demanded that regulatory powers keep the same scope as market actors, class conflict extended to a national level, and the country overall faced pressures for a national military. Yet Americans found their responses constrained by earlier institutional choices. Political parties now had vested interests in the local spoils of a decentralized system, and the political elite fought to block the rise of central administration. Although structural pressures eventually produced a national administrative state, it emerged in a much more partial and messy way than in other industrializing countries. An organizational legacy limited Americans' ability to respond to changing structural challenges.

Skocpol and Skowronek's logic was clearly a rationalist variant of institutionalism. Their actors pursued individual interests in greater power, security, and wealth given their available options, and the organizational constraints they confronted were objectively present. Yet unlike the rationalist institutionalist school that was emerging concurrently in economics and Congressional studies, they pictured a complex and fairly unpredictable world in which rational people were constantly confronted by unforeseen consequences of their earlier choices. Major institutions arose through incremental processes and tended to cope with a wide range of cross-cutting imperatives, and so were often poorly suited for new challenges. Institutional adaptation was limited because the transaction costs to substantial institutional change were often massive, and because small groups of people often possessed coercive power to defend existing arrangements. It followed that path dependence was a pervasive dynamic of political action. At any given moment rational actors would seek to construct or alter institutions to best further their foreseeable interests, but even powerful people usually found themselves captive to some unintended consequences of past action.

More recent historical institutionalist work has stretched the bounds of the school beyond rationalist foundations. To some degree this is probably a reaction to rationalist institutionalism, as these more inductive, methodologically qualitative scholars try to stress what is special about their own approach. To some degree it has happened simply as students of the early historical institutionalists moved into different logics while holding on to the label (or as early historical institutionalists themselves moved in new directions) (Hall 1989; Katzenstein 1996; Blyth 2002; Orren and Skowronek 2004; Thelen 2004). From both sources comes the notion that today's historical institutionalism incorporates both the rationalist logic of a path-dependent obstacle course and claims about how institutions reach more deeply into the ideational process of 'preference formation'. The most prominent edited volume on historical institutionalism summarizes their 'core difference' with rationalist institutionalism in the claim that 'not just the *strategies* but also the *goals* actors pursue are shaped by the institutional context' (Thelen and Steinmo 1992). Their school, they suggest, sees institutions not simply as an external obstacle course but also as a web of rules and norms of authority that reaches into how actors define themselves and what they seek.

My typology suggests that historical institutionalists deserve both more and less credit for uniqueness than they sometimes claim. They are more unusual than they realize in relying consistently on distinctively institutionalist logic. Only some self-labeled rationalist institutionalists can say the same. Yet it does not make sense historically or logically to say that their school is defined by a focus on how institutions affect both strategies and deep 'preference formation'. Historically speaking, this definition does not apply to some of their canonical works, like the very rationalist early books by Skocpol and Skowronek. Peter Hall and Rosemary Taylor add that '[m]any of the arguments recently produced by this school could readily be translated into rational choice terms', citing Ellen Immergut and some of Hall's own work (Immergut 1992; Steinmo 1993, 1994; Hall 1994; Hall and Taylor 1996; Hall and Soskice 2001). Much of historical institutionalism pictures institutions as a very real obstacle course and does not engage issues of preference formation or norm-based action. Logically speaking, as Hall and Taylor note elsewhere, the historical institutionalists who do delve into norms, ideas, and preference formation have not set out a distinctive synthesis. They draw on both rationalist organizational-obstacle-course thinking and sociological-institutionalist-style thinking to create 'something of an amalgam but not one that represents a fully realized alternative to either of these approaches' (Hall and Taylor 1998: 958). This amalgam may be powerful in some concrete arguments, but it is not a distinct new logical position.

In terms of explanatory logic, then, historical institutionalists are a broad school.[8] All employ some institutionalist causal segments. They concede to various degrees that institutional path dependence operates within some bounds of structural logic. Some are additionally interested in norms, ideas, and other aspects of ideational logic. Like the confusion around wide-ranging 'rationalist institutionalism' confronted in the previous section, this compound logic is often difficult to classify clearly. As we saw above, compound approaches that are difficult to classify can run into substantive criticism. Just as loose structuralists are often accused of dangerously ad hoc flexibility, some historical institutionalists seem to move fairly opportunistically between institutional and ideational arguments. They suffer less from strong attacks on this score because historical institutionalists—unlike their formal rationalist brethren—are widely seen as very strong empirical researchers. They are rarely accused

---

[8] Breakdowns of literature by methods rather than explanatory logic tend to portray historical institutionalists as a somewhat tighter group, since they all undertake qualitative, macro-historical, empirically detailed research (Pierson and Skocpol 2002).

of simply speculating abstractly about the conditions that might have motivated certain actions. But sometimes they advance claims about how institutions and ideational factors cause certain actions without being explicit about how we would know when and how much action reflects one or the other. This can leave ambiguity about what they are really arguing.

One brief example suffices to illustrate the point. Victoria Hattam offers one of historical institutionalism's most explicit and well-regarded invocations of both institutional and ideational factors in her work on working-class organization in the USA and the UK:

> The argument...has two interrelated components: one institutional and one interpretive. The institutional argument claims that differences in state structure lead to differences in English and American labor strategies. Particular configurations of institutional power provided very different incentives and constraints for workers in the two countries and eventually channeled labor protest along different paths.... The second leg of the argument adds an interpretative component that emphasizes the *changing significance* of state structures for working-class formation both over time and across organizations. We will see that particular ideologies and cultural traditions were themselves constitutive of economic interests and political power.
>
> (Hattam 1992: 156–7, her emphasis)

Hattam's institutionalist claim is that differences in state organization encouraged workers to mobilize politically in the UK but to avoid electoral politics in the USA. Both the USA and the UK enacted legislation to criminalize labor movements as conspiracies. In the USA, powerful courts voided later legislative attempts to override these statutes, so workers rationally saw little incentive to seek legislative action. In the UK, the courts tended to defer to the legislature, so workers were attracted to party mobilization by rational hopes to legalize union activism. Her ideational argument is that the divergence did not occur until a broad ideological shift in the second half of the nineteenth century. Earlier workers in both arenas focused more on gaining political participation than on rights to unionization and strikes. Since this goal made no challenge to the balance of power between courts and legislatures, the situation remained fairly similar in both countries. Only when new ideas shifted workers' goals to unionization did they challenge something over which courts had jurisdiction—and so different institutional positions of courts led to different outcomes on either side of the Atlantic.

Many reviewers have found this argument elegant and important.[9] Yet like most historical institutionalist work that draws on both institutionalist and ideational claims, Hattam is vague about why and how much the institutionalist parts of the story are institutionalist. (The same applies to how much the ideational parts are ideational, but I focus on institutionalism here.) Several reviewers point out, for example, that Hattam is unclear on how much the American Federation of Labor's turn away from political activism was a straightforwardly rational reaction to the institutional obstacle of the judiciary. They note that other movements in American history have not been deterred by similar judicial stonewalling (on abolition or civil rights), and more broadly that political activism can be either discouraged or galvanized by nonmajoritarian repression. Hattam's logic-of-position argument is not fleshed out enough to nail down to what extent the workers' position vis-à-vis courts rationally dictated a turn away from politics, as opposed to at least partly reflecting their interpretation of their position. Her invocation of interpretive logic to explain other aspects of the workers' strategic choices encourages us to wonder why she did not see such dynamics there as well.

I am not expert enough on nineteenth-century American politics to evaluate how strongly these objections threaten Hattam's argument, but that is not the point. The point is that historical institutionalists who combine institutional and ideational logics often leave this kind of ambiguity. Historical institutionalists who use a consistently rationalist obstacle-course vocabulary—again, like the major books by Skowronek, Skocpol, or Steinmo—do not have this problem. Others might object that ideational elements *should* matter in their accounts, but at least their readers know what they are arguing (for such objections, Dobbin 1994; Sewell 1996). Those who introduce ideational claims alongside institutionalist claims, on the other hand, force themselves (or should) to be very careful and explicit about how much each one is operating. This is the price to pay for being allowed to draw on multiple theoretical sources.

Being explicit about when action reflects objective institutional conditions or ideational interpretations does not require a vast general theory about when institutions or ideational elements matter. It just requires enough explicit logic and methodological precision to nail down when we see evidence of institutions or ideational elements mattering (Parsons 2003). With that in mind, I expect that most historical institutionalists

---

[9] See reviews in the *American Political Science Review* 88: 3 (September 1994), 764–5; *American Historical Review* 99: 4 (October 1994), 1396–7; *Journal of Economic History* 54 (March 1994), 216–18; *Industrial and Labor Relations Review* 48 (April 1995), 598–600.

will sympathize with this call for more explicit attention to the relative importance of institutions and culture or ideas. Several citations above underscore that I am echoing their own self-analyses (Hall and Taylor 1996, 1998; Immergut 1998; Collier 1999; Lieberman 2001). I must also repeat my support for combined arguments. This call for attention to the lines between institutional and ideational claims is not meant to discourage a compound approach. Advocates of compound explanations must be especially careful, though, about how multiple claims fit together.

Supporting Institutionalist Claims

To support an institutionalist causal segment we need two kinds of evidence. First, in a temporally and conceptually proximate sense, we must document how and to what extent actions flow directly from institutional conditions. This task is similar to the steps that support a structural claim. We need to document the pattern of institutional constraints or incentives around the time of the action, provide a logic by which position in this pattern would dictate certain actions, show that the pattern of action corresponds to the institutional patterns, and (since this is a rationalist logic) offer at least some evidence that actors exhibited broadly rational decision-making and actually followed the logic we have posited.

The other set of steps to support an institutionalist claim reflects the man-made, particularistic nature of this kind of cause. As the introductory chapters stressed, institutions are consequences of earlier actions. Even once we demonstrate their apparent proximate causal importance in a pattern of action, their effects only become distinctly institutional to the extent that we show that the institutions do not reduce to other conditions. We must show that at some point in the past, extra-institutional conditions were insufficient to cause people to create or maintain this institutional pattern of action rather than some range of alternatives. In other words, we must document the contingency which was resolved by the particularistic logic of institutional path dependence. Only given this sense of historical alternatives can we substantiate and specify a distinctly institutionalist causal claim.

Documenting contingency may seem a tall order, but it is no more difficult than documenting causality. Arguing that a certain set of structural conditions left a certain range of options open, for example, is just the mirror image of arguing that structural conditions constrained or propelled people toward a certain course of action. At first glance it may seem harder to support the negative claim that no causal vectors shut down contingency than to argue positively for one causal vector, but these arguments follow the same process. Arguing positively that some range of variation traces to one cause requires us to show, in principle, that no other cause accounted for some of that variation. In other words, positive causal arguments themselves depend directly on negative claims about the contingency of competing causes. In neither kind of claim can we ever address all potential causes. There is always room to suspect that some cause has escaped our notice. We usually truncate our search for causes by focusing pragmatically on the fairly small set of competing claims that scholars have advanced on similar topics. While one of the concluding points of this book is that we must extend this set further than most scholars do—working harder to debate a range of abstractly plausible alternative claims—we can never come close to chasing down every imaginable hypothesis. This is fine: ultimately we are debating other scholars, not Truth itself. Respectable support for causal claims forces us to carve out a range of causal effect for one cause vis-à-vis other active hypotheses (plus, perhaps, a few arguments that may not be present in a specific debate but which have substantial grounding in broader theoretical approaches). Respectable support for claims about contingency forces us to mobilize evidence that a similar range of actively competing or broadly legitimate hypotheses fail to explain across a certain range of actions (Mahoney 2000).

Conclusion

This chapter began by noting an implicit consensus on how to define *institution* but considerable disagreement on how to link institutions to action. To allow *institutionalist* to designate a clear and distinct logic of explanation, I first considered in the abstract what kind of claims would give the most direct and irreducible force to institutions. To separate institutionalist claims from ideational or psychological interpretations, they must employ a logic where rational individuals confront intersubjectively present, man-made organizations, rules, or conventions. To separate institutionalist claims from structural causality, these constraints must be unintended legacies of past choices made amid structural ambiguity or unpredictability, not intentional solutions or adaptations to structural conditions.

Next I argued that this kind of institutionalist causal segment does not match cleanly to any of the schools that claim the institutionalist mantle. Sociological institutionalists focus on ideational dynamics in which institutions affect action by shaping interpretations of legitimate or conceivable behavior. The most common logic in rationalist institutionalist work is one of 'structure-induced equilibrium', with institutions cast as by-products of structural conditions. Other rationalist institutionalists take institutions seriously as constraints but ignore path dependence, effectively treating inherited institutions as a loose extension of structure. Only to the extent that rationalist institutionalists include unintended consequences—which many do to some degree—do they employ distinctly institutionalist logic. Historical institutionalists are the most consistent advocates of institutionalist claims, but often mix them with ideational logic. To realize the promise of this compound logic, historical institutionalists must be more careful about the relative contributions of its components.

The last section noted that institutionalist claims demand a two-step demonstration. First they must link institutional positions to action, using evidence much like that needed to link structural positions to action. Then they must do the reverse for extra-institutional conditions—showing that at some point structures, ideational elements, and psychology (and perhaps other preexisting institutions) did not link clearly to patterns of action, thereby establishing a range of contingency that institutions later resolved. The product is an argument with a very distinctive feel, in which rational people unintentionally construct their own future. It exhibits the combination of positional thinking with particularity that defines the second box of my master matrix.

4

Ideational Explanation

Ideational argument is another rich tradition in thinking on politics, but has never held the status of structure (a term practically everyone wants to claim) or institutions (the rage of the past few decades). There has been an ideational or cultural upswing in political science since the 1990s, and it probably enjoys a stronger footing in the discipline than ever before. Yet when many political scientists hear the word 'culture', they still share Goering's famous inclination to reach for a gun. For many reasons they suspect that ideas, norms, and culture are not amenable to serious causal argument. Methodologically, intangible ideational elements seem less measurable than structures or institutions. Theoretically, ideational claims are inherently particularistic—about the invented beliefs of particular humans—and obstruct the scientific goal of generalization.

There are also historical reasons for skepticism. Many ideational scholars themselves posit tension between ideational elements and causal claims. No less an authority than Weber saw a divide between causal explanation and the understanding (*Verstehen*) necessary to access ideational meaning. Many scholars echo this view, partly exempting them from engaging structural or institutional claims (and vice versa). Another historical problem is that the best-known exemplars of ideational argument in political science are not well regarded. The notion of 'political culture' in particular has 'what many consider a shady past', as sociologist Margaret Somers (1995) puts it. The most famous works in this vein play into criticisms of ideational thinking as static, monolithic, and tautological—the kind of view captured in jokes like the one about Hell being where the British cook, the Germans entertain, and the Italians run everything. They hint that all people from these places think the same way and always will, and that the culture that explains their behavior can be read in circular fashion off the behavior that we want to explain.

Of course there may be some fairly static, monolithic bits of culture out there. The joke is funny because it captures something. But there are other ways to think about how ideational elements cause action. Unfortunately they are scattered especially far and wide across the social sciences and history. Together with its suspect methodological status and the 'understanding/explanation' debate, this dispersion of the ideational literature still makes it fairly easy to dismiss within political science.[1]

Thus this chapter faces a different challenge from the first two. Unlike structure, a widely acceptable definition of 'ideational elements' is not hard to find. Unlike institutionalism, scholars share basic ideas about how such elements could affect action. Rather than deep ambiguity about ideational logic, it is confusion about how to make an ideational explanation in practice that most often troubles its proponents and opponents. The application of ideational logic suffers from debates over what causal arguments are, from methodological challenges about showing ideas or culture and their effects, and from a fragmentation of ideational scholarship. An attempt to set ideational explanation alongside the other logics requires first a buttressing of the causal status of the whole category—not just delineating its boundaries but firming up its content—and then the construction of an interdisciplinary way to organize variations within it.[2]

As a final introductory point I must admit some awkwardness in the category's label. While it works well semantically for structure to cause certain actions in structural claims, institutions to cause certain actions in institutionalist claims, and psychology to cause certain actions in psychological claims, here I employ the dry and inelegant phrasing that 'ideational elements' cause certain actions in ideational claims. A more mellifluous option would be to label the causes in this category simply as 'ideas'. But that would confuse things substantively, since 'ideas' is best employed to designate just one kind of ideational element that is different from practices, symbols, identities, or culture. So 'ideational elements' and 'ideational explanation' will have to do, with the understanding

[1] As one anecdotal indication of this dismissal, the most recent decadal 'State of the Discipline' volume in political science touched on ideational factors only in a chapter on constructivist thinking in international relations (Katznelson and Milner 2002).

[2] This 'buttressing' may seem a biased contrast to my calls for narrower uses of structural and institutional labels. In my view it simply reflects the different challenges around each set of terms. Structural and institutional vocabularies are crowded with causal logics. Ideational explanation is widely dispersed and buried in methodological and epistemological confusion. Like with structure or institutions, I just seek to extract a distinct logic of explanation from the cacophony of academic discourse. Whether anyone uses this logic is up to them.

that these phrases cover any particularistic interpretive material of any scope. The dynamics of idiosyncratic personal beliefs may be very different from those of deep interpretive assumptions shared by all humans in the twenty-first century, but relative to structural, institutional, or psychological causes they share a connection to action through the same basic causal logic.

Defining Ideational Explanation

Just as a definition of institutionalist explanation raised different problems from a definition of structural explanation, so nailing down ideational explanation faces its own obstacles. The initial problems for structural or institutional explanation are more easily resolved here. Unlike with structure, a basic definition of ideational elements is not terribly problematic. Most definitions of the closely related term 'culture' give us overlapping and compatible lists of ideational elements: they include practices, symbols, norms, grammars, models, beliefs, ideas, and/or identities that carry meanings about the world (Geertz 1973; Bourdieu 1977; Swidler 1986; Sewell 1999). Unlike institutions, the link from a basic definition of ideational elements to the core logic of ideational explanation is short and direct. We can talk about structure without being structuralists or institutions without being institutionalists, but we cannot even discuss many ideational elements without implying a certain causal logic. We might recognize that a pattern of material structures or man-made institutions exists but then debate whether or not it influences action. But when we say that people hold certain culture or beliefs, we are not just making a descriptive statement that leaves open the causal dynamics. It makes little sense to call something a 'belief' unless we also mean that someone *believes* in it: that they use it to assign meaning and interpret the world around them.[3] Thus the very notion of ideas, culture or beliefs leads us straight to the core logic of ideational explanation. It explains actions as a result of people interpreting their world through certain ideational elements.

For the most aggressive ideational claim this definition might suffice, without worrying about boundaries with other logics. We might argue that an action is 'all culture', flowing entirely from ideational

---

[3] The same is not true semantically of other ideational elements like practices or symbols; we could describe something as a 'practice' without implying that it is something that people 'believe' in. I return later to nonideational uses of these other terms.

elements that dictate end goals, modes of analysis, broad strategies, and detailed practices. Ideational instructions might be so powerful that someone could interpret any objective structural or institutional situation as encouraging (or at least allowing) the same actions. Her thinking might not reflect any hard-wired psychological dispositions. This would make ideas or culture the only thing connecting the individual to action, with no role for structure, institutions, or psychology. Such people could invent and live by any beliefs and practices at all, no matter how self-destructive or absurd. Their only limits would be physical possibilities—they could not dream themselves to survive without food, live forever, or fly into space without the right technology—but even physical limits might not discourage them from trying (perhaps perishing repeatedly in the attempt). We might see societies with cultures based around suicide, opposed to reproduction, or where leaders were selected for stupidity or insanity. Such societies might not endure for long, but to explain their appearance we would need a logic in which ideational elements explained everything.

In practice nobody quite makes such arguments about real action. Just as strongly structural theorists like Marx allow for other dynamics when they turn to empirical cases of action, even the strongest ideational theorists like Foucault implicitly admit some limits to interpretative flexibility.[4] In philosophy or science fiction it may be interesting to imagine people who make up their world with no connection to objective reality—as Descartes muses, and *The Matrix* plays out—but any serious attempt at explaining action allows for some intersubjective bounds. We have not seen people who entirely ignore that they confront a physical setting, needing food and air and so on, and in fact most people seem highly sensitive to their environment. That still leaves a tremendous range of variation that might be caused by ideational elements, of course. We have seen societies where ritual suicide is common. We have seen societies where reproduction is surrounded by many barriers. We have seen near-absolute power handed to individuals widely recognized as insane or stupid. Still, even in strikingly crazy moments like China's Cultural Revolution or the Holocaust, no serious argument sees people acting with total disregard for at-least-relatively-objective things like geography, available

---

[4] Many scholars argue that we are incapable of accessing these limits—even to an epistemologically pragmatist standard of intersubjective consensus, without any claims to 'real' objective knowledge—and that this can justify treating everything as if it were ideational and interpretive. But even strong proponents of this view in the abstract typically acknowledge some ability to access the world in their empirical work, if only tacitly (Alcoff 1993; Bunge 1993; Wendt 1999: 106).

technology, population patterns, and even man-made things like major salient organizations. People may invent a stunning range of beliefs and practices, but they do not quite do so in infinitely flexible ways.

Even a basic sense of ideational explanation, then, requires attention to boundaries with other logics. The best point of departure is to consider the relationship of ideational claims to rationality, since regular objective rationality is integral to structural and institutional claims and regular irrationality is the core of psychological claims. Ideational claims can feature either 'a-rationality' (often called 'multiple rationalities'[5]) or irrationality (or both). One way to make space for an ideational causal segment is to assert that the objective conditions around certain people are highly ambiguous or uncertain, such that even rational people depend to some degree on interpretive filters to organize their preferences, priorities, and problems. This argument would suggest that the particular interpretive filter that they adopt is arbitrary—they could rationally adopt a wide range of interpretations, and just inherit one from preexisting culture or creatively invent it—but it then shapes how they act. The other way is to assert that people are partly irrational (at least with respect to any coherent rationality we can reconstruct). They may be unable or indisposed to hold consistent preferences, accurately perceive external conditions, or match solutions instrumentally to problems (or perhaps all three), and so to some degree depend on ideationally defined formulae to shape their thinking and action.

Structure, Institutions, and A-rational Ideational Claims

We can explore the ideational boundary with logics of position most directly by considering ideational claims that are consistent with rationality. A-rational ideational claims share some characteristics with institutionalist ones. Both delineate themselves from structural claims by starting from ambiguity in the objective environment. Both then see people themselves creating the constraints that resolve the ambiguity and channel their action along a certain path. One big difference is that institutionalists only see ambiguity in environmental conditions at the starting point of their arguments, while a-rational ideational claims see ambiguity throughout. For institutionalists, the situation external to the individual eventually clarifies thanks to the unintended consequences of

---

[5] This phrase is consistent with my description (Lukes and Hollis 1982), but I think 'a-rational' is a more explicit term. These arguments' first claim is that there is no clear rational course of action in the absence of interpretative filters.

earlier institution-building. The organizations and rules that resolve the ambiguity are intersubjectively present and clear, such that any rational person parachuted into this position would be oriented in similar directions. In a-rational ideational claims it is the actor's interpretation of the situation, not the situation itself, which ultimately indicates a way forward. Rather than seeing a clear path because they unintentionally box themselves into a man-made but real obstacle course, people narrow their choices as they take on a certain subjective way of interpreting things. Other people parachuted in with other interpretive filters might still see the situation as ambiguous, or could see it as pointing in other directions.

But if differences about interpretation draw a basic distinction from both structural and institutionalist thinking, there are still semantic problems on this boundary. Careful readers will have noticed that my definitions of ideational elements and institutions overlap. Both include 'practices', and in fact the overlap goes farther. Many elements in my ideational list—practices, norms, grammars, models—could fit with an institutionalist claim. We have seen that given ambiguity or unpredictability, objectively rational people might adopt certain informal ways of acting (practices, norms, models, etc.) and then maintain them for institutional reasons that have nothing to do with interpretative dynamics. This is true even of terms like symbols or identities that sound more purely ideational. An objectively rational person could join a group and find that to communicate certain notions he must refer to a certain symbol. The symbol might link certain connotations and rule out others and so might channel his action in certain ways. But this would not necessarily mean that he or anyone else is actively interpreting the world through the meanings invoked by the symbol. It might just be a conventional way of communicating that is hard to change across a dispersed group of people: an informal institution, affecting action in an institutionalist way.

There are many examples of work in this institutionalist vein that get labeled misleadingly as cultural or ideational. A prominent one is Robert Putnam's work on 'civic community'. His study of civic life in Italy is sometimes seen as shoring up the poorly specified literature on the cultural foundations of democracy. Putnam argues that the density of associational life in Italy's regions—their interconnectedness, trust, and 'social capital'—corresponds to variations in economic development and government performance. In short, a dense associational life is 'the key to making democracy work' (Putnam 1993). David Laitin celebrates Putnam's analysis as a robust 'narrow theory of culture' (Laitin 1995; see also Finnemore and Sikkink 2001). Yet Laitin also notes that Putnam assigns no role to meaning or interpretation. His social networks and norms originate in a 'critical juncture' of regional institutional divergence in the twelfth century, and coalesce in quite rational, self-reinforcing path-dependent dynamics thereafter. Putnam himself avoids the word 'culture', drawing largely on institutional theorizing. Without taking anything away from Putnam, I would label his work as institutionalist. His explanation is built around norms and practices, but they relate to action in an objective way rather than an interpretive one.

How can we clear up this overlap between institutions and ideational elements to dispel confusion about arguments like Putnam's? It is simply unavoidable that many components of both institutions and ideational elements—practices, norms, and so on—can relate causally to action through two different logics. The best solution follows prevailing usages of these terms. I have noted that social scientists largely agree on the definitional components of institutions and ideational elements. The common definition of institutions leaves open how institutions relate to action, however, whereas ideational elements are typically presented in ways that directly imply interpretive dynamics. It thus makes sense to continue to allow *institution* to apply to any sort of informal practice or norm or symbol (though only rationalist and path-dependent claims about such things are institutional*ist*). Ideational elements, on the other hand, should only include the subset of institutions that relate to action in an interpretive way. The result is a rephrased and broader version of Powell and DiMaggio's description of sociological institutionalism—which I labeled an ideational approach—as focusing on conventions that 'take on a rulelike status in social thought and action' (Powell and DiMaggio 1991: 9). Ideational explanation addresses the subset of institutions (practices, symbols, norms, grammars, models, identities) *through which people interpret their world.*

This overlap between institutions and ideational elements has important implications. I can only flag them briefly here. If practices, norms, symbols, and so on can relate to action in different ways, then the same practice, norm, or symbol might affect some people in an institutional way and others in an ideational way. Within the same group, some people may engage in a practice because they take it for granted and never conceive of an alternative, or because they value it as legitimate, while others may simply be bound into it by social expectations and the transaction costs of shifting the group to another convention. Some of Putnam's institutionally civic communities may actually have some ideationally civic people in them. Even more complicated, these dynamics could run parallel to each other vis-à-vis the same individual. A certain practice could both set limits on how someone interprets the world and surround her with intersubjectively present constraints or incentives. If she somehow became 'enlightened' and altered her interpretive framework, she might still see fairly overwhelming reasons not to change her behavior. In behavioral terms we would see no shift, despite a change in causal logics that could alter what we would expect of her future behavior.[6] The methodological implications are daunting: we may need a great deal of information to trace varied relationships to practices or norms. In many situations we may be unable to do so, but this hardly exempts us from making the attempt.

We will see below that the varieties of ideational thinking present different ways to imagine such combinations. For the moment, let me underscore the basic implications of an a-rational basis for ideational claims. On the one hand, a virtue of a-rational foundations is that an ideational claim can retain some of the drive implied by rational actors, rather than beginning from a relatively aimless image of action. It limits just how weird people's thinking can get. On the other hand, the potential cost of building an ideational claim on a-rationality is that it subordinates the claim to structural or institutional segments. Ideational elements only affect action within the range of ambiguity permitted by structural and institutional conditions. This may not be a huge concession: we might argue that this range is very wide, especially as we consider the complex assumptions that may lie behind even the simplest political actions. Still, we have much experimental evidence that people are fairly irrational, so there are good reasons to think that ideational thinking need not always be bound by rationality. Overall, ideational claims built on a-rationality take the safer route in methodological and theoretical terms—limiting just how creatively people can imagine their world—but also take a relatively modest view of what ideas, norms, or culture can do.

Psychology and Irrational Ideational Claims

The arguments that claim the most causal variation for ideational elements fall on the irrational side of the category. By breaking with rationality ideational claims concede less to logics of position. Their actors

---

[6] If the pattern of behavior were shaken up by some sort of shock, for example, we would expect the 'believers' to react differently from those who had merely felt constrained by convention.

can misrepresent or ignore even salient structural or institutional conditions. Interpretation that is less chained to the objective world can invent a wider range of meanings and action. But if the strictures of objective observation and rational calculation no longer bound human action, this may not mean that no regular, universal patterns shape human thinking. There can be either particular or general patterns of irrationality. This distinction forms the boundary between ideational and psychological claims.

Culture and psychology have been hopelessly conflated in much social science literature. The few who use the terms fairly clearly converge explicitly or implicitly on the solution I advocate: that we define ideational or cultural claims as particular and psychological claims as general (see Chapter 5). Ideational logic suggests that certain historically situated people develop their own ways of interpreting the world around them, and that this shapes how they act. Any ideational claim is framed around particular people: Chinese people, workers in nineteenth-century England, inhabitants of a certain Ukrainian region, members of the German Social Democratic Party, religious Muslims, and so on.[7] Psychological claims suggest that all people tend to interpret the world through certain patterns of irrationality, and that this shapes how they act. They need not be totally universal—some variants divide people up into a variety of psychological types who interpret similar situations differently, like leader-types and follower-types—but they are never framed with respect to a particular historical group of people. Any argument that bounds its claims to a particular group (*these* historically situated people interpret things in a certain way) leaves the realm of psychology and enters that of culture and ideas (as does the growing literature in 'cultural psychology': Fiske et al. 1998; Nisbett 2003).

The basic distinction is fairly simple to apply. Wherever we see broad generalization in an argument about culture or ideas we know that psychological logic is actually at work (unless it traces rationally to objective structural or institutional conditions). A good example is Karl Polanyi's argument about 'market society' in nineteenth- and twentieth-century Europe (Polanyi 1944). For Polanyi, this period is the story of the advance of a powerful ideological project—the creation of free markets—and then of broad social reactions against it. Polanyi's book is often seen as the classic assertion of an ideational approach to political economy. It helped

---

[7] Again, it is possible that a particular ideational element could spread to all human beings, making it *look* universal, but it would still have once been the contingent invention of certain people rather than a regular general reflex of humankind.

found the view that markets are not natural, given, obvious ways to organize exchange, as economists often imply. Polanyi saw the rise of the market project as an irrational ideological movement that was not even in the objective interest of its leading proponents. But it is less often noted that his view of the fall of market society is a psychological argument that sharply limits the overall impact of ideational elements in his analysis. As markets reorganized European societies, he argues, people everywhere rose up against them in defense of universal needs for social bonds and stability. This new marketized world simply did not fit with 'human nature'. In the long term, hard-wired human psychology trumped an attempt at cultural creation. Europeans were forced back to the more socially embedded approaches to political economy showcased in communism, fascism, and social democracy.

One of Polanyi's critics provides a nicely contrasting example of an irrational but more fully ideational argument. The historian William Reddy's study of the French textile industry suggests that 'market society' never arose in nineteenth-century Europe. He argues that functioning labor markets never actually appeared in this period—but people *believed* they did, and these beliefs shaped their actions. Labor markets only generate efficiency if workers are allocated to jobs in competitive, price-sensitive ways. But as power looms entered French textiles, inefficient weavers accepted an 80 percent wage cut—and starvation in large numbers—rather than seeking other jobs. Meanwhile, women and children joined the workforce as employers sought docile workers. Despite being perceived as more desirable than men, however, they received lower wages. Across several patterns of labor allocation, Reddy (1984: 10) argues, 'the wrong competitor won'. Rather than markets matching productivity to wages, a web of norms and practices (about professions, location, gender, and so on) continued to determine the conditions of labor and production. But at the same time, the spread of abstract ideas of 'market culture' meant all increasingly *believed* that spreading social disintegration was the product of efficient free markets. This led people to accept an astounding degree of dislocation and suffering in the name of 'progress' and efficiency—and eventually paved the way for something closer to real labor markets to emerge.

Reddy displays how an irrational ideational argument without psychological generalizations can claim broad causal scope. Not only are people convinced by 'market culture' to do things that destroy their lives, but their beliefs at one level directly contradict the situation on the ground and their other norms. Their action is broadly and deeply organized by a mix of ideational elements. At the same time, Reddy underlines that even irrationally based ideational claims need a boundary with logics of position. His actors are far from fully irrational. Workers' pursuit of basic material security and comfort is just channeled by perception of certain options as illegitimate (like shifting jobs radically) or legitimate (defending 'rights' to a decent living in a given trade). In the long term, after much suffering, workers accept more flexible labor decisions. Employers, meanwhile, are quite rationally delighted to capitalize on the norms that lead weavers to cut their wages and allow women and children to be paid less for better work. Reddy lays an ideational obstacle course over his actors, ruling out certain paths and sometimes boxing them in to narrow options, but within those bounds he sees a good deal of instrumental action. He argues not that people are aimlessly irrational in general but that he can show how ideational elements steered them in certain directions—some of which look quite irrational.

Just how successfully Reddy makes and supports clear causal claims for culture or norms is not my current concern (for a mildly critical review, Biernacki 1995: 19). The point is just to use these examples to picture one kind of argument. Basing an ideational claim at least partly in irrationality moves back the threshold versus structural or institutional claims, allowing interpretation to trump even clear constraints. How much of that space gets claimed for ideational segments depends on how much the argument attributes importance to psychological patterns. A final point to note is that many ideational claims effectively take an agnostic position on the a- or irrationality of any given ideational element. This works by taking on certain competing structural or institutional claims, but not the whole notion of rationality in general. They point to salient structural or institutional conditions, play out how we might expect objectively rational people to respond to them, marshal evidence that a given action is either ambiguously related to those objective signals or contradicts them—and leave it at that. This amounts to showing that the action is a- or irrational with respect to salient competing arguments, but remaining agnostic on the hard-to-demonstrate issue of overarching rationality or irrationality (Parsons 2003: 16–17, 239).

I return briefly to issues of demonstration at the end of the chapter. Having offered a basic definition of ideational logic and sketched its boundaries, I now turn to a step that the previous chapters were able to skip. Unlike structural or institutional logic, ideational logic faces basic challenges to its explanatory status.

Challenges to Ideational Explanation

Skepticism about ideational explanation features three main objections. First, many ideational claims do something other than explanation. This view is often offered sympathetically by ideational scholars themselves, but whatever its intentions it legitimizes a certain lack of engagement with nonideational scholarship. Second, even if ideational claims can explain, they are so hard to verify empirically that we should venture them only when all others fail. This casts ideational argument as speculation that we do when we cannot nail down what is really going on. Third, even if some ideational causal segments are amenable to some demonstration, they tend to be so superficial and static that they are hardly worth considering. Explaining actions with culture or ideas, this suggests, is akin to saying 'he wanted it because that is what he wants', or 'they did it because that is what they do'.

The first objection is the only one that any sophisticated social scientist today asserts explicitly and strongly. Still, a glance at any selection of recent publications suggests that political scientists still subscribe widely to a combination of the others. Arguments that are mainly structural or institutional routinely neglect ideational alternatives, whereas ideationally-focused claims that achieve prominent publication fight off many structural or institutional competitors (except where they self-excuse from this fight by reason of the first objection, and publish only in culture-friendly venues). This is not just a problem for proponents of ideational claims. Viable explanations can be drawn from this category of logic, and so scholarship that ignores it neglects our scientific duty to explore alternatives. I am under no illusion that more attention to ideational elements will mean more agreement on how much they matter, but our debates are less scientific to the extent that we exclude them for bad reasons.

Challenge: Ideational Argument is not Explanation

Many scholars would not locate ideational claims in a survey of explanatory logics. The three reasons to do so have sterling pedigrees, coming from Hume and Weber. Hume supplied two reasons in his definition of causation: for A to be a cause of B, A must exist independently of B, A must occur before B in time, and all instances of A must be followed by the appearance of B (Hume [1748] 1975). The first apparent problem for ideational claims arises in chronological succession and independent existence. As the IR constructivist Alexander Wendt develops most clearly, many ideational elements do not seem to have this kind of relationship to action (Wendt 1998, 1999). We might be tempted to argue that the norm of sovereignty causes the existence of the state, but the two are not chronologically or ontologically separate. At the very moment certain people came to believe in the norm of sovereignty, they looked around and saw states. The second apparent problem concerns Hume's last requirement, that a real cause always produces its effect. This has usually been understood as implying a mechanistic causal generalization or law. Such a requirement does not seem to fit with the particularistic format of ideational logic. Weber added a third problem by distinguishing between an argument's 'adequacy on a causal level' and 'adequacy on the level of meaning' (Weber [1922] 1958). His point (as it is most commonly understood from his vast scholarship) was that we could have a strong knowledge of causality—being confident that under certain conditions, certain people would take certain actions—without understanding the significance of what they were doing as they understood it. The disconnect could lead us to misinterpret the whole situation. Weber's conclusion was that we need both causal and interpretive information to truly capture human action (Turner 2000).

Taken together, these points lead many scholars to locate ideational claims in a realm of interpretation that is distinct from causal explanation. Ideational theorists like Martin Hollis and Steve Smith tend to perceive the two as equally important, or interpretation as a more fundamental prerequisite to causal explanation (Hollis and Smith 1990). Scholars of more structural or institutional leanings tend to downgrade the interpretive realm, at least semantically. King, Keohane, and Verba (1994: 37) class it as description that can help set up our real business of explanation. In a partial attempt to bridge this divide, Wendt argues that some ideational claims fit a standard model of causality (someone believes something at time t, causing them under certain conditions to act in a certain way at time $t + 1$), but also that we should extend the notion of explanation to include a non-causal logic of 'constitutive explanation':

If we want to explain how a master can sell his slave then we need to invoke the structure of shared understandings existing between master and slave, and in the wider society, that make this ability to sell people possible. This social structure does not merely describe the rights of the master; it explains them, since without it those rights by definition could not exist. By way of contrast, even if a parent in the antebellum American South had the physical capability and desire to sell their child, they could not do so because the structure of that culture did not recognize such a right. These explanations are not causal. It's not as if the social structure of slavery exists independently of the master's right to sell his slave and causes that right to come into being. Rather, the master's right is conceptually or logically dependent on the structure of slavery, such that when the latter comes into being so does the former by definition.

(Wendt 1998: 113)

In my view the language of constitutiveness is very insightful. It offers a powerful way to conceive of the deep subjective background conditions to certain actions. But I do not agree that this insight leads to a kind of argument that is meaningfully distinct from causal explanation—whether 'constitutive explanation' or a more separate kind of 'understanding'. A few fairly simple moves can set aside each of the Humean and Weberian bases for this distinction, erasing the notion that ideational claims are somehow not in direct competition with causal scholarship about the same actions.

The first is to recognize that the problem of inseparability is not distinctive to ideational elements. Wendt offers the initial step. He notes that the issue of constitutiveness is not limited to the 'understanding' realm of culture but is even part of 'hard science' inquiry as well. In all realms, scholars ask not just causal 'why?' questions but also 'constitutive' questions. He suggests that causal 'why?' questions ask about how something came about, and constitutive 'how?' or 'what' questions ask what makes up entities or systems in a static sense. For example:

Constitutive questions usually take the form of 'how-possible?' or 'what?' 'How was it possible for Stalin, a single individual, to exercise so much power over the Soviet people?' 'How is it possible for Luxembourg to survive in an anarchic world next door to Great Powers like France and Germany?' 'How is it possible for a gas to have a temperature?' And 'how is it possible for the Earth to keep the moon in its orbit?' are all requests for information about the conditions of possibility for natural and social kinds. A related logic underlies what-questions: 'What kind of political system is the European Union?' 'Was Serbian behavior during the Bosnian Civil War "genocide"?' 'What are comets made of?' And 'what is ball lightning?' What we seek in asking these questions is insight into what it is that instantiates some phenomenon, not why that phenomenon comes about.

(Wendt 1998: 105)

Wendt's examples indirectly provide the other steps of this first move. In three ways he and similar scholars present ideational causes and effects as less separable than they could be. First is the simple presence of definitions and assumptions, as is most obvious in the questions about what we call the EU, genocide, or ball lightning. Certainly we must make ontological assumptions and define concepts to characterize outcomes and possible causes, and in so doing we exclude some dynamics and so begin to 'explain'. But this is part of the logical structure of causal explanation, not a new kind of endeavor, and the only upshot is that we should try to use open-minded definitions. Second is an even simpler problem of abstraction. Wendt cannot separate causes and effects partly because he has not expressed interest in specific effects. The further we get from specific actions—the more our 'outcomes' are potentials or general states of affairs: explaining that *a* man *could* sell *a* slave—the less we have anything to explain and the more our 'outcomes' become inseparable from initial definitions and ontological assumptions. If Wendt rephrased his questions to explain actions—that *some* man *did* sell *his* slave at some point—his substantive point about culture and norms would stand but the problem of inseparability would be much less severe. He could still argue that the seller could not have sold the slave without ideational elements in place that made this conceivable and legitimate. Now, however, we could presumably see that those elements were demonstrably in place the day before the sale. Space would open up between ideational cause and action-effect. Third is a related issue of specifying causes and effects. Wendt cannot separate 'the social structure of slavery' from 'a man's right to sell a slave' because they are the same thing. These are two different labels for the same set of norms, beliefs, or practices in the antebellum South. Taking his cause as the presence of these norms in a certain group and his effect as a specific action would go a long way toward solving the problem.

In sum, we can get at Wendt's insightful point without leaving the realm of causal relations. Some man sold a slave at some point, as opposed to pursuing general well-being in other ways that could have made sense in his objective environment, be*cause* he and his neighbors interpreted their world through norms of slavery. If he had inhabited other norms—just as, arguably, if he had inhabited a different position in markets or institutions—he would have acted differently. If we ask the right questions this cause is adequately separable from its effect in any specific action. The same is not true in reverse—the effect cannot exist without the cause—but it does not have to be. We may be able to separate norms of slave-selling from any given exercise of such rights, but the action might still make no sense without the cultural elements that make it an option. This is fine: a world where effects could exist without their causes would be a strange place. An act of slave-selling also is not ontologically separable from various nonideational conditions that define such an action: the availability of people to sell, buyers with something to exchange, the means of coercion for seller and buyer to retain control of the slave, a meeting-place, and a basic way for buyer and seller to communicate. Classic causal logic does not ask that we imagine an effect without its causes; it just asks that we ascertain the cause and effect without using the same information for both. Documenting an intangible ideational cause separately from its action-effect may be a bit harder than doing the same with structural or institutional causes (as I discuss below), but it is not impossible. On the one hand we can look at earlier patterns of behavior, written and spoken utterances, and perhaps (with care) after-the-fact interviews to establish the beliefs and norms of the seller and his interlocutors. On the other hand we can document the action: bringing another person to a meeting-place, handing over that person in chains, taking some pieces of metal in return, and perhaps displaying signs of pleasure. Then we can debate how much we need the former to explain the latter, and how much other demonstrable conditions tell us why this person did this and not something else.[8]

That disposes of inseparability, but other obstacles remain. Even a clear, separable demonstration of the proximate influence of certain beliefs or norms (or identities, practices, symbols, etc.) cannot fully support an ideational causal segment. Most logic-of-position claims do not suggest that people have no beliefs or norms; they just argue (to some degree) that beliefs or norms are epiphenomenal derivations of objective positions. This means that all ideational claims require two arguments. First they must show the proximate causal role of preexisting ideational elements. This involves a demonstration that the ideational elements do not just reduce to other immediate conditions, but focuses on conditions just prior to the action in question. The second step is to show more deeply that these ideational elements reflect their own distinct dynamic, establishing their autonomy vis-à-vis longer-term or overarching objective conditions. In other words, an ideational claim must document its particularistic foundations, showing how much ideas or norms have autonomy from other causes. Helpfully, Chapter 3 laid out a kind of explanatory segment with a similar two-stage format. Just as an institutionalist claim must show both that actions flow from man-made constraints in a proximate sense

---

[8] Some might not call such norms a 'cause' if they do not arise or shift just prior to the action. This just requires a common distinction in philosophy of causality between 'standing conditions' and 'instigating conditions' that arises with all sorts of causes. Most causal arguments invoke some of both (Little 1991: 26).

and that those man-made constraints arose in the past with some range of autonomy from material conditions, so an ideational claim must show that actions immediately reflect certain elements of culture or ideas or norms and that these elements arose with some range of autonomy from preexisting objective conditions.

The particularistic parallel to institutionalism helps ideational logic resolve Hume's second objection, about the general nature of causality. Institutionalist claims are just as vulnerable to requirements for general laws as ideational ones, since both begin from the non-necessity of man-made arrangements. If certain institutions or ideational elements were strongly explicable themselves—if they followed as the obvious or unavoidable responses to preceding conditions—then their effects are just the derived effects of the preceding conditions. To generate distinctive institutionalist or ideational causal segments we must separate the man-made arrangements from other causal conditions by positing some contingency in their creation or endurance. Humeans might conclude that institutional and ideational claims are not explanations, since they partly jump over contingency rather than moving from initial conditions to action via necessary, general causal relations. As Chapter 1 laid out, however, separating such arguments into two conceptual stages erases this problem. At the proximate stage of explaining a specific action, an ideational claim should be able to make a standard causal claim that preexisting ideational elements caused the action (relative to some range of variation, like all causal claims). In the second stage, the ideational claim shows that these elements arose amid objective ambiguity or irrationality, generating new causes in a broader sense. There is no conflict with Hume (or any other version of causality) at this stage because this claim is not ultimately a causal one that aspires to meet Hume's conditions. It does contain some standard causal features, as suggested in the observation of Chapter 3 that contingency is the mirror image of causality. It argues in classic causal style, but negatively, that certain constellations of other causes do *not* dictate action over some range of options. But its claim about how this range is narrowed to one set of ideational elements is contingent, not causal. The whole point is that the selection of certain ideational elements *cannot* be explained by preexisting conditions: they were contingent over a range of options. This is why, in opposition to a simple reading of Hume, 'particular explanation' is not a contradiction in terms.[9] At one point, taking ideational (or institutional)

---

[9] For a reading of Hume that allows him to be consistent with particular explanation, see Davidson (1963).

elements as our dependent variable, we argue that their form was under-determined. We then take the established form as an independent variable at another point and argue that it exerted causal pressure on later actions.

Lastly we confront the Weberian problem of meaning. It implies not just that ideational elements are hard to separate out as causes or that 'explanation' must follow general laws (though Weber did subscribe to this simple reading of Hume), but that accessing causality and accessing meaning involve different kinds of knowledge. We may be able to highlight the causes of human behaviors (through *Ërklarung*, explanation) without accessing how the actors understand their action (with *Verstehen*, understanding), and vice versa. In subscribing to this notion, Weberian scholars like Hollis and Smith often also argue that arguments involving meaning posit a fundamentally different mode of cause–effect relationships. They suggest that standard causal explanations of human action, modeled on the hard sciences, approach behavior as a world of 'natural kinds' with 'necessary and constant' cause–effect relationships, like gravity compelling falling apples. Ideational scholarship, by contrast, posits action shaped by 'social kinds' that do not feature such relationships. Certain beliefs might incline someone toward a line of action, but the beliefs do not force him to action in the same way that gravity pulls apples. In other words, since meanings detour arguments to run through human cognition, they cannot have the same causal format as a mechanistic or biological stimulus/response model (Taylor 1985; Hollis and Smith 1990). Ideational claims belong in their own noncausal realm both because they depend on meaning-style-knowledge and because they operate by different deep rules.

There is certainly no avoiding the fact that meanings constitute a methodological problem of the first order. Understanding the actor's point of view requires different methods from trying to chart the constraints, incentives, and forces pushing them from the outside. But Weber's disciples are wrong to see problems of meaning and nonmechanistic causality as driving a line between ideational and nonideational claims about action. Rather than separating explanations of action from 'constitutive' or 'understanding' approaches, this line sets off *any* intentional explanation of action from explanations of other things. With the exception of the most instinctual psychological mechanisms, all the explanations considered in this book share a different kind of causal relationship from the dynamics of falling apples, earthquakes, or chemical reactions. Logic-of-position claims may treat structural or institutional conditions as 'natural kinds', but they connect those conditions to action through human cognition, via rationality. Even the strongest structural claim cannot coherently insist that people react to structural positions in the same physical way that the apple is compelled by gravity. They incorporate meanings as well: to offer a causal claim with a mechanism (as opposed to a model that just correlates structural positions to action without claiming to capture what is going on) they must posit and show that people assign the right, intersubjective, rational meanings to structural conditions. As noted in Chapters 2 and 3, this means offering rhetorical evidence of how people saw their situation. With the exception of instinctual-psychological claims, any coherent account of human choices passes through cognition and actors' understandings. Logics of interpretation set different limits on cognition from logics of position, but neither is more mechanistic than the other.

Assuming we accept a requirement for explanations to offer causal mechanisms, the only alternative to this view is a bit ironic: to suggest that nonideational claims are noncausal themselves. Only if nonideational explanations do not claim to capture what really happens when people take action—advocating a noncausal extrapolation-by-correlation model of theorizing—does it make sense to say that they short-circuit actors' understandings (Friedman 1953; Waltz 1979). Otherwise we are all trying to explain why certain people really made certain choices, not just why automata that look like these people might make similar choices. We all share a cognitively routed kind of causality that makes claims about how people interpreted their situation. This does not change the fact that ideational claims add an additional level of causal and methodological complexity in suggesting that actors' interpretations can vary widely for nongeneral-law reasons. But it does mean we can set aside the Weberian attempt to locate ideational logic in a special realm.

To sum up, we should not let confusing debates over causation and constitution prevent us from recognizing the possibility of ideational causal segments. Three moves offer solutions to these problems. First, we must ask careful, specific questions about causes and effects. Second, we must recognize that any intentional explanation of action takes cognitive pathways and so appeals to actors' understandings. Third, we must note the similarity of ideational claims to the particularistic logic of institutionalism. The notion that certain ideational elements constitute action is similar to the notion that actions today cannot be explained without seeing how actors bound themselves into institutional arrangements over time. In both cases the point is that today's actions are embedded in the man-made consequences of earlier actions, and that to explain today's actions we must study not just immediate decision-making but how people became embedded in a certain man-made framework. These notions differ in that ideational elements are subjective while institutions are intersubjectively present, leading to the differences between institutional and ideational logic discussed above. But the two logics confront similar Humean challenges and share a core solution. Like institutionalism, ideational claims open space for their distinct dynamics with a 'negative explanation' in the past—showing that particular ideational elements were *not* the necessary reaction to pre-existing conditions across some range of alternatives—but then build a more conventional causal explanation on the consequences of this earlier development.

Challenge: Ideational Explanations Are Too Hard to Verify

Even if ideational explanation makes sense in theory, it might be infeasible in practice. For many social scientists (and political scientists in particular), ideational claims are so difficult to demonstrate that they belong in a speculative category. As David Elkins and Richard Simeon summarized (1979):

Several characteristics of political culture pose special problems for measuring and describing it. First, it is often hard to disentangle from structural or psychological variables. Second, it is an abstract concept, not a concrete thing. It cannot be directly seen, heard, or touched; therefore it must be inferred from other clues. Third, for most of the members of a society, culture is unconscious, inexplicit, taken for granted; hence we cannot easily ask people about it directly. Fourth, while individuals participate in a culture, as a collective attribute of society, we do not describe a culture by simply aggregating all the individuals. How then do we find it?

Although I avoid the old vocabulary of 'political culture' (for reasons discussed below), Elkins and Simeon pose the problem well. Demonstrating causal claims is hard enough when they rest on tangible material resources or organizations. Is it feasible to base one on intangible ideational elements? Can we overcome Weber's problem of meaning—putting ourselves in the subjective place of our actors—well enough to make interpretations into the building blocks of concrete claims?

Without denying that culture, ideas, norms, or identities are relatively intangible sorts of causes, the first step to countering this objection is to recognize that even the most concrete structural claims rely on intangibles. Elkins and Simeon mention the example of gravity. In the social

113

sciences the major structural notions of 'mode of production', 'market', or 'distribution of power' are not directly observable things. The evolving material constraints and incentives invoked by Marxism, liberal economic theory, or realism are not visible as though we were watching the physical operation of a bicycle. Instead, each of these theoretical traditions points to a variety of incomplete bits of observable evidence of the presence of its larger construct, and fills in the gaps by appealing to a stylized model (Bunzl 1995). This is all the more true of the man-made constraints and incentives invoked by institutionalist claims. Moreover, as noted above, all structural and institutional claims depend on the nondemonstrable concept of rationality to link their constraints and incentives to action. Ideational claims are not different in requiring us to look inside actors' heads and make some claims about decision-making processes that we can never fully access. Structural or institutional claims that skip this step—failing to offer at least some evidence of roughly objective rational-looking decision-making—simply correlate a pattern of constraints and incentives to actions without making a causal claim (Blyth 2003).

That said, ideational elements are still less tangible than structure or institutions. The structures in structural claims may be hard to see all at once, but at least in the hardest structural claims (about the most fully non-man-made structures, like geography) the causal claim begins from something material that has a physical existence. This is less true of structural claims that rest more on 'material' patterns—in quotes, things a scholar only treats as physical givens but which might be more man-made and institutional, like the property rights in 'modes of production' or 'markets', or the kinds of authority often built into a 'distribution of power'—but still these arguments incorporate *some* ostensibly physically present elements. Institutional constraints may also include physical patterns in organizational manifestations like buildings and the location of people and resources. All structural and institutional claims are also relatively tangible in their insistence on the objective reality of their causes. Even for the elements of institutional claims (or 'material' structural claims) that have no physical manifestation, they are at least claiming that these conventions or norms are unambiguously *there* in social behavior and would be perceived similarly by any actor. Ideational claims, by contrast, take as point of departure that to some degree 'there is no there there'. They focus on causes that have no physical existence, and whose significance is only visible through a particular subjective lens.

Yet this still does not mean that ideational elements are much more difficult to document than structures or institutions. Though the significance of any ideational element is subjective—we can only see it through the subjective views of its adherents—the facts that the adherents perceive it and attribute certain meaning to it are potentially as objective as anything else we might claim. As Durkheim observed long ago in writing of 'social facts', I must enter your subjectivity to understand and describe your beliefs (or norms or identity), but whether or not you believe something is an intersubjective fact (Durkheim [1897] 1951). It is by no means obvious that it is unusually difficult methodologically to describe people's beliefs (or norms or identity) or to document how strongly they believe in them. It may well be easier to get a strong sense of an American's beliefs (or, given careful surveys and statistics, even the whole population of American beliefs) about terrorism, globalization, or abortion than it is to be confident about how much they are objectively threatened by terrorism, how they stand objectively to gain or lose from globalization, or what kind of objective conditions could lead people to different views of human fetuses. Documenting what George W. Bush believed about Iraq's weapons of mass destruction would probably be easier than documenting whether Iraq really had or sought weapons of mass destruction. We have plenty of respectable methods for gathering information about people's subjective perceptions, from archival work on original documents to surveys to interviews to participant observation. Of course, in using these methods we must grapple with our subjectivity as observers, but that problem is separate from whether the object of our study is subjective culture or ostensibly objective structures or institutions. Whatever our object of study, we must be wary of our human tendency to perceive things and gather information in skewed ways.

The real challenge to demonstrating ideational claims is not that measuring ideational elements is so much more difficult than measuring other things, but that specifying the degree of their autonomy from structural and institutional conditions is very hard. Again, this second stage is critical to show that apparent beliefs, practices, or norms (etc.) are truly 'ideational' rather than just congealed rational responses to objective conditions. Yet this just requires the reverse of making specific structural or institutional claims, so it implies no unique challenges. To lay the foundations for causal claims about the effects of ideational elements, we must trace their origins or change over time prior to the action we seek to explain, making a negative argument that some combination of structural and institutional ambiguity, unpredictability, or actors' irrationality permitted a range of interpretations. The more specific we can be about this range of real or potential interpretive variation (arguing either that similarly positioned people did interpret things differently, or that they could have), the more strongly we can argue that their adherence to one interpretation within this range led them to a certain action (see Parsons 2003 for an empirical example). Ultimately, the same difficult challenge is posed equally to all claims. Strong structural, institutional, or psychological claims obviously need to be as precise as possible about how tightly their constraints dictate certain actions. The mirror image of the same task lays foundations for the causal autonomy of ideational elements.

Challenge: Ideational Explanations Are Superficial, Static, and Maybe Tautological

Even if we allow that causal ideational explanation is possible in theory and feasible in empirical terms, it might not be a very plausible, powerful route for explanation. A common gut feeling among social scientists, and especially political scientists, is that culture and ideas are just too close to action to explain it. Describing culture is often difficult without referring to the actions it might explain, creating risks of tautology: we know that people adhere to a certain idea because we see them acting consistently with it, and we know that they act this way because they adhere to this idea. Even if we can establish people's beliefs or norms prior to and independently from the action, it may seem unsatisfying to rest our explanation on interpretations without looking for something more concrete. It feels like asserting that someone acts like a capitalist just because they want money and prefer to avoid direct labor, without considering something like Marx's picture of the underpinnings of such action. As the famous comparativist Barrington Moore wrote in his landmark 1966 book *The Social Origins of Dictatorship and Democracy*:

To explain behavior in terms of cultural values is to engage in circular reasoning. If we notice that a landed aristocracy resists commercial enterprise, we do not *explain* this fact by stating that the aristocracy has done so in the past or even that it is the carrier of certain traditions that make it hostile to such activities: the problem is to determine out of what past and present experiences such an outlook arises and maintains itself.... To speak of cultural inertia is to overlook the concrete interests and privileges that are served by indoctrination, education, and the entire complicated process of transmitting culture from one generation to the next. A member of the Chinese gentry in the nineteenth century, we may agree, usually judged economic opportunities in a way very different from that of a twentieth-century American businessman farmer. But he did so because he grew up in a Chinese Imperial society whose class structure, system of rewards, privileges, and sanctions penalized certain forms of economic gain that would have destroyed the hegemony and authority of the dominant groups.

(1966: 486; his emphasis)

Hopefully the preceding sections are persuasive that Moore is wrong to deny the basic possibility of causal ideational claims. He is stating his bias as a dyed-in-the-wool structural thinker as though it were a logical argument. But if there are not good logical reasons to take Moore's position, many political scientists today hold it partly for historical reasons. They see ideational claims as suspect, not because they have studied their foundations and found them weak, but because the main ideational arguments they know suffer from problems.

When political scientists think of culture and ideas in their discipline, the names that jump to mind are giants of a generation that is now retired (or close to retiring): Gabriel Almond and Sidney Verba (authors of the pathbreaking 1963 study *The Civic Culture*), Samuel Huntington (of *Clash of Civilizations* fame), Lucien Pye, Harry Eckstein, Ronald Inglehart, or Aaron Wildavsky (Almond and Verba 1963; Pye and Verba 1965; Eckstein 1966; Pye 1968, 1981; Inglehart 1977; Douglas and Wildavsky 1982). Of these, the first two are easily the most common reference points for ideational argument in political science today. *The Civic Culture*'s survey of attitudes about democracy in five countries inspired a large literature that received renewed attention in the 1980s and 1990s (Wildavsky 1987; Eckstein 1988; Inglehart 1988, 1989; Ellis, Thompson, and Wildavsky 1990; Wilson 1992; Diamond 1993). Although Huntington's article (1993) and book (1996) were written for policy audiences and 'not intended to be a work of social science', his thesis of increasing civilizational conflict is not only the best known recent exemplar of ideational logic, but also possibly the best known political science argument of any sort in the past several decades (Huntington 1996: 13). But for different reasons, both these works do more to confirm than to dispel skepticism about ideational explanation. They pay little attention to how we would show ideational elements as autonomous causal forces—leaving unclear how much the actions they investigate are 'cultural'. This leaves their claims ambiguous and perhaps tautological. Given little attention to the extent of culture's autonomy, they seem to read back its shape and effects from the actions it is meant to explain. They also present a view of national or civilizational cultures as static and monolithic, with little room for contestation or change.

The main problems with *The Civic Culture* concern ambiguity in what it claims about culture. Almond and Verba set out to show that 'there exists...a pattern of political attitudes and an underlying set of social attitudes that is supportive of a stable democratic process' (Almond and Verba 1963: vii). Some countries—notably Britain and the USA—sustained democracy better than others partly because they developed this 'civic culture'. It mixed a healthy dose of modern, rational citizen participation with a bit of traditional 'subject orientation' to keep the masses from participating too much and overwhelming democratic institutions. But 'every political system is embedded in a particular pattern of orientation to political actions'—a 'political culture'—and only a few alighted on the civic one (Almond 1956). The other countries surveyed (West Germany, Italy, and Mexico) tended toward more traditional 'parochial' or 'subject' political cultures, and so their democracies were more likely to be instable or impaired. The key weakness with these claims was that Almond and Verba quite explicitly refused to make an argument about how much these patterns of attitudes were substantively 'cultural'. In *The Civic Culture*, Almond summarized later, 'It is quite clear that political culture is treated as both an independent and a dependent variable, as causing structure and being caused by it' (Almond 1989*a*: 29). Political culture is 'a relatively soft variable' of considerable 'plasticity' (Almond 1983):

> The relaxed version of political culture theory—the one presented by most of its advocates—is that the relation between political structure and culture is interactive, that one cannot explain cultural propensities without reference to historical experience and contemporary structural constraints and opportunities, and that, in turn, a prior set of attitudinal patterns will tend to persist in some form and degree and for a significant period of time, despite efforts to transform it.... This is all we need to demonstrate in order to make a place for political culture theory in the pantheon of the explanatory variables of politics.
>
> (Almond 1989*b*: 146)

This might have been true if political culture theorists tried to specify at least some of the specific contributions of cultural elements within this interactive process, 'bracketing' some causal arrows that started with culture. Instead later work in this vein has largely defended Almond's vague dialectical position (Pye 1981: 20–2; Inglehart 1988; Almond 1989*a*, *b*; Lijphart 1989; Diamond 1993). The problem is that asserting a dialectic does not demonstrate the importance of one side of the dialectic. As critics never tire of pointing out, this literature makes little attempt to speak to just how much culture has any distinct effects of its own (Barry

1970; Jackman and Miller 1996; Pateman 1989; Gendzel 1997; Formisano 2001). Frequent accusations of tautology arise from the absence of such an attempt, since vague dialectics obviously lend themselves to tautology (Elkins and Simeon 1979; Laitin 1995; Biernacki 1999). Almond and Verba provide intriguing evidence of certain attitudes, but the evidence of these attitudes' effects largely amounts to pointing to the 'contemporary structural constraints and opportunities' that also partly explain the attitudes. The ideational role in the whole circle is lost.

Huntington's *Clash* suffers from a different ambiguity. His claim is stronger and clearer, but in writing for a broad nonscholarly audience he makes little effort to support it. My readers will know the basic argument:

It is my hypothesis that the fundamental source of conflict in this new [post-cold war] world will not be primarily ideological or primarily economic. The great divisions among humankind and the dominating source of conflict will be cultural. Nation states will remain the most powerful actors in world affairs, but the principle conflicts of global politics will occur between nations and groups of different civilizations. The clash of civilizations will dominate global politics. The fault lines between civilizations will be the battle lines for the future.

(Huntington 1996: 22)

For Huntington, major ideological conflict ended with the Cold War. Technology and global economic interaction are weakening states or nations and also local identities as objects of loyalty, and so people are increasingly focused on the 'real' and 'basic' units of regional civilizations. Moreover, the dominance of one civilization—the West—provokes growing civilizational awareness and assertiveness in the demographically burgeoning East and South. Other noncivilizational conflicts will continue to occur, but civilizational conflicts will dominate the overall pattern of violence and carry the main threat of escalation to global confrontation.

To some degree it is inappropriate that this argument received so much academic attention, with reviews in most academic journals (including very theoretical reviews of cultural scholarship). Huntington wrote for a policy audience, flagged that his book was 'not social science', and admitted that the article pointed to evidence 'casually' (Huntington 1996: 258). Still, the book is full of theoretical paradigms and predictive models, references to academic predecessors, and tables and figures, and this reception may have been inevitable for any work from one of Harvard's most celebrated social scientists. In any case, reviewers consistently found Huntington's empirical support unconvincing (e.g. Evans 1997; Jervis

1997; Tiryakian 1997; Rosecrance 1998). In the present, at least as much violence goes on within Huntington's civilizations as between them. Historically, he offers no evidence that other cleavages trumped civilizations in the past but have faded away recently. Overall, Huntington produced a work of inspired punditry that has garnered major academic reactions. He was very successful at generating renewed attention to culture and fomenting debate. But an unfortunate side effect was to exacerbate the widespread perception that ideational arguments in general are mostly smoke and mirrors.

Perhaps just as damaging for ideational theorizing as the direct weaknesses of *The Civic Culture* or *The Clash of Civilizations* is their rather crude model of ideational logic. They present images of consensual cultural blocs, organized on systematic, coherent, and fairly permanent principles that define the core nature of a people. Their caveats note internal variations and conflict, but these are cast not as features of culture but as caveats about its weakness. Most of the 'political culture' literature holds this view at a definitional level. Almond began from the notion that 'every political system [meaning country] is embedded in a particular pattern of orientation to political actions' (Almond 1956). Pye noted that this implied 'an underlying and latent coherence in political life' (Pye 1972). The main branch of the political culture school, following Almond, uses surveys to seek the majority or median view in a polity. Others, like Pye, take a more top-down and qualitative route of reasoning back from observed practices to the overarching 'national character' that 'we feel must have existed for the... political system to have developed as it has' (Pye 1968: viii). The latter is Huntington's approach, though he focuses more on arguing that civilizations are conflictual than on detailing the principles by which they operate. The problem with either emphasis is not that there is nothing to find along these lines—many countries surely have some national elements of culture, and Huntington can hardly be wrong to see cultural civilizations in human history—but that culture overall is defined as operating primarily at these vast levels in a consensual way. Especially for readers who are not familiar with a wider range of ideational scholarship, a reasonable inference is that ideational theorizing is useful to the extent that we see slavishly single-minded large groups of people in the world. The more people scheme and strategize, debate, adopt new positions, organize at a variety of levels, or simply do not know what to do, the less ideational factors matter. Since people obviously do all these things—and political scientists pay special attention to them—this sets up ideational logic for a fall.

Again, I do not mean to rule out that there are overarching national or civilizational ideational elements in our world. There may even be some fairly static and consensual ones. We might also excuse Huntington from sharp criticism given his target audience, and give credit to Almond and Verba for their pioneering attention to culture. But it is not difficult to see how the salience of these examples has contributed to widespread doubts about ideational argument. The next section returns to my mapping task to give a wider sense of the options for ideational logic.

Varieties of Ideational Explanation

Just as I made no attempt to chart all structural variants or to parse every nuance of institutionalism, so any real attempt to summarize ideational thinking would overwhelm this book. What I can offer is a fairly simple way to highlight variations within the category, with brief attention to the most common variants.

Generally, ideational schools of thought vary in almost as many ways as explanatory schools. They ask different questions, use different methods, and focus on different levels of analysis. But just as I have argued that the most fundamental variation in arguments overall concerns basic causal logic, so it is most useful to chart ideational claims in terms of the basic relationship they posit between ideational elements and action. These vary on four main dimensions:[10]

(i) Affective Versus Cognitive Ideational elements might dictate certain actions by defining emotional rewards—crudely put, by telling someone what feels good psychologically—or by defining what she can conceive of doing under certain circumstances. Affective views are often signaled by a vocabulary of 'values'. They imply that the actor is somewhat conscious of her beliefs or norms; it only makes sense to say that she values something out of emotional preference if she could conceive of alternatives. This may only be an ill-defined emotional attachment, such that she could not really defend her preference logically. But on some level she consciously prefers her practices or beliefs, having 'internalized' a commitment to them, and would tend to defend them against alternatives. Cognitive ideational claims, on the other hand, are signaled by terms like maps, grammars, models, practices, or the phrase 'taken for granted' (Swidler

[10] For a map of cultural approaches that arranges them in distinct models rather than along dimensions of debate, see Sewell (1999).

121

1986; Powell and DiMaggio 1991). They imply a less conscious role for interpretation, taking ideationally constructed descriptions of the world and normative prescriptions as the only imaginable ways to do things (or the only imaginably appropriate and legitimate way). This is a less internalized view: ideational elements are shared rules and practices that individuals have learned to use, but they have not ever been persuaded internally that these are good ways to do things. It leaves people somewhat more open to changing their culture or ideas if they become aware of alternatives—though even if alternative practices or beliefs came to someone's attention, she might not have the meanings at her disposal to comprehend them.

(ii) Ends Versus Means Ideational elements might cause action by defining end goals, indirectly leading people to choose certain actions, or by defining courses of action directly as conceivable or appropriate. 'Ends'-focused arguments suggest a somewhat higher degree of awareness of the objective world. They imply that once people have their goals, they choose the means to pursue them in a fairly unconstrained, instrumental fashion. The most famous example is Weber's argument in *The Protestant Ethic and the Spirit of Capitalism*, in which certain beliefs about salvation made it rational for Protestants to become intensely capitalistic in this life (Weber [1930] 1958). Once religious beliefs defined their end goal, Protestants figured out concrete ways to get there. 'Means'-focused views leave less room for conscious thinking between ideational elements and action. They see the most important ideational elements as practices or 'strategies of action' that are conceivable or appropriate in certain kinds of situations (Swidler 1986). People may be free to rationalize these actions by connecting them to different goals, or they may simply have no clear idea of their goals—but in this view such rationalizations are secondary to the conceivability or appropriateness of certain actions themselves.

(iii) Tight/Consensual Versus Loose/Contested The ideational element or elements relative to any given arena of action might define imaginable or valued actions fairly specifically or might be fairly loose and ambiguous. An individual might see some slice of the world through a 'tool kit' that comprises several options—leaving some room for relatively instrumental choice between them, within the bounds of the set of imaginable or appropriate tools—or he might only see one well-defined option (Swidler 1986). In a slightly different vocabulary, culture might only define 'points of concern' rather than specific options, selecting certain

issues or themes as important to argue about and defining others as unimportant or non-existent (Laitin 1986). Tightness could conceivably vary with partial independence at group and individual levels; a group might share a fairly loose set of ideational elements on some issue, but individuals within the group might adopt stricter packages of beliefs. In any scenario where group culture is relatively loose, we might expect contestation within ideationally defined bounds.

(iv) Coherent Versus Incoherent The various ideational elements around an individual might form a systematic, coherent whole, without logical contradictions, or they might be highly incoherent and logically incompatible. This coherence could vary independently at group and individual levels. We might imagine a group's shared culture as quite incoherent—a French person might draw on a variety of conflicting beliefs, norms, or practices that are equally 'French'—but see any individual as arriving at a more systematic subset to guide their precise behavior. We could even imagine a systematic group culture but relatively incoherent individual beliefs. If the coherent group culture were relatively loose, it might allow for multiple mini-interpretations that individuals could mix up incoherently. Views that emphasize individual-level coherence imply a relatively conscious view of ideational factors, with people avoiding inconsistencies in their overall set of goals or practices. Group-level coherence or incoherence has less of a logical relationship to consciousness, except in a scenario where tight coherent group culture only leaves room for tight coherent individual beliefs (and so implies a fair degree of consciousness).

While broad schools of thought and specific arguments take certain positions along these dimensions, we need not insist that ideational elements in general reflect one position in this map. Any dimension could be left as an empirical question. We could say that some ideational elements are affective, some cognitive; some define ends and some means; some are tight and some loose; some clusters of elements are coherent but others incoherent, and leave it to the researcher to figure out how to characterize any given bit of ideationally informed action. Furthermore, positions along the first two dimensions are not mutually exclusive with respect to one action. We might have a mix of affective and cognitive reasons for choosing an action, and ideational elements might define both our ends and our means. Of course, the less ideational theorists take overarching positions on these four issues—refusing to insist that ideational factors in general fit somewhere on this map—the weaker and less distinct their broad theoretical claims become. Still, one imaginable view is that the ideational factors in human action overall are highly varied on all these dimensions.

But again, theoretical schools do tend to take positions. There are some loose logical links across these various issues, and two patterns in particular form the most common variants of ideational logic. First, views that emphasize affect, ends, and coherence all imply a relatively high degree of consciousness and have tended to go together historically. Such views also often emphasize tight, consensual culture at both group and individual levels. This affective/ends/tight/coherent stance emerged implicitly from a fairly rational view of action. If we picture fairly rational people, it seems easiest to expect that ideational elements might just attach emotional rewards to certain end goals, and that these goals would be fairly clear, consensual, and consistent across the people who shared them. This view implies that ideational elements stand somewhat apart from action and from actors' immediate perceptions of the environment. Culture sets broad priorities, but once given these preferences, people figure out how to implement them in relatively direct interaction with objective conditions.

This picture of culture, norms, and ideas emerged with some of the earliest explicit semi-ideational arguments, from Durkheim. After Durkheim it passed with some changes through Weber and came to dominate ideational thinking in political science into the 1970s. Durkheim saw culturally informed action as quite rational: 'rationalist', interestingly, was a label he preferred for his work (Harris 2001: 473). To summarize crudely, he saw ideational elements as existing mainly to meet affective psychological needs. We want emotionally to be part of a group and a larger meaning. A cultural 'collective consciousness' gives us our ends in life, making us feel that we live at least partly in the service of higher goals. Since these meanings derive from principles that functionally serve our psychological needs, culture is highly coherent. It is also tight and consensual, as implied by Durkheim's use of evolutionary metaphors that treat groups and societies as 'organisms'. Contestation within a group is like sickness in an organism (see Lukes 1973; Jones 1986). I argue in Chapter 5 that Durkheim's deep reliance on psychological needs actually locates most of his claims in the psychological category. But to the extent that ideational logic did enter his framework, it was of this affective/ends/tight/coherent variety.

Weber kept a similar view of the relationship of ideational elements to action, but departed from the Durkheimian framework on the sources and overall role of culture in human life. He dropped Durkheim's metaphor of societies as evolving organisms. While in much of his writing he replaced it with a similar progressive story of 'rationalization' from tradition into modernity, he also hinted that culture might be a cyclical phenomenon. Every so often cultural meanings break down, to be reshaped when a 'charismatic leader' provides a new vision of meaning (Weber [1930] 1958: 181–2; Janos 1986: 28). He also replaced Durkheim's emphasis on organic solidarity with a view of meanings partly as tools of domination, hinting at possibilities for greater contestation. Yet Weber retained Durkheim's basic view of the culture-action connection. In *The Protestant Ethic*, once Protestants came to value a new view of their life goals, they rationally shifted to adopt new practices that would get them instrumentally to that goal. Weber made this nicely explicit in his famous metaphor of ideas as 'switchmen' on the railroad tracks of life. Culture sets the ends we value, determining which tracks we follow, but rational-instrumental pursuit of these goals pushes us along them (Weber [1922] 1958: 280).

Most of the older generation of ideational theorists in political science learned this view of culture in the 1950s and 1960s, mainly thanks to Harvard sociologist Talcott Parsons (who first translated Weber into English). Although scholars like Almond and Verba, Pye, or Wildavsky allowed for a cognitive dimension to culture, their vocabulary implied an affective, ends-focused core.[11] Almond and Verba's political culture consisted of individuals' 'psychological orientations' toward political structures (which meant institutions and some other things). This suggested that the political structures were intersubjectively real and apparent to people. Rather than operating at a cognitive level of basic perception, culture's role was to tell people how to feel about those structures, and to assign end goals around them (Dittmer 1977). When combined with the resolutely national and consensual emphasis of this generation of literature—with which most postwar political science snuck back past Weber to something like Durkheim's view of organism-like consensual societies[12]—the overall

[11] The broader Parsonian paradigm also included cognitive dimensions in its definitions but effectively sidelined them (Powell and DiMaggio 1991: 17).

[12] Following Talcott Parsons, much of postwar American political science downplayed the notion of top-down domination in Weber in favor of a focus on bottom-up legitimacy. This line of thinking flowed as much from an implicit belief in pluralism (with its metaphor of politics as a market in which social groups fluidly coalesce and recoalesce into majorities on various issues) as from Durkheim's metaphors of organisms, but both metaphors shared an emphasis on interdependent, nonconflictual, ultimately consensual societies. Organic metaphors and Durkheimian language were an explicit part of the 'structural-functionalist' school that dominated this era (Janos 1986).

view of culture fit well in the affective/ends/coherent/tight position on my map.

Although this school enjoyed a 'renaissance' in political science in the late 1980s, the second major strand of ideational logic surged to the fore around the same time. It coalesced around the opposite set of logical links, between cognitive/means/incoherent positions that fit less well with rationality and conscious instrumental action. In contrast to an affective view of ideational elements as shaping the inputs into rational decision-making (attaching emotional weight to certain options) cognitive views depart more from rationality in arguing that ideational elements shape our ability to perceive options at all. An emphasis on means-focused ideational elements also cuts out rationality; actions are chosen not as instrumental routes to ideational goals but just because this is how things are done. Incoherent patterns of contradictory beliefs or norms obviously further weaken the role of rationality. On the other hand, this cognitive/means/incoherent stance has also often come with a loose, contestable view of culture, norms, and ideas that reintroduces some scope for instrumental action. People may irrationally 'take for granted' the maze of incoherent bounds on the options they consider, but on any given issue those bounds may be loose enough to permit some degree of strategizing, choice, and innovation.

This view drew on some hints from Weber, but only emerged explicitly in sociology in the 1960s (Powell and DiMaggio 1991: 18). Several strands of sociological theory came together—most notably from Harold Garfinkel, Peter Berger and Thomas Luckmann, and Pierre Bourdieu—to replace the affective notion of moral commitment with a cognitive notion that ideational elements are taken for granted (Berger and Luckmann 1967; Garfinkel 1967; Bourdieu 1977). This 'shifted the image of cognition from a rational, discursive, quasi-scientific process to one that operates largely beneath the level of consciousness, a routine and conventional "practical reason" governed by "rules" that are recognized only when they are breached' (Powell and DiMaggio 1991: 20). People may not consciously value many of their own ideas and norms. They have never been asked to think about most of it. Instead they have just become aware of the finite set of courses of action that are comprehensible and legitimate in an arena, perhaps along with thin rationalizations that they mouth if pushed to justify their actions. They may react emotionally to deviation from these practices, but this reflects a distress of incomprehension more than conscious defense of things they value. Again, this takes an obvious step away from rationality—the main ideational impact is to block off rational decision-making, not weight the inputs to it—but it also opens another door to instrumental action. If ideational elements are more taken-for-granted practices than internally valued goals, individuals gain some distance from them. Rather than being socialized into notions they value, they are given a finite range of things they can legitimately do. Within that range they may manipulate and recombine their 'tool kit' of courses of action. Especially if the tool kit is incoherent, with different practices and rationalizations available in the various arenas of life, they may find many chances to mix and match.

This kind of thinking entered political science in the early 1990s, by way of the sociological schools of 'practice theory' and the 'new socio-logical institutionalism' (NSI). Practice theory developed mainly from the work of Bourdieu (1977; also DiMaggio 1979; Brubaker 1985). It pictured culture as a set of practices that defined cognitive limits on the means of action. It is best known to American political scientists through Ann Swidler's metaphor of the 'tool kit' of 'strategies of action' (Swidler 1986). Sociological institutionalism had a particularly strong impact after the 1991 publication of Powell and DiMaggio's *New Institutionalism in Organizational Analysis* (whose introduction provides the framework for much of this section). It entered political science most directly in IR, where scholars like Peter Katzenstein, Michael Barnett, Martha Finnemore, and Jeffrey Legro were drawn to the NSI focus on the 'isomorphism' of organizations and practices—how models or practices emerge and proliferate across 'organizational fields' (or arenas of action). Appealing especially to the work of Stanford sociologist John Meyer, they began to explore how norms and practices proliferated across international and national arenas (Meyer and Hannan 1979; Legro 1995; Finnemore 1996; Katzenstein 1996; Meyer et al. 1997). Around the same time, similar thinking percolated into work on American political development and comparative political economy. Though research on US political history referred less explicitly to NSI, scholars like Victoria Hattam and Gerald Berk drew on it to understand America's trajectory (Hattam 1993; Berk 1994). They and colleagues in comparative political economy also increasingly interacted with NSI sociologists writing on political subjects (and often publishing in political science venues), like Frank Dobbin, Neil Fligstein, David Strang, Richard Biernacki, and John Campbell (Fligstein 1990; Strang 1991; Dobbin 1994; Biernacki 1995; Campbell 1998). By the late 1990s, practitioners of cognitive-style ideational thinking were probably as numerous in political science as adherents of the older affective current.

The uptick in ideationally focused political science in the 1990s also included strands that fit less cleanly into the two common constellations. In IR, Alexander Wendt (1987), Nicolas Onuf (1989), and Friedrich Kratochwil (1989) set the foundations of 'constructivism' in the late 1980s. Their main point was that the nature of state interaction is not dictated by objective conditions—whether in realism's security-focused battle for relative gains or in liberalism's wealth-focused search for absolute gains—but instead is 'socially constructed'. They adopted a cognitive, means-focused ideational logic, but their emphasis on basic principles defining periods of the international system carried a connotation of strong coherence. Just how coherently they saw ideational factors overall, and how tightly they thought norms or ideas usually define action, was difficult to tell because they shied away from empirical claims (Checkel 1998). In comparative politics, the 'ideas' school also emerged in the late 1980s from scholars like Peter Hall (1989), Kathryn Sikkink (1991), Sheri Berman (1998), and Kathleen McNamara (1998). Their main point was that in the complex world of policymaking, specific choices often trace more directly to packages of ideas than to objective structural or institutional conditions. Their focus on fairly precise policy ideas gave them a clear position on coherence and tightness: the ideational elements they traced had high individual coherence ('believers' took up consistent packages of ideas), low group coherence (groups were often split by competing policy ideas), and were quite tight (packages of ideas led closely to certain policy choices). Their picture of crusading advocates of fairly conscious beliefs also suggested at least a somewhat affective approach. In the opposite move from constructivists, though, they shied away from abstract micro- and meta-theorizing and stressed specific empirical arguments, so their overall position on affective/cognitive or ends/means debates remained a bit blurry.[13]

What is at stake in these differences over ideational elements? Again, we need not insist that all ideational dynamics occupy one pole on these dimensions. They may vary a good deal. But for two reasons we should be as precise as we can on these measures. First and most obviously, if ideational dynamics overall may vary in these terms, claims about the effects of any specific ideational element need to specify how it works. 'Culture matters' is not a claim worth considering; we need to know

---

[13] The same moderate criticism applies to my previous work (2002, 2003).

how some piece of it matters. Second, only in nailing down the shape of relevant ideational elements in an arena can ideational claims illuminate processes of change. To see the openings for change in an ideational claim we need a clear view of how tightly and coherently ideational elements dictate previous actions, and of the affective/cognitive and ends/means mechanisms by which people are tethered to those actions. A map of such openings is the closest thing that ideational claims can offer to structural or institutional analysis of the constraints and opportunities available to actors in an objective obstacle course. Ideational claims, especially irrationally based ones, may not insist that people perceive and choose highly specific reactions to such 'openings', as would a rationalist logic of position. But this makes them all the more dependent on specifying what they do claim about the constraining or empowering dynamics of ideational elements.

Supporting Ideational Claims

Once we set aside the epistemological reasons for excluding ideational claims from causal debates, support for such claims holds few special mysteries. Much of the common-sense basics of support for ideational claims are already visible in the literature even despite the epistemological confusion. Even many ideationally inclined scholars who try to separate their work behind a Weberian veil tend to offer more empirically based comments on causality than they admit. Though they characterize their own claims as noncausal, they typically feel free to criticize more classically explanatory scholarship as inadequate. This implies that they do claim some purchase on causality (Biernacki 1999).

Basic empirical support for an ideational claim does not look radically different from the similar tasks in preceding chapters. I suggested earlier that support for particularistic institutionalist claims showcases much of the model for ideational ones. Institutional claims must show both that action reflects institutional positioning and that the actions that produced the institutions were not straightforward responses to preexisting causes. Ideational claims must show both that actions reflect certain interpretations rather than direct objective positioning, and that the interpretations are not just derived from objective positioning. In the former stage, ideational claims connect actions to ideational elements much like structural or institutional claims connect actions to material or institutional positions. Ideally, an ideational claim first documents the 'presence' of ideational elements prior to the action, including their content and distribution across the people under study. Second, it shows that the people it claims followed these ideational elements—the 'believers', if you will (though that word may be less appropriate for certain ideational elements)—oriented their action similarly to each other and differently from others. Third, it provides an argument about how these ideational elements oriented action this way, mainly on the dimensions discussed above (mostly affective or mostly cognitive? by dictating ends or means? etc.). Fourth, as distinctly as possible from the initial evidence of preexisting ideational elements, it provides evidence that during the action, people's thinking followed the process laid out in the third step.

In their second stage, establishing the autonomy of ideational elements as causes, ideational claims must detail the limits of competing logics' ability to account for the ideational elements in question. Given that empirical ideational claims always allow for some intersubjective reality, and that most allow for some general psychological predilections among humans, they effectively need to make their competitors' arguments as far as possible in order to delineate the causal space within which ideational elements were decisive. How different could these ideational elements have been? If possible, what were historically active alternative interpretations that were somehow crowded out? In addition to this largely negative focus—documenting the range over which other logics do not explain these ideational elements—our ideational claim would ideally relate the story by which these ideational elements came to fill that space. By definition this will be a story largely about contingency and agency—it will focus on historical accident or creative invention—but it is important to fill in the argument.

Like in the similar sections in Chapters 2 and 3, this basic sketch of support for ideational claims does not even begin to address the methods by which ideational claims can go about presenting convincing evidence. The justification for stopping here is partly about feasibility. This is a book on mapping substantive claims, and I can only give the brief attention to methods that is necessary to flesh out logical categories. But I also see less of a need to spill ink on the more strictly methodological side. Without making light of the challenges of interpretation of culture and ideas (or of any other aspect of reality), I think we have many plausible tools to access both the objective and interpretive aspects of political action. Our main problems lie not in how to find and check evidence for our arguments, but in formulating clear and distinct arguments to begin with.

Conclusion

This chapter stands out in tone and size. Rather than just cutting away confusing or overlapping terms to reveal a clean category, I spent many pages defending the mere existence of ideational explanation. In my view this is a reflection of the odd historical place that ideational thinking occupies in the human sciences. A generation hence, I like to think, a new version of this book may look more balanced. We may have dispensed with some bad reasons for having narrow, falsely 'scientific' debates that exclude ideational claims. I doubt we will agree much more on how the world works, but more common recognition of plausible alternatives would constitute some progress.

Three paragraphs can sum up the main points. First, ideational causal claims trace actions to some constellation of practices, symbols, norms, grammars, models, beliefs, and/or identities through which certain people interpret their world. For these ideational elements to gain autonomy as distinct causes of action, they must be the consequence of earlier contingent actions—not just a reflection of other conditions. This makes ideational explanation a particularistic logic, beginning with an unexplained creative or accidental act but then explaining later actions as its consequences. It can rely on 'a-rational' foundations, seeing the opening for interpretation in an objectively ambiguous world, or on irrational foundations, seeing people as unable or indisposed to recognize the objective world. Even in irrational variants, though, no coherent ideational claim sees people as entirely free to interpret things subjectively. All ideational claims must interlock with other logics to frame the space for their own claims.

Second, the common reasons for skepticism about ideational explanation are misplaced. Conceptually, the notion of a separate real of 'constitutive' scholarship or dynamics is built on imprecise questions about causes and effects, not on some weird mode of relationships that somehow exist alongside the chronologically bound, stepwise creation of the present from the past that characterizes the rest of our universe. The notion that ideational claims are not explanation due to their nongeneral format overlooks the possibility of two-stage particularistic logics. Methodologically, there are no broad reasons to dismiss ideational causal claims as impossible to document. Ideational elements are indeed intangible. But all arguments rely on some intangibles, all intentional explanations of human action invoke some meanings, and at least some beliefs, norms, practices, or symbols are quite easy to document in plausible ways. Historically, many political scientists have downplayed these conceptual and methodological possibilities because some well-known but weak ideational arguments discredit the category.

Third, a helpful way to organize the varieties of ideational argument is to consider where they fall along four dimensions. We can characterize the relationship between any ideational element and an action as mostly affective or mostly cognitive, mostly relating to the ends of action or mostly relating to the means, relatively coherent or relatively incoherent with other relevant ideational elements (at group and individual levels), and relatively tight or relatively loose in connecting to specific actions. The most prominent ideational claims over the last century fall into two broad positions on these dimensions. From Durkheim and Weber into much of anthropology, Parsonian sociology, and postwar political science runs a strand of affective/ends/coherent/tight analysis of culture. Since the 1960s, a strand of cognitive/means/incoherent/loose analysis emerged from the work of Bourdieu, Garfinkel, Berger and Luckmann, and others. Recent schools of ideational thought in political science—most notably constructivism and the 'ideas' literature—are harder to locate, since they respectively need to spell out more empirical claims and more ontological foundations.

5

Psychological Explanation

Psychology is an unusual term. It refers both to a set of phenomena (as in, 'our psychology makes us act this way') and to the discipline that studies them. Definitions of the discipline are easiest to find. Psychology is 'the scientific study of the human mind and human behavior', investigating the internal contours of individuals' judgments and decisions (McGraw 2006). But not all claims we can make about mental processes can usefully be called psycholog*ical*, invoking psychology as a distinct set of phenomena with causal implications rather than as a broad subject for study. A glance into volumes on political psychology, for example (like Kuklinski 2002), often turns up some claims that are clearly ideational (with individuals' mental processes depicted as the beliefs or values of some historical group) or structural or institutional (with individuals' mental processes presented simply as rational: automatic, objective, utility-maximizing responses to an accurately perceived environment).

To be distinct from ideational claims, psychological logic must refer to mental motives or rules that are hard-wired in physiological terms. Few psychologists today defend a strongly hard-wired view of action—most emphasize the interrelationship of 'nature and nurture'—but the distinctly psycholog*ical* components of their arguments focus on nature. In most versions these hard-wired motives or rules are universal to all people, as 'human psychology', though in some they vary across groups or individuals. To be distinct from structural or institutional claims, psychological logic must invoke hard-wired mental processes that do not simply match clear costs, benefits, and probabilities to a fixed hierarchy of preferences via objective rationality. This is not to deny that rationalist arguments invoke a highly specific model of psychology. But as we have seen, the point of espousing that model is to set aside some variation in action from variation in mental processes, directing our explanatory attention to variation in objective environmental conditions. Only to the extent that people think in hard-wired ways that are different from simple rational models do we need a distinct psychological category of explanatory logic.

This means that distinctly psychological claims can do either of two things that logics of position do not do. They can either argue that people are hard-wired to employ irrational decision-making, or they can argue that hard-wired psychology explains some of the preferences of rational actors. Practically all psychological claims take the former route, focusing on how people interpret their environment in irrational ways. They try to show that people are hard-wired to take cognitive shortcuts, be overwhelmed by emotion, sift information in biased ways, misperceive clear signals, and so on. Only a small minority of psychological claims focus on hard-wired preferences. This small subset is an a-rational variant of psychological logic, since in principle it is just about what rational actors choose to pursue. But again, while a-rational hard-wired preference-definition has received some attention from psychologically inclined scholars, contemporary work is almost entirely focused on irrationality.

A psychological causal segment, then, argues that people take certain actions because they interpret their world in hard-wired (and almost always irrational) ways. In contrast to the revisionism of the other chapters, this is a mainstream definition.[1] But like the other chapters, this one confronts its own set of challenges. Unlike structure, psychology's basic meaning is not very problematic. Unlike institutionalism, psychological explanation is often defined as I suggest. Unlike ideational explanation, the disciplinary status and 'hard science' experimental credentials of psychological logic mean it is rarely dismissed entirely. But in its own way, psychological logic suffers from even greater marginality in political science than ideational logic. Common political science typologies like 'interests, institutions, ideas', or 'structure, culture, rationality' ignore it.[2] This may be partly due to a division of labor—psychological scholarship is marginal in political science *because* it has its own discipline—though the reverse dynamic seems more common. Structural or ideational incursions

---

[1] For one of many conventional summaries that take this basic view, see Kahler (1998).

[2] The most recent 'State of the Discipline' volume has no identifiable 'political psychology' chapter, though it is mentioned in chapters on public opinion and citizen participation.

into political science, for example, have often moved from strongholds in economics, sociology, or anthropology.

I see three deeper reasons for this marginality. Two are bad reasons that run parallel to common skepticism about culture and ideas. First, as a logic of interpretation, psychological claims rely more directly on intangible evidence than structural or institutional competitors. Second, like ideational explanation, psychological approaches in political science suffer from a historical problem of weak standard-bearers. Due to the origins of political psychology in Freudian psychoanalysis, personality studies of political leaders are still 'sometimes mistakenly identified as *the* psychological approach' to politics (Sears, Huddy, and Jervis 2003: 4; their emphasis). The reputation of psychology in some quarters has yet to recover from the delegitimation of psychoanalysis. Fortunately these two objections are easy to dismiss. Chapter 4 has already defended interpretive explanations, and the briefest glance across recent political-psychological scholarship turns up a thriving variety of post-Freudian theories.

The third objection is more fundamental. The deepest skepticism about psychological claims in political science concerns their thin and distant relationship to specific actions (and especially to variation in action). While serious scholars might argue that British politics is different from Mongolian politics almost entirely for structural reasons, almost entirely for institutional reasons, or almost entirely for ideational reasons, no one is likely to argue that the major source of variation between the two arenas is psychological. Again, some scholarship points to variation in psychological dispositions across groups, and a great deal of research documents that individuals can have radically different psychological inclinations (see Alford and Hibbing 2004). But even if we picture the most detailed psychological dispositions—with inherited proclivities, say, to risky behavior, violence, or conservatism—the explanatory material that psychological claims build around action is inherently less variegated and rich than elaborate descriptions of structural positions in markets or military competition, complex obstacle courses of man-made institutions, or the often-bizarre idiosyncrasies of cultural practices. The dispositions revealed by psychological analysis are just that: dispositions. The degree and direction of their activation tend to depend heavily on other factors. They seem far from real political action when compared to the sharp imperatives of a structural threat of war, institutional pressures to defend a bureaucratic budget, or specific ideologies or rituals.

But the flip side of this objection suggests the promise of psychological claims in political science. They are distant from action because they are prior to other logics, showing the hard-wired dispositions that people have 'before' (analytically, not chronologically) they are set down in structural, institutional, and/or ideational settings. To the extent that scholars can document politically relevant contours of human irrationality—like tendencies to form sharp in-group/out-group boundaries, to exaggerate low probabilities of large losses, or to calculate demands only relative to salient reference groups—the proponents of other logics must engage how (and how much) causal variation these dispositions leave to other causes. If we all tend toward in-group identity formation and the creation of out-group enemies, for example, to what extent can any constellation of structural incentives, institutional orders, or beliefs and norms sustain peaceful interaction? In addition to the point of departure that universalistic psychological theories could offer, psychological claims of individual variation might fill in the last steps of general theorizing. Universal psychological dispositions could set a range of human needs, emotions, and cognitive tools. Structure, institutions, or culture and ideas could fill in the conditions to which these needs and tools get applied. Individual-level psychological theories could explain why individuals apply the needs and tools in different ways. If psychological theorizing were as successful as it could be, it could provide the broad framework and the most specific individual analysis, with other logics contributing middle-range claims in between.

Some political psychologists are convinced of the appropriateness of this format for social science theorizing. Many proponents of structural, institutional, or ideational claims are less sure. As in the previous chapters I remain agnostic, aiming only to present the logical core, boundaries, and main variations of a distinct kind of explanatory claim. Though I see this chapter as the least revisionist—using most terms as intended by these scholars—it too leads to reclassifications of prominent literature. Most notably I argue that some of the canon of ideational theorizing, from Durkheim through some later 'cultural' scholars, belongs in this category. I also note that much of the research done by 'political psychologists', especially in the large literature on public opinion, does not use psychological logic to explain anything. As with my preceding remarks, this is a point of clarification rather than a criticism. Just how much hard-wired psychology explains in politics is too big a question for this book, but I would like us to pose it more clearly.

Defining Psychological Explanation

Mapping out a distinct category of psychological causal segments first requires a longer defense of the dominant—but contested—move of placing irrationality at its core. This helps clarify the category's boundaries with rationalistic logics of position. Nailing down the boundaries more fully then demands more attention to the unusual distance of psychological claims from action, as well as elaboration of the confused boundary with ideational claims.

Distinct Psychological Claims Are Not About Rationality

Some political psychologists object to the emphasis on irrationality in their subfield. Jonathan Mercer and Rose McDermott argue that a huge amount of recent neurological and experimental research calls for an extension of political psychology beyond irrationality. Subjects with brain damage only to emotional centers cannot make everyday decisions, getting trapped in absurd overanalysis of costs and benefits. This implies that even seemingly rational behavior depends on emotions. Drawing on a wide range of evidence and theorizing, McDermott summarizes, '... accurate emotional processing constitutes an inherent part of rationality itself; emotion facilitates quick, effective, and accurate decision making' (McDermott 2004*b*). Thus, concludes Mercer, the standard view of psychology as about irrationality 'is coherent and logical, but wrong', and '[p]olitical psychology is—or at least should be—as much about accurate judgments as inaccurate ones'. Mercer further suggests that rationalist theorizing that does not recognize emotion and other psychological processes stretches the bounds of plausibility. Structural or institutional claims that picture human beings as mechanical cost-benefit calculators, he argues, can only be mostly normative (telling us how people *should* behave under certain conditions, but not explaining how they do) or correlative (offering a stylized model that may match outcomes but not plausible causal mechanisms for explanation) (Mercer 2005).[3]

I find McDermott and Mercer persuasive that emotions are relevant to the extent that we do seem rational. I also emphasized in Chapters 2 and 3 that rationalist explanation always relies on some degree of 'as if' argument, as Mercer suggests. Even if people *were* acting rationally,

---

[3] See also Cosmides and Tooby (1994) and Crawford (2000). A powerful criticism of rationality is Rabin (2000).

we could not fully document it in any real-world situation. Yet just how much recent research renders implausible causal claims based on classical rationality requires more debate. More attention to emotional bases may better flesh out the mechanisms of rationality. Such research only really challenges rationalist logic-of-position claims, however, to the extent that it leads us to expect and document divergence in real action from rationalist lines. Only with this kind of demonstration—of a range of effects of psychological dynamics on real-world actions that are distinct from simple rational response to an objective structural or institutional environment—will rationalist arguments be compelled to qualify or alter their claims. In other words, Mercer and McDermott are right that recent research offers a new picture of rationality, but their point only impacts explanatory debates if it does more than shore up structural or institutionalist claims with more realistic micro-foundations. If we want 'psychological explanation' to designate a distinct kind of causal segment, it must refer to claims about how action departs from simple rationalist expectations for hard-wired reasons.

Thus we return to the position that distinct psychological claims do one or both of two things. They can claim that we must pay attention to psychology because action reflects hard-wired preferences. This may not directly challenge rationalist claims, since people might pursue these preferences in otherwise-rational response to a structural or institutional environment. The more direct path to a distinct psychological causal segment—and by far the most common route—is to focus on irrationality. The core of psychological logic consists of claims that people arrive at certain actions because they analyze, categorize, perceive, judge, desire, feel, or instinctively need in irrational ways.

The Foundational but Distant Nature of 'Hard-wired' Argument

Confirming an irrationality-focused core for psychological claims helps delineate their boundary vis-à-vis rationalist logics of position. But that boundary and the one with ideational claims can still seem difficult to draw sharply. No interesting psychological claim holds that normal people are totally irrational, fully ignoring all objective aspects of their structural and institutional environment. There is always something there for people to misinterpret. Many psychological claims also depend strongly on connections to ideational elements to fill in the ways in which hard-wired psychological dispositions get activated in particular societies or settings. I made the same point about the other logics: practically all claims rely on some help from other logics and can only be clear in specifying their relative roles. Yet psychological claims depend the most on other logics because they operate at such a remove from action. No interesting political action can be seen as even close to fully determined by psychological causes. Thus a sense of the boundaries of the category requires close attention to just how far 'hard-wiredness' might go, and how it might interact with other factors.

'Hard-wired' psychological dispositions are lodged in physical brain structure and processes. These in turn are presumably the result of genetics, though they may change with age or injury, and might be altered by other environmental impacts (like exposure to toxins, or perhaps even to television!). Many such features will be shared across all human beings, but some will vary with individuals or groups. Although there is obviously much more to be said about the physiological states and mechanisms of hard-wired psychology, this basic observation is sufficient to serve as the foundation for psychological logic. The more a causal claim about action goes beyond physically based mental processes inside a person's skull—pointing either to his position in external conditions, or to 'socially constructed' interpretations with no physiological basis— the more its psychological causal segment interacts with (and concedes to) other logics. One sign that most psychologists accept this basic view is their widespread skepticism about the developing subfield of 'cultural psychology'. As I noted in Chapter 4, it is commonly and correctly understood as a very different enterprise from mainstream psychology (Fiske et al. 1998; Tedeschi 1988; Nisbett 2003).

Let me be clear: few psychologists today (and even fewer political psychologists) use a language of genetic or physiological determinism. As I mentioned at the outset, most stress the interaction of hard-wiring with environmental conditions, picturing a world of both nature and nurture. But again, the parts of their arguments that we can usefully call distinctively psychological are those that ascribe some range of causal effects to hard-wired motives or rules. One example of recent work that is nicely explicit about this—and also about the acute challenge of connecting such effects to concrete political action—uses twins to study inherited political leanings. After studying survey research on thousands of identical twins in the USA and Australia, John Alford, Carolyn Funk, and John Hibbing come to the striking view that 'political attitudes are influenced much more heavily by genetics than by parental socialization' (Alford, Funk, and Hibbing 2005: 164). Purely biological inheritance appears to account for much of the variation in some broad political attitudes. But Alford, Funk, and Hibbing hasten to add that they are not biological determinists. Genes interact in complex and poorly understood ways, and genetic makeups only 'generally influence the extent to which organisms are responsive to particular environmental conditions'. At most their results sketch two broad personality types—labeled 'absolutist' and 'contextualist', and mapping broadly onto American notions of conservative and liberal—and they stress that many factors can trump such broad attitudes in voting choices or other political action. Overall, their results suggest that hard-wired personality types are important, but also that tracing effects in any case will immediately lead us into complex interaction with other causes (for a similar broad-audience argument, Ridley 2003).

To see what happens when scholars do connect psychological claims to concrete actions, consider some prominent examples. Two of the best-known psychological theories in political science are 'prospect theory' and 'relative deprivation'. The core observation of Daniel Kahneman and Amos Tversky's prospect theory—documented exhaustively in classroom experimentation in the USA—is that people are risk-averse when focused on gains and risk-seeking when focused on losses. When asked if they prefer a certain gain of $1,000 or a 50-percent chance at $2,500, most people choose the former; when forced to choose a certain loss of $1,000 or a 50-percent chance of a loss of $2,500, most choose the latter. The most straight-forward rational thinker would do the reverse.[4] Advocates of prospect theory in political science argue that it helps to explain many political actions: the Japanese decision to attack Pearl Harbor (a desperate grab for a low probability of avoiding loss), the American decision not to unseat Saddam Hussein in the first Gulf War (a cautious choice focused on acquired gains), or the intractability of territorial conflicts in Ireland or the Middle East (driven by deep-seated aversion to total loss on both sides) (McDermott 1998, 2004c).

The phrase 'relative deprivation' was coined by psychologist Samuel Stouffer in the 1940s, but has older intellectual roots. Stouffer was puzzled to find that African-American soldiers during World War II appeared to be happier when stationed in the American South than in the North. He reasoned that the soldiers evaluated their own condition by reference to local African-Americans, and so demanded less in the South where local

---

[4] A mathematician would value a 50-percent chance of gaining or losing $2,500 at +/− $1,250, and so would choose taking the risk to gain more and the certain loss of less.

black populations were worse off (Stouffer et al. 1949). In so doing he echoed a comment Marx made a century earlier:

A house may be large or small; as long as the surrounding houses are equally small it satisfies all social demands for a dwelling. But let a palace arise beside the little house, and it shrinks from a little house to a hut. The little house shows now that its owner has only very slight or no demands to make; and however high it may shoot up in the course of civilization, if the neighboring palace grows to an equal or even greater extent, the occupant of the relatively small house will feel more and more uncomfortable, dissatisfied and cramped within its four walls.

(Marx [1849] 1978)

Marx never developed this observation much, probably because the notion of inherently relative demands—that people only felt exploited if treated worse than salient reference groups—fit awkwardly with his structural logic. But the early twentieth-century economist Thorstein Veblen picked up the idea to explain patterns of economic consumption and conflict around them, arguing that the masses base their consumption and demands on imitation of elites (Veblen 1915). Others invoked a similar dynamic globally as an 'international demonstration effect' that simultaneously drives and blocks Third World development. Spreading knowledge of First World wealth leads poorer populations to alter their aspirations, creating demand for development but also dissatisfaction that foments unrest and instability (de Schweinitz 1964; Cohen 1973; Bendix 1979). In parallel, a wide range of postwar scholars in psychology, sociology, anthropology, and political science followed Stouffer's lead, especially to explain prejudices, social unrest, and revolution. According to Ted Gurr, for example, rebellions occur not when people suffer some absolute level of immiseration or oppression, but when they are denied whatever standard of living they see as appropriate for people like themselves (Gurr 1970; Crocker, Major, and Steele 1998; Walker and Smith 2002).

Prospect theory and relative deprivation both provide distinct, plausible, broadly important expectations about action. Actual causal claims based on them, though, invoke hard-wired psychology only at a highly abstract level. As they get into concrete cases they quickly shift to other kinds of causal segments that orient or activate psychological dispositions. Prospect theorists are frank that they have no systematic view of 'framing effects' that dictate what people perceive as gains or losses (or how people rank them as large or small in situations without easy dollar-amount labels) (Fischoff 1983; Levy 1994). Relative deprivation theorists similarly rely on other logics about whom people see as 'like themselves', and what entitlements the actors and their reference groups ostensibly deserve.

In McDermott's application of prospect theory, for example, she argues that when Iranians took over the American embassy in 1979, President Jimmy Carter 'could only have seen himself operating in a domain of losses' (McDermott 1998: 47). Falling domestic popularity and a seemingly insoluble international crisis were relatively objective conditions that made the status quo unacceptable. The beliefs of individual advisers led to internal debates about how to respond, however, with some stressing analogies to hostage situations during World War II and others drawing parallels to the Bay of Pigs invasion or the Israeli raid at Entebbe. Overall, McDermott suggests that the irrational regularities of prospect theory set a background propensity for risky strategies in bad times; Carter's apparently rational reactions to objective conditions framed a 'domain of loss' and defined the policy problem; and the beliefs of individual leaders about appropriate historical analogies inclined them toward certain risky options.

Andrew Janos offers a sophisticated political application of relative deprivation, making it the core of a long-term explanation of eastern European development. Once western Europe took a lead in agricultural production and industrialization, he argues, the psychological dynamics of relative deprivation undercut eastern European economic growth, political stability, and cultural pride. Rising trade and travel in the nineteenth century spread British standards for consumption, but productivity was slower to change. Even with slowly rising incomes, eastern Europeans 'felt they were becoming poorer with every passing year' (Janos 1989). Marginal rates of saving and private investment fell to boost consumption. Nationalism and other forms of political resentment increased. The mood shifted to the 'sense of malaise, self-pity, and gloom that permeates both public and literary life in these countries after the middle of the nineteenth century' (Janos 1989: 224). Like in McDermott's use of prospect theory, relative deprivation offers a foundational decision rule, but other causes fill out the argument. The objective fact of a western lead in production, together with the arrival through trade of large quantities of goods long seen as luxuries—textiles, soap, candles, dishes, glassware—brought a new reference group to the attention of eastern Europeans and reset their definitions of acceptable (and even necessary) consumption. Other structural, institutional, and ideational factors affected how this sense of 'backwardness' played out. But an impression of deprivation relative to the West defined the core trajectories of eastern European societies.

A distinct psychological logic forms the heart of these arguments, but their psychological components alone do not strongly narrow down causal possibilities. In this sense psychological claims are similar to rational-choice theory without a substantive environment or assumptions about preferences. On the other hand, they differ from rationalism in carrying both more and less substance. They carry more substance in offering a distinct source of causal variation, which is why psychological logic holds a place in this typology but 'rationalism' does not. Once again, the point of rationalism in explanatory theory is to distill 'mental processes' to the simplest, most invariant stimulus-response functionalism, attributing variation entirely (over the scope of their claims) to variation in the objective environment. Psychological claims assert that interpretation imparts its own irreducible dynamics to action. They usually carry less substance than rationalism, however, in leaving the causal terrain more open. If we think of rational choice as a psychological model itself—departing for a moment from my terminology—it is typically presented as a full model of decision-making, as least with respect to some scope of salient conditions and choices. Psychological claims do not tend to offer comparable general models of all decision-making. Instead they advance just one way (or a set of ways) in which decision-making is skewed by hard-wired inclinations. They offer a partial model of decision-making that leaves the door open to other variation in interpretation. Other psychological rules might be out there: if people have some irrational patterns of thinking, they may have others. Their thinking might also depend on ideational rules, attitudes, or practices. Thus psychological claims tend to be more selective than rationalist ones in what they tell us about decision-making, and they also fit more easily with other claims about interpretation.

Confusion on the Ideational Boundary

One more clarification stakes out the category's basic boundaries. Though my distinction between general, physiological psychological claims, and particularistic, 'socially constructed' ideational claims is fairly standard, the logic of some prominent scholarship nonetheless contradicts its self-described and commonly understood position on this line. Some major 'psychological' schools are logically ideational, and major works on 'culture' are logically psychological.

The most important example on the 'psychological' side is the behaviorist tradition that follows from Pavlov, Watson, and Skinner. It set the foundations for the field of political socialization, which is one of the largest components of what is usually called political psychology. Pavlov's famous dog makes clear why this label is confusing. The dog was not hard-wired to salivate at the chime of a bell; it was taught to do so. The core logic of this tradition is that habits learned at some point (usually early in life) condition behavior in lasting ways. With respect to party loyalties, for example, the argument runs that the flexible, open minds of young people absorb political attitudes from their families and social contexts, gradually producing more inflexible ideological commitments with age (Hyman 1959; Campbell et al. 1960; Jennings and Niemi 1974, 1981; Converse 1976; Miller and Shanks 1996; Sears and Levy 2003). Certainly it makes sense to locate this research within psychology as a discipline, as part of the study of mental processes. But for my purposes of categorizing causal logics, these scholars argue that the shape of mental processes is caused not by hard-wired psychology but by social context (and usually culture: prevailing beliefs, norms, and identities).

Another large literature to which the same point applies is the work on framing, metaphors, analogies, or 'operational codes' that usually appears in surveys of political psychology, especially in IR (though it also frequently surfaces in surveys of ideas and culture). Alexander George's work on operational codes, Ole Holsti and James Rosenau's work on 'belief systems', Yuen Foong Khong's study of historical analogies, and similar work begins from psychological discussions of the cognitive limits that lead people to rely on shortcuts to decision and action (George 1969; Holsti and Rosenau 1979; Tetlock and McGuire 1986; Khong 1991). But beyond this point of departure, these scholars present particular codes, frames, analogies, or belief systems as assembled from cultural elements, individual innovation, and salient events, without emphasizing any hard-wired limits on how people might arrive at lenses through which they interpret the world. In other words, these arguments invoke abstract psychology on cognitive limits mainly as a background reason why culture and ideas determine what people do. Psychological limits negatively rule out rational processes of calculation, but are not presented as precluding any particular action. There is nothing wrong with such a move, of course, but its explanatory claims belong almost entirely in the ideational category.

On the 'ideational' side, many 'theories of culture' stretching back to Durkheim rely strongly on psychological logic. A common entry point for such logic is through theorizing on how culture and ideas respond to basic human needs. If the needs are psychological, then psychology may ultimately explain why culture arises and takes certain forms (and actions that ostensibly follow). For Durkheim, societies only remain orderly if united by a 'collective consciousness' of shared beliefs, symbols and attitudes that gives meaning to action and organizes social life. In preindustrial societies, he thought social order required a consciousness built around religion and kinship, with fairly uniform beliefs across individuals and an emphasis on custom, obligation, and affective attachments to the group. To hold together more 'advanced' societies with more of a division of labor—economically, with people offering goods and services in a market rather than fending for themselves, and socio-politically, with differentiated institutions for governance, religion, and so on—the consciousness had to focus more on contractual, institutional, and legal ties between individuals. Durkheim generally argued that these psychological needs, conditioned by economic phases, explained the presence and shape of cultures in a functionalist way. Traditional and advanced ideal-types were 'normal' cases, implying that the right kind of culture usually arose as needed. Biological metaphors of societies as 'organisms' further implied self-regulating forces, like a body's immune system, that kept societies 'healthy' and encouraged cultural adaptation to economic change. As his clearest biographer concludes, he proposed 'a social-psychological theory about the social conditions for individual psychological health' (Lukes 1973: 215; Jones 1986; Morrison 1995). Durkheim did note 'pathological' cases where collective consciousness weakened (most famously in his study of suicide), but he was never clear about why (Durkheim [1897] 1951). His clearest, most consistent point was that psychological needs caused certain cultural forms and their evolution over time.

Inglehart provides a contemporary example of similar thinking. Inglehart is a latter-day 'modernization theorist' whose lineage traces from Durkheim through Weber (where it took a more solidly ideational turn), through Talcott Parsons (where ideational logic was again muted in favor of structural and psychological claims), to the modernization theory of scholars like Daniel Lerner and Daniel Bell (see Lerner 1958; Bell 1973; Janos 1986). In Inglehart, Durkheim is almost fully reborn, with an explicitly functionalist view of evolving social 'organisms' (Inglehart 1997: 11–18). The shape of the organism—the culture and values of its individual components—reflects a combination of human inclinations that evolve with underlying economic change. There is a structural component, since these inclinations seem to be partly rational responses to the fulfillment of basic needs in a changing landscape. One claim is that people focus on 'materialist' values at modest levels of wealth but dabble in 'postmodern' concerns (the environment, feminism, and so on) in the more secure comfort of advanced economies. But the main logic portrays people who interpret their world through values and beliefs, which fits poorly with rationalist structuralism. Rather than seeing people who react directly to their surroundings, Inglehart suggests that all human beings tend to share similar interpretive filters under certain structural conditions. Like with Durkheim, human thinking and action is first bounded by a small set of psychological possibilities, each of which functions best in certain economic phases. Ideational logic enters only in residual international variations.

In a slightly subtler vein, some 'cultural' scholarship drops the underlying structural evolution of Durkheim, Parsons, or Inglehart but retains their goal of typologizing cultures into finite variants. This preserves a psychological focus on the *limits* of ideational variation. Probably the best-known example in political science is the 'cultural theory' of Wildavsky. He saw 'only a limited number of cultures that between them categorize most human relations.... What makes order possible is that only a few conjunctions of shared values and their corresponding social relations are viable in that they are socially livable' (Wildavsky 1987). He founded his view in work by anthropologist Mary Douglas that posited five (and only five) kinds of cultures: fatalist/apathetic, collectivist/hierarchical, individualist/competitive, egalitarian, and autonomous/retreatist (Douglas 1970, 1992). Wildavsky and his collaborators argued that once we classify people in one of these groups, we can explain many of their political attitudes. Psychological needs for coherence and consistency apparently prevent enduring mixes of these principles. There is room for ideational logic in this approach, since the reasons why any group ends up in one of these boxes might reflect particularistic social construction. But these scholars' main concern is with showing how real-world attitudes and actions that seem complex and surprising—like messy debates between Right and Left—clarify once we realize that they boil down to a limited number of psychological possibilities (Ellis, Thompson, and Wildavsky 1990; Ellis and Thompson 1997; also Hofstede 1984; Schwartz 1999). Recently they have labeled their view a 'theory of constrained relativism' (Thompson, Verweij, and Ellis 2006). Their focus is not on how culture causes variation, but on how psychology constrains it.

These are just a few salient examples of confusion on the psychological/ideational boundary. More extended treatment of any of these works might reveal more nuance between their psychological and ideational components. But together with the treatment of the same boundary in

Chapter 4, these snapshots serve my purposes. They show that just as with structural or institutional claims, we cannot take scholars at their word when they call their work cultural or psychological. Instead we must define the terms ourselves and trace how causal claims boil down to socially constructed or hard-wired interpretive elements (or other things). Yet again I stress that this is not a substantive criticism. None of these arguments is weaker just because its logic is more or less distinctively psychological than its author claims. If these scholars described their claims a little more clearly, though—or if we can clarify their logic for them—we would be better able to engage debates about whether they are substantively right or wrong.

Variants of Psychological Explanation

A full chart of psychological claims is even further beyond this book's scope than comprehensive maps of structural, institutional, or ideational thinking. Such scholarship fills an entire discipline. Its overall terrain is also less familiar to me (as to most political scientists) than the other logics. Its role in political science has been more erratic than the incursions of structure, institutions, or culture, figuring strongly and explicitly only in the subfields of public opinion and foreign policy.

Accordingly my ambitions are modest. I signal several substantive divides in this literature. I then apply them to the main bodies of work that are typically seen as political psychology. The resultant survey is more abstract and skeletal than many good overviews of political psychology (Hermann 1986; Sears 1987; Kuklinski 2002; Monroe 2002; Sears, Huddy, and Jervis 2003). Still, it is novel in the way this book is novel overall. Other overviews are almost all built around historical schools and dependent variables rather than distinctive causal claims. While lineages and big questions are critical to knowing the field, they can obscure a sense of substantive options when offered as a first cut. To the uninitiated, such surveys can come across as unstructured lists of research on anything involving 'mental processes': so-and-so was interested in this, the school of so-and-so was interested in that (though see Larson 1985: 24–65; Sullivan, Rahn, and Rudolph 2002). I try to highlight how scholars in this vein make different causal claims about action.

Though the physiological foundations of hard-wired psychology give its elements a different status from socially constructed ideational elements, the ways in which these elements can relate to action share many similarities. Three of the four distinctions between psychological claims parallel the ideational dimensions in Chapter 4.

(i) Affective Versus Cognitive Versus Instinctual Just as ideational elements can be affective or cognitive, so people could be hard-wired to depart from rationality and straightforward preferences in feeling certain affective needs or in using limited or non-rational cognitive processes to analyze information.[5] Affectively people might be hard-wired to feel positive emotions vis-à-vis (or to 'like') chocolate, certain body types in mates, or risky action in their teenage years. Cognitively people might be unable to calculate desires without reference groups, or tend toward exaggeration of low-probability losses or gains, or only actually formulate preferences and choices when forced to by explicit questioning. In psychological logic there is also a third possibility. It is best captured by 'instincts' though psychologists often use the word 'motives' (which is also often extended to include affective attachments) (Weiner 1992; Gollwitzer and Brandstätter 1995; Pittman 1998). When a fruit fly engages its mating ritual, it is usually seen as acting in an automatic, machine-like mode without emotion (the fly does not perform the ritual because it feels good) or cognitions (of which the fly is not capable). Human beings may have similar instincts or urges that short-circuit affect and cognition.

Affective, cognitive, and institutional mechanisms in psychology can relate differently to rationality, but have less distinct ties to consciousness than do affective or cognitive ideational claims. Psychological affective claims might just define preferences in otherwise-rational thinking; cognitive claims are about patterned irrationality; and instinctual claims sidestep evaluative or analytic thinking entirely. For none of these mechanisms does it necessarily matter whether or not someone is conscious of her psychological dispositions. Recall that particularistic ideational claims are founded on the possibility that the same person could act differently given other ideational elements. This means that the level of consciousness of alternative beliefs or practices matters a great deal. Psychological claims, whether affective, cognitive, or instinctual, do not have this contingent basis—they follow a general logic that the physiological organization of any given person has certain causal consequences—and may operate irrespective of consciousness. This is most obvious with instincts, which may move us whether we note them or not, but can

[5] To use more psychological terms, someone's psychological makeup could tell him something about positive/negative, attraction/aversion, approach/avoidance distinctions or about true/false distinctions (Zajonc 1998).

also be true of affect or cognition. If affection for chocolate or cognitive rules like prospect theory are hard-wired rather than culturally learned, it might be that no amount of conscious enticement with vanilla would matter. No amount of conscious study of mathematics would dispel unease at small risks of painful death or excitement at small chances of winning the lottery. Consciousness could conceivably give people the opportunity to counter their desires or mitigate biases in indirect ways—avoiding chocolate shops, or tasking employees to challenge leaders' biases—but it may not be possible to unlearn that which is not learned.

(ii) Ends Versus Means Hard-wired psychological dispositions might define what people want or like (informing the ends they seek) or how people choose strategies and actions in pursuit of ends (informing means). Unlike in ideational claims, this dimension has fairly weak logical links to affect, cognition, or instinct. For example, relative deprivation is usually seen as a cognitive logic about how people define what they want, setting end preferences. Genetic inclinations to conservatism might be seen as affective commitments to certain strategies or practices (or general views of risk or change) irrespective of ends. Instincts too could be about either ends or means. Not only might we instinctively seek certain ends, like to reproduce, but we might be pre-programmed for patterns of action like the fruit-fly ritual. A psychological ends-means distinction does, however, relate to different degrees of rationality like the same distinction about culture. If the main point of a psychological claim is that we are hard-wired to seek the end of healthy children, it can still be coherent to suggest that we pursue that goal via the most instrumentally rational actions given our environment. If the main point is that we are hard-wired affectively or instinctively to keep our children nearby—a reflexive action, not an end—then we might do so even when a local threat puts them at risk. The former claim allows for more rationality than the latter. Arguments about means-focused interpretive elements, whether psychological or ideationally, define action more proximately and less rationally than arguments about ends (Pittman 1998: 566–70).

(iii) Coherent Versus Incoherent Psychological claims might picture people with a consistent set of wants, cognitions, and instincts or a jumble of incoherent imperatives and processes. Here again the logical links across dimensions are weaker than with ideational claims. In ideational logic coherence tends to imply a more rational-affective-ends approach, with ideational elements defining what otherwise-rational people pursue. This

is one option in psychological claims—again, like hard-wired desire for chocolate—but other links are just as plausible. For example, the large literature on 'cognitive dissonance' pictures people as coherent 'consistency seekers': motivated at a deep level (perhaps by both cognitive limits and emotional comfort) to render consistent their actions and their world. This notion seems to fit with quite rational actors, but the main point of this research has instead been that people push coherence to an irrational level—reading more coherence into the world and their actions than is objectively warranted (Festinger 1957; Pittman 1998: 556). Incoherence, on the other hand, has an obvious logical link to a strong view of irrationality (whether it reflects incoherent affects, cognitions, or instincts). It is difficult to posit more irrationality than psychological claims in which people hold a mess of inclinations which only coalesce into plans of action when they must decide on something. In between strong coherence or incoherence views, some psychological claims suggest that people seek to simplify and routinize their thinking and action, imposing at least some coherence, but that their 'schemas' or 'frames' are always somewhat compartmentalized and inconsistent (and some might err on the side of irrationally exaggerated coherence).

(iv) Individual Versus Universal As I have noted, some psychological claims focus on universal dynamics of 'how humans think', and some on differences between how individuals think. This is partly just a question of focus, since the two kinds of claims are compatible. Our hard-wiring probably features some universal components and some variable ones. These focuses are distinct, however, in that they ultimately compete. The more individual variation we see in psychology, the less universal psychology explains. Surveys of psychological work often include a third focus between these two, noting the large literature on group dynamics. But the psychological component of group arguments always reduces to either universal or individual logic. Group-level arguments either focus on human tendencies to form groups in certain ways, or (more rarely) on how groups are made up of people who share individual-level inclinations.

As with ideational claims, debate on these dimensions does not mean that psychological claims overall must occupy one position. Only on coherence is a general view necessary: either someone's (or everyone's) psychology exhibits some degree of coherence or it does not. Otherwise we could have some affective psychological constraints and some cognitive, some of ends and some of means, and some universal and some individual. If it is conceivable that psychology overall varies on these dimensions, however, any claim about certain elements of psychology must occupy a specific position to be clear. At a very deep level this may not be possible, since especially cognition and affect are increasingly seen as related at their foundations. For example, we might seek cognitive consistency because it feels good. Even some experimental psychologists point out that such rock-bottom questions may ultimately concern philosophers more than social scientists (Sniderman, Brody, and Tetlock 1993; Pittman 1998; Zajonc 1998). Still, at an observable level there seem to be distinct mechanisms of cognition, affect, and instinct, and clear psychological claims need to specify which they employ as best they can.

I made the same point about ideational claims in Chapter 4, but then observed that links across the dimensions configure most work into two broad approaches. Affectively focused ideational claims imply a more conscious and rational view of action, in which ideational elements define fairly conscious end preferences. The image of conscious values and instrumentally pursued ends also implies that these preferences (and actions that follow from them) are relatively coherent. Thus there are logical links in ideational scholarship—and even stronger historical links in claims that have appeared together—that create an affective/ends/coherent view and a cognitive/means/incoherent view to oppose it. But as I noted above, political-psychological work turns out to be more diverse because the logical and historical links across these dimensions are weaker. Coherence and ends-focused scholarship tend to go together, but affective/cognitive and individual/universal commitments vary on their own.

More helpful for this organizational task is that one approach dominated the first few decades of explicit political psychology, and that more recent scholarship concentrates on public opinion and foreign policy. I can cover most of the literature by sketching where the pioneers and these subfields fall on my map. This prevents this section from discussing more far-flung examples, like relative deprivation work in economic development or the 'theories of culture' from Wildavsky or Inglehart. It also leads us to revisit some work that is not psychological by my definition, especially on public opinion. But the point of the section, like of the book overall, is to illustrate a useful breakdown rather than to apply it exhaustively.

Lasswell and the Origins of Political Psychology

Starting with the pioneers also permits some elaboration of my initial claim that early work in political psychology, like on 'political culture', left psychological logic with a weak reputation from which it is still recovering. The subfield's founding father was Harold Lasswell, who sparked a generation of work on 'personality and politics' based on Freudian psychoanalysis (Lasswell 1930, 1935, 1936, 1948). Lasswell took the notion from Freud that most human action is partly motivated by unconscious psychological needs. These needs vary extensively, however, with early life experiences. To understand behavior, he looked to how early experiences left people imprinted with certain personalities. At the elite level, the result was the 'psychobiography' of leaders (George and George 1956; Erikson 1958; Mazlish 1972; Winter 2003). But societies could also develop typical personalities through shared experiences. This made work on public opinion into the study of how 'private affects were displaced onto political objects' (Lasswell 1930). For example, Lasswell argued that Hitler performed a 'maternal function' for German society in certain ways. Some of the Germans' human psychological needs went unfulfilled in the early twentieth century, and this partly explained their turn to the Nazis (Lasswell 1977). A famous related example is *The Authoritarian Personality*, whose authors ascribed authoritarian inclinations (and other undesirable dispositions) to parents' failure to provide psychologically appropriate mixes of discipline and affection (Adorno et al. 1950; also Lane 1962).

Lasswell's approach did not fall from favor because anyone fully rejected the basic notions that people share some psychological needs or that personalities vary with experience. Its basic logic was not absurd or incoherent. In my terms, the Lasswellian tradition invoked universal psychological logic to portray people as driven by instinctual bundles of urges, with a focus on at least semicoherent ends.[6] Within these parameters, individual or group variation followed from nonpsychological logics. Either objective-structural experiences (i.e. German interwar suffering) or cultural elements (i.e. parenting styles) led people to repress or develop instinctual urges in particular ways. The result was the major instance of an a-rational psychological logic of preference-definition. To understand anyone's behavior, this approach told us to seek the combination

---

[6] Freud tended to see affects or emotions as derived from instincts, and in general psychoanalytic approaches dissolved the affective logic of like/dislike or good/bad into a language of instinctual needs (Stein 1991; Weiner 1992; McDermott 2004a).

of human psychological requirements and individual experiences that created a desire for certain kinds of relationships or positions. Given these ends, their actions followed fairly logically.

Instead, the delegitimation of the school flowed mostly from messy, hard-to-demonstrate, often-tautological applications of its basic notions. Like psychoanalysis more broadly, Lasswellian research seemed to trace any behavior to a flexible mix of 'needs' and selective readings of experiences.[7] It interpreted a person's psychoses from his actions and words and then used the psychoses to explain the same actions and words. Even worse, perhaps, was a confused entanglement with an erratically functionalist view of culture. Only the universal-needs side of the argument clearly featured hard-wired psychology. The emphasis on personality shaped by experiences usually seemed cultural. It cast variation in what people wanted as the result of what they experienced early in life. Yet these personalities and culture were also partly explained by psychology. Much like contemporary anthropologists like Ruth Benedict, Lasswell offered 'a view of internal psychology as little more than a barely contained caldron of urges set for life in instinctual concrete, and culture as a defense against them.... In other words, culture was a solution to the problem of how groups might live in the physical and psychological circumstances in which they found themselves' (Renshon 2002). Individuals and peoples developed personalities that functionally addressed their psychological imbalances. But as in Durkheim, this psychologically based cultural functionalism was murky. Perhaps Hitler assuaged some psychological challenges for interwar Germans, but was Nazism really psychologically functional in a broad sense? How much did interwar German needs reflect universal urges, historically formed German personalities, or the immediate objective challenges of a country in crisis? It did not help that even Lasswell's defenders admit his writing is 'difficult to read and understand' (Eulau and Zlomke 1999; see also Rogow 1977).

Today Lasswell has practically disappeared from view (Eulau and Zlomke 1999; but see Ascher and Hirschfelder-Ascher, 2004). He is most often cited in the still-active school of elite personality studies, though few scholars retain a similar framework. Stanley Renshon applies an explicitly psychoanalytic approach to American presidential leadership (Renshon 1996, 2003). In a related vein is James David Barber's typology

[7] For a summary of criticisms of Freudian approaches, see McDermott (2004a: 156–9, 203–6).

of presidential personalities, though he focused on documenting certain inclinations (formed by distinctions between 'active' versus 'passive' individuals and 'positive' versus 'negative') rather than seeking the sources of personality in interpretive biographies (Barber 1992). But most politically oriented studies of personality have changed in two major ways since the 1960s. First, they are more empirical and less aggressively interpretive. Studies of leadership have become much more typological than deeply theoretical à la Freud. Rather than positing an overarching set of needs to which personalities and cultures can be traced through the filter of early experience, leadership scholars trace correlations between markers of psychological traits or motives, class the correlations into typologies, and then suggest with a variety of caveats that these personality types do not reduce to other factors and so explain some variation in action (Simonton 1987; Winter 1987; Post 2003; McDermott 2004a; Goethals 2005). Second, their theoretical content focuses more on cognitive and means-focused elements than on instinctively or affectively defined preferences. In Margaret Hermann's version of 'trait analysis', for example, typologies of leaders' personalities are organized largely around cognitive measures like conceptual complexity (how simplistic is their world view?), self-confidence (how do they evaluate themselves relative to others?), task versus relationship orientation (do they focus more on solving problems or building relationships?), and in-group bias (how strongly do they distinguish their group from others?) (Hermann 2003).

Psychology and Foreign Policy

It is in foreign policy studies that personality claims remain most prominent. At first glance they can seem to dominate psychological work in IR. Hermann offers the notion that 'individuals matter' as the first proposal in a summary of 'political psychology as a perspective on politics' (Hermann 2002). Janice Gross Stein premises her overview of psychological approaches to international conflict on the impact of leaders (Stein 2002). Both moves might seem to imply that individual-level variation in leaders' personalities is the main thrust of these literatures. But as Stein goes on to capture well, most recent psychological claims in IR are actually universalistic. They focus on leaders not because they claim that psychology varies with individual leaders, but because it may be in the choices of leaders that the impact of universal psychology is most easily visible. Since the 1970s they also heavily privilege cognitive mechanisms over affect or instinct, to the point that one prominent advocate summarizes this literature as a 'cognitivist' alternative to the rationalist-structural IR orthodoxy of realism (Tetlock 1998; for discussion of affective work, Lebow 1981; Mercer 2006).

At the origins of this more universal and cognitive literature stands Robert Jervis's 1976 book *Perception and Misperception in International Politics*. Jervis set a research agenda about the 'menu of systematic strategies of simplification' through which leaders confront a complex world.[8] The basic approach is to take experimental findings of cognitive shortcuts and biases and seek evidence of them in real-world political action. Prospect theory informs the most developed examples. Another focus has been the 'fundamental attribution error': we tend to infer from others' potentially threatening actions that they are bad by nature, but see our own similar actions as imposed by circumstances. Thus Cold-War-era US leaders pointed to Soviet defense spending as evidence of hostile intentions, but saw their own buildup as defensive or driven by domestic politics (and seemed to expect even Soviet leaders to see this) (Jervis 1976; Nisbett and Ross 1980; Kahneman, Slovic, and Tversky 1982; Fiske and Taylor 1984). Political scientists have also looked for biases of availability (interpreting ambiguous information simply in terms of what is most easily remembered), representativeness (exaggerating similarities between events and prior classes of events), or anchoring (estimating magnitude or degrees by comparison with easily available but inappropriate initial values) (Kahneman and Tversky 1972, 1973; Tversky and Kahneman 1973, 1982; Ross and Sicoly 1979; Taylor 1982; Tetlock 1998; Stein 2002).

A smaller but salient line of psychological research in IR focuses on small-group dynamics. The study of group interaction is often seen as different from Jervis-style research on internal biases and heuristics, but it too departs from observations of universal cognitive dispositions.[9] The central notion is that to organize a cognitively challenging environment, humans grasp at available distinctions to create social categories and form 'ingroups' and 'outgroups'. The distinctiveness of this work lies less in truly group-level dynamics than in greater attention to affective elements. In the 'social identity theory' (SIT) developed by Henry Tajfel and John Turner, affective evaluations are quickly attached to cognitive

---

[8] The phrase is Janice Gross Stein's (2002: 293) but aptly captures Jervis's perspective. One of the strongest hypotheses in the book is that where leaders appear to 'like' someone or something affectively, this is usually because they have cognitively analyzed that it will benefit them (Jervis 1976: 120–2).

[9] The separation between these two focuses traces to a dependent-variable division in psychology between cognitive psychology (focused on internal mental processes of individuals) and social psychology (focused on how people behave in interaction).

categories because we are motivated to see our own identification as positive. This leads not only to 'cold' cognitive errors—applying various biases to 'us' and 'them'—but also to 'hot' affective attachments to the group and its norms and practices (Janis 1972; Tajfel and Turner 1986; Turner 1987). In IR, Jonathan Mercer uses SIT to argue that there are hard-wired psychological reasons, not rationalist-structural ones, to share neorealist expectations of pervasive and enduring international conflict (Mercer 1995). Donald Horowitz invokes the same foundations for ethnic conflict (Horowitz 1985: 141–50). This literature remains mostly a theoretical elaboration of experimental findings, however, with only a few detailed applications to empirical cases in politics (Levy 2003: 272; McDermott 2004: 153–88; Rosen 2005).

Overall, psychological claims in IR today mirror the dominance of cognitivism in psychology since the 1970s. Most hypotheses and claims are cognitive, means-focused, and pitched at the universal level. They tend to posit moderate coherence. To some degree people are cast as consistency-seekers who operate through heuristics, but these cognitive devices may not be consistent across issues or arenas.[10] Of the two significant IR focuses that occupy other places on my dimensions, one might be best seen as an inheritor of past traditions and the other as a harbinger of future research. Personality studies are distinctive in their focus on individual-level variation and in retaining a Lasswellian echo of instinctual and affectively based ends alongside cognitive dynamics. Small-group work incorporates affective dynamics more directly, reflecting a shift back towards emotion in psychology, but is just beginning to produce empirical claims in IR (Zajonc 1998; McDermott 2004a; Mercer 2005).

Psychology and Public Opinion

Some of the same breakdown applies in the huge literature on public opinion. To the extent they exist, psychological claims about public opinion are mainly universal and cognitive. As Donald Kinder notes in an excellent summary of this US-focused literature, it is 'the proverbial "average American" who occupies center stage', and 'emotion is conspicuous by its absence' (Kinder 1998: 814). The main substantive difference between psychological arguments in the two subfields concerns the dimension of

---

[10] One well-known line of argument on elite decision-making emphasizes high incoherence, however: the 'garbage-can model', in which leaders haphazardly connect whatever problems appear before them to a logically separate stream of 'solutions' (metaphorically mixing problems and solutions together in a garbage can and taking whatever comes out: Cohen, March, and Olsen 1972).

coherence. The central debates in public opinion hover around the pole of incoherence. They concern whether 'average Americans' are almost totally incoherent or if they manage to achieve at least some coherence. The phrase 'to the extent they exist' above hints at a side effect of this emphasis. Even though the public opinion literature is often labeled altogether as 'political psychology', it features few strong psychological causal segments. The main positions either employ psychological claims negatively—suggesting that the typical person's psychology is so incoherent that there are not many opinions to explain—or argue that despite psychological incoherence people end up calculating in roughly rational ways.

Increasing flows of survey data in the 1950s shifted public opinion research away from Lasswellian interpretations and toward quantitative empirics. But if this literature was psychological in a disciplinary sense right from the start—focusing on mental processes—it rarely explained public opinions with hard-wired logic. Early voter studies in the 1950s, Angus Campbell's influential *American Voter,* and later work by Philip Converse painted a striking picture of voters with almost no knowledge or interest in politics, few policy preferences, and little cognitive structure to hold these things together (Berelson, Lazarsfeld, and McPhee 1954; Campbell et al. 1960; Converse 1964). Given near-complete incoherence, these scholars explained any fairly stable opinions through institutional inertia or cultural 'taken for grantedness' (without quite using that phrase). People retained party affiliations and a few incoherent views just as they went to the same family church for generations. Neither cognition, affect, nor instinct was necessary to explain the patterns. The main competitor to this view was still less psychological. Rationalist scholars like Anthony Downs did not directly contest an image of incoherent citizens, but noted that it was rational for busy 'average Americans' to see their votes as unimportant and leave politics to politicians (Downs 1957). This more rational image was later bolstered by arguments that instability in opinions reflected vague surveys and measurement error, not opinionless citizens (Aachen 1975; Erikson 1979).

As time went on, shifting opinion and party affiliation in the USA sapped at simple inertial explanation (Nie, Verba, and Petrocik 1976). At the aggregate level, party affiliations and views showed trends that were neither simply inertial nor incoherently random. At the same time the early findings of voter ignorance were repeatedly confirmed (Delli Carpini and Keeter 1996). Both on the 'non-attitude' and rationalist sides of the literature, scholars turned to more elaborate psychological models of cognitive processing. On the one hand, John Zaller and Stanley Feldman argued that 'non-attitudes' reflect incoherence across too many views more than an absence of views. When asked to commit themselves, they suggested, people tend to average across whatever set of relevant ideas come into their heads. The selection of ideas that come to them is largely decided by recent salient information and the framing of the issue by elites, media, and surveys or ballot questions (Zaller 1992; Zaller and Feldman 1992). On the other hand, Milton Lodge and his collaborators offered an 'online' cognitive model that bolstered a more rationalist theory. People may not know much about politics, but this may not mean their views are random or irrational. They might learn a new piece of information, factor it relatively rationally into overall judgments on a candidate or issue, 'update' their online view, and then forget the information. They would have fairly consistent and rational views without being able to answer factual or analytic questions behind them (Lodge 1995; Kinder 1998: 812–14).[11] In parallel, another current of research arose to square widespread incoherence with seemingly sophisticated votes at the 'macro' aggregate level. Its dominant claim is that the mass of ignorant voters are random and largely cancel each other out; a small number of sophisticated voters shift the whole pattern, both directly in their own shifting votes and indirectly as 'opinion leaders' (Stimson 1991; Page and Shapiro 1992; Erickson, Makuen, and Stimson 2002).

Though this literature delves deeply into non-classically rational mental processes, it ascribes little causal force to psychological logic. The 'macro'-level research ultimately portrays opinions driven by well-informed and relatively rational elites, and the 'online' model suggests a sort of rational end-run around ignorance. Zaller and Feldman's work invokes psychological causes mainly negatively, as did the earlier work by Campbell and Converse. In their view, the study of individual psychology shows us that most people are either too ignorant or too cognitively limited to hold opinions in a rational way. They are hard-wired *not* to hold stable, coherent, strong views, rather than being hard-wired to think something in particular. To the extent that they arrive at views and make choices, these are determined mainly by the information that flows to them from leaders and the media. The bottom-line explanation for patterns of opinion or voting is built around the shape of institutional or ideational channels for the provision of information.

---

[11] Other arguments about how seemingly incoherent people take shortcuts to rational views are Popkin (1991) and Sniderman, Brody, and Tetlock (1993).

The same is largely true within a recent turn to affect in public opinion, which is better developed than similar thinking in IR. The best single predictors of candidate support are generally positive or negative feelings, and opinions and voting decisions more broadly correspond powerfully to emotional responses (Conover and Feldman 1986; Sullivan and Masters 1988; Marcus and MacKuen 1993; Nadeau, Niemi, and Amato 1995; Marcus 2000). But again, if detailed studies along these lines invoke elaborate mental processes, they mostly use psychological claims negatively to argue that people do *not* evaluate and act in a mechanistic rational way. When they turn to more positive claims about why people arrive at certain views and actions (and why action varies overall), they tend to step beyond psychological logic. An older current studies political socialization, suggesting that people gain affective attachments in their early years. People are hard-wired to rely on emotions in decision-making, but socialization studies stress that social setting and culture determine which affective attachments people adopt (e.g. Sears 2001). A more recent variant offers elaborate neuroscientific bases for the role of emotion, but similarly invokes a 'learning' model in which the affects people hold reflect their experiences and cultural setting, not hard-wired inclinations (Marcus and MacKuen 2001).

Despite increasingly explicit attention to mental processes, then, the opinion literature does not feature many strong psychological claims. The clearest exception is the fairly new focus on genetic dispositions discussed earlier, which suggest inherited proclivities to liberalism or conservatism and possibly other views. As my initial presentation stressed, though, even this neatly ideal-typical psychological claim only invokes hard-wiring at considerable distance from opinions about the world, let alone from specific action. Moreover, as scholars working on genetic inclinations note, they are a small minority that confronts deep skepticism from most opinion experts (Alford, Funk, and Hibbing 2005). In sum, perhaps the most striking thing about research on the 'political psychology of public opinion' is that the distinctive causal role of psychology within it is small and contested.

Once more I must stress that these are points of categorization, not criticism. Clearly these claims are not less correct just for avoiding psychological determinism. Indeed, this largely negative and distant role for psychological logic follows reasonably from the most widely agreed point on public opinion: that most citizens everywhere are ignorant and incoherent about politics. If most people do not have strong, consistent opinions and rarely take explicitly political actions, then of course we cannot produce strong psychological claims (or any other kind of strong claims) to explain their opinions or actions. There is nothing very solid to explain. The study of leaders' mental processes in IR tends to feature somewhat stronger psychological claims for the simple reason that leaders do tend to have opinions, and they also take concrete, overtly political actions whose causes we can try to tease out. Even in a context of opinionated individuals who undertake discrete actions with substantial impact, though, the IR literature also underscores how psychological claims tend to rely especially heavily on other causal logics. Psychological dispositions only generate expectations about how people act when plugged into structural, institutional, or ideational contexts.

Supporting Psychological Claims

Once again, I cannot seriously discuss evidence for psychological claims, but will briefly sketch what we would look for. We are back on the 'general' side of the master two-by-two matrix, and so can avoid the challenges of particularism that complicated Chapters 3 and 4. Psychological claims share with structural ones the basic notion that an intersubjectively real, regular set of conditions puts either deterministic or probabilistic causal pressure on action in certain directions. Contingency only enters such claims in making them weaker (meaning less deterministic, not less convincing). It is admittedly logically possible to create a particularistic psychological claim. An accidental knock on the head might alter a president's psychological inclinations and her subsequent policies. But politically relevant real-world examples are practically nonexistent.

Supporting general psychological claims to explain specific actions involves four steps. First, separate from the action in question, we require a conceptual claim and empirical support for some psychological disposition—an instinctual motivation, affective attachment, or cognitive process. If the claim is universal, we need experimental and/or broad statistical evidence of these dispositions. For claims about individual personality, we would want experimental and/or broad statistical evidence of a range of individual personalities. (Most work in psychology stops here, without explaining specific actions; most psychological claims by political scientists pick up from this step and apply the psychologists' claims to explain specific actions.) Second, we need a conceptual claim about the mechanism by which this disposition led to the action in question. This means taking as clear a position as possible on the dimensions above, and also being as specific as possible about the range of variation that is consistent with the claim; what alternative actions could this mechanism have allowed? Third, ideally we require evidence of this mechanism in a range of cases that vary across structural, institutional, and ideational factors. Cross-cultural controls are often especially important, both because psychological claims so frequently rely partly on ideational claims and because a growing number of classic psychological 'findings' seem to reflect a Western context (Nisbett 2003). Failing comparable real cases, we could look to counterfactual cases to tease out psychological effects (Tetlock and Belkin 1996; Lebow 2000). Fourth, and most difficult, we need the most precise process-tracing evidence the author can offer on how and how much the psychological dispositions interacted with nonpsychological factors to produce this action. What narrowed down the range of possibilities permitted by hard-wired instructions?

This last step is very challenging, but once again, the distance of psychological claims from action make it an integral part of such arguments. Only once the claims are linked to action through other causal segments can we see how psychology mattered. Still, this is only a difference of degree with most arguments. Psychological claims may stand out for their dependence on other logics, but practically all explanations confront the same challenge of interlocking 'how much' questions. As the book's conclusion will stress, we must all learn to make each other's arguments better.

Conclusion

This chapter made four points. I defined psychological logic as claims about the causal effects of hard-wired mental processes that depart from a simple rational model. In most cases they point to irrational biases, misperceptions, instincts or affects. They can also explain preferences prior to rational action. Arguments that psychology can illuminate rationality are right on substance—rationality is a certain model of psychology— but less helpful with respect to terminology. If we want 'psychological explanation' to mean something distinctive, as opposed to just referring to the mental-process elements of any claim at all, then its core must be claims that go beyond simple rationality. Unlike the other definitions in this book, this one also has the advantage of reflecting common usage.

Second, despite mainstream use of this definition, a great deal of literature applies the 'psychological' label very loosely. Confusion is especially common on the ideational-psychological boundary. Many 'cultural' arguments are mostly psychological. Theorizing from Durkheim to Wildavsky or Inglehart explores the causal effects of psychology in limiting ideational variation—why certain ideational elements have to go together under certain conditions—more than ideationally caused variation. Much self-labeled 'psychological' work is mostly ideational. Arguments about political socialization or operational codes often employ psychology to make the negative point that people are cognitively limited, relying on culture and ideas to explain action more positively. More broadly, it is common practice to describe as psychological any argument that mentions mental processes, especially in the public opinion literature. But this obscures that many—indeed most—claims about public opinion explain opinions and actions mainly in structural, institutional, or ideational terms.

Third, just as ideational claims can be charted on several dimensions, so psychological claims vary most importantly in how they relate psychology to action: via cognitive, affective, or instinctual mechanisms, ends versus means, coherence versus incoherence, and at universal or individual levels. The logical and historical connections across these dimensions are weaker than in ideational logic, producing psychological claims that are all over the map. That said, early Lasswellian political psychology was mostly instinctual, ends-focused, semicoherent, and universal (with individual variation explained as a reaction to nonpsychological experience and social context). Since the 1970s, the large majority of work has been cognitive, means-focused, and universal, with fairly strong coherence in international relations but strong incoherence in public opinion. Individual-level personality studies continue to be a secondary strand in the literature, and recent genetics-based claims bolster them in a new way. Affective dynamics are also garnering increasing attention.

Fourth, both to explain the low salience of psychological work in political science (and especially political science typologies) and to capture its distinctive challenges in empirical support, the most important feature of psychological claims relative to others is the distance of psychological dispositions from action. Once again, this is only a question of degree—almost all empirical arguments combine my categories—but scholars who are most interested in psychological causal segments rely on such combinations in especially immediate and unavoidable ways.

Conclusion

This book has offered a first cut into the universe of explanatory claims we might make about action. I presented a mix of deductive and inductive arguments that the deepest debates about action reflect positional/interpretive and general/particular divides, and that the core connotations of four common theoretical labels—structural, institutional, ideational, and psychological—match up well to the resultant four categories of causal logic. I suggested that all explanatory arguments about action, to the extent that they are clear, can be broken down into causal segments that sort into these categories. To excavate these debates from the many contradictory ways in which scholars employ these terms (and others), I have had to ask that almost all theoretical schools alter their vocabulary in some way. With a few exceptions these calls for relabeling have not carried substantive criticism. No one is wrong just because they define certain terms in certain ways. Unless we all refer to some interrelated terms of debate, though, deciding how wrong or right anyone is—or even what anyone claims to begin with—is harder than it should be.

This framework only provides a first cut. We need many other distinctions to capture the stakes in any explanatory fight. For purposes other than basic teaching and theorizing about explanation, other distinctions may be more important. Some major historical debates have gone on entirely within one causal category, and this typology does little to illuminate them (except in clarifying what they do not debate in sharing the same causal category). My first cut is also very abstract—or crude—in leaving much to say about how to differentiate or combine causal claims in practice. Beyond simple remarks on the evidence for each kind of causal segment, I went no further than abstract claims that the segments are ontologically and epistemologically compatible and that their demonstration usually requires interdependent claims across logics that bound and specify each other. This choice partly reflects the limits on what can fit in a reasonably sized book. But it also flows from my impression that social science literature is increasingly strong on methods but still weak (and perhaps, of late, even increasingly confused) on the range of plausible options in substantive argument. If we can clarify that range and reduce the communicative costs of decentralized terminology, I have little doubt that today's scholars will mobilize clever ways to mount sharp empirical battles between different substantive claims. Still, the contribution of this framework does depend on that concrete translation by others.

At the abstract level of my project, two important tasks remain. How we chart the universe of basic explanatory options has important implications for how we judge theoretical contributions and progress, and for some basic issues about research design. Both are subjects that deserve their own books, and neither was in my sights when I began constructing this typology. But I would be remiss not to quickly underscore the framework's implications for philosophy of science and practical methods.

Defining Progress

This book suggests that our most basic enterprise in the social sciences and history is to build empirically supported claims about how much human actions reflect structural, institutional, ideational, and/or psychological causes. My efforts have focused on giving the clearest possible meaning to the previous sentence, and on overcoming objections to the inclusion of some of these alternatives in the competition. It follows that to proceed with any rigor, we should engage this competition without prejudging the results. Ideally we would craft research that puts these alternatives (and their relevant internal variants, and combined claims) in competition. We would reward scholars who come out with the most convincing and important logical and empirical claims, irrespective of which kinds of causal segments they employ and whether they use them fairly 'purely' or in combination.

Unfortunately this conclusion fits poorly with the prevailing standards for progress in the social sciences. Borrowed from the 'hard' sciences, today's mainstream standards basically reflect positivism, the nineteenth-century epistemology that portrayed the discovery of objective general laws of everything as the feasible goal of scholarly work. In principle, most social scientists espouse something like the more nuanced epistemology of 'sophisticated methodological falsificationism' developed by Imre Lakatos. It still prioritizes general theorizing above all, but surrounds the search for laws in intelligent caveats that recognize our ultimate inability to access objective Truth. Although real proof or falsification of any theory is thus impossible, Lakatos argued that science still advances through pragmatic falsification (reasonable rejection rather than airtight disproof) and increasingly general theories. 'Progressive' scholarship occurs either when an existing theory is extended to account for new empirical facts, or a new, broader theory accounts for the empirically corroborated aspects of previous theories and new facts as well. Advancing knowledge requires ever-more-general theory: 'There is no falsification before the emergence of a better theory' (Lakatos 1970).

Though Lakatos seemed to doubt the viability of such general theorizing in historical explanations of human action, his writings largely define progress in the 'soft' sciences today (Lakatos 1971; Elman and Elman 2002). In codifying the standards of political science, King, Keohane, and Verba (1994) make generality the single most important measure of progress, stressing that '[g]ood social science attempts to go beyond these particulars to more general knowledge' and that '[t]he question is less whether, in some general sense, a theory is false or not... than *how much of the world the theory can help us explain*' (101, their emphasis). They echo the advice of an earlier methodological landmark, Adam Przeworski and Henry Teune's *Logic of Comparative Social Inquiry* (1970: 4):

The pivotal assumption of this analysis is that social science research, including comparative inquiry, should and can lead to general statements about social phenomena. This assumption implies that human and social behavior can be explained in terms of general laws established by observation. Introduced here as an expression of preference, this assumption will not be logically justified.

The deepest problem in the social sciences today, however, is that this assumption cannot be logically justified. Przeworski and Teune's position may be defensible in the physical and mathematical sciences that Lakatos studied, where the alternative to deep general laws may well be just randomness. Even where contingencies leave room for particular dynamics in complex natural systems—perhaps with contingent leaps in processes of protein folding, the collapse of stars, or avalanches—the range of possible resolutions to such contingencies might be fairly narrow. The resulting world might be better described as hard-to-predict variations on general themes than in a vocabulary of deep particularity or uniqueness. In such natural subjects, then, it might be plausible a priori that only ever-more-general scholarship represents an improved, organized understanding of what is going on. When we turn to human action, however, we cannot disregard other possibilities between general laws and chaos. Human beings might—just might—have fairly free reign to construct their own

165

worlds. By accident or creativity they might generate a variety of partly unique arenas and actions that are not the necessary, predictable and explicable results of preexisting conditions. The resultant world could be highly organized, and even predictable to some degree within its confines, but generalizing theories about 'human action' might account for very little of its patterns or variations. This would be the particularistic planet imagined by strong institutional or ideational claims.

Besides drawing on weak analogies to the hard sciences, the common identification of progress with generality builds on many of the confusions encountered earlier: that particularistic claims incorporating contingency are not explanations, that ideational claims lie in a separate realm, and that 'interest'-based arguments enjoy an especially concrete, demonstrable, almost-physical causal quality. Given the number of common oversights that tie into this view and their provenance from revered forefathers—Hume, Weber, and most of the pioneers of postwar social science—its endurance is not surprising. But if we take seriously the goal of engaging a competition between all the plausible ways of accounting for human action, we cannot avoid the conclusion that this view is deeply unscientific. One of the great debates in the social sciences concerns the generality of patterns of action—are there many general dynamics out there?—but prevailing standards presume that we learn something only to the extent that one side wins the debate. They reject some logically plausible, historically well-developed hypotheses about what might be true in the name of what general theorists hope to be true. Certainly many of us share that hope to some degree. The goal of general theory is an attractive one, and the potential for particularistic dynamics forces us to admit that some components of our world may have been highly contingent. Nonetheless, we cannot permit this hope to seduce us into prejudging our answers so severely.

What are better standards for social science progress? We should laud as most valuable and 'progressive' the arguments that demonstrate reasonably specific causal force over the widest range of important outcomes, whether their causes are general or particular. In other words, a valuable contribution has three components. First, it accounts for what many people see as major variation in something important, telling us why one thing happened and others did not. The variation might be factual across multiple cases (why did democracy result here and not there?) or counterfactual (why did China stagnate instead of industrializing first?). Whether the logic is general or particular, accounting for variation can legitimately include the delineation of some contingency. Second, it accounts for variation in reasonably specific ways. A scholar might speak rhetorically to wide variation without connecting clear mechanisms to concrete, distinct outcomes. This can be taken too far, obviously—we do not need to know many specific details about outcomes—and often this criterion creates trade-offs with accounting for wide variation. But the best arguments do both, spelling out clear causal mechanisms that lead to very different outcomes and justifying how they capture the defining character of the outcomes to a satisfying degree of precision. Third, it must do better than competitors at demonstrating its claims empirically. As almost all philosophers of science now agree, this will always be debatable. We can only draw provisional conclusions that rest pragmatically on intersubjective truth, trying to convince as many people who are as different as possible that our claims are better than others. Still, some arguments *are* better than others.

These three points should sound familiar, since the standards I criticize also instruct us to seek clear claims that trace to wide variation in reasonably specific outcomes with good empirical support. The crucial difference is that I have left out what they make the first priority. There is no extra credit—let alone the most fundamental credit—for doing these things in a general framework. Since the generality of our phenomena is an open question, we must stop rewarding the scope of a claim separately from its empirical bases. General claims only deserve credit for *documented generality*: the range of empirical outcomes for which they have made precise claims and offer direct empirical support. Particular claims deserve equal credit for *documented particularity* across similar ranges of outcomes and degrees of precision. Our battles should concern what causal mechanisms we claim happened somewhere and what evidence we have for it, not whether or not we can embed our claims in otherwise-unsupported general frameworks.[1]

A Caveat on Falsifiability

One caveat moderates my heresy. It concerns falsifiability—that obviously desirable quality of an argument that some imaginable evidence could show it to be wrong. Arguments that are clearer about how they can be wrong give us greater confidence when they appear to be right. While we should not insist that our claims be general, we should insist that they be falsifiable. There are some reasons to think that general claims will tend

[1] For a concrete example and discussion of perverse consequences of Lakatosian standards in European Union studies, see Parsons (2003: 30).

to be a bit more clearly falsifiable than particular ones, and this justifies reinstating at least a small premium a priori on generality in theoretical contributions.

General claims can be falsified in either of two ways. Since they make claims across a number of instances of action, they might be wrong about a 'cross-case' pattern. The correlation they expect between certain causes and effects across relevant cases might not show up. Since they also make claims about causal mechanisms in each case, they might be wrong in 'within-case' process-tracing (Collier, Brady, and Seawright 2004). The explanatory relationships they posit might not exist even given causes and effects that appear to vary together across cases.

This twofold basis for falsifiability is less present—though not entirely absent—in particular claims. Again, they are 'particular' in the sense that their claims about one arena do not imply that even identical conditions would produce similar results (unless by accident they hit upon similar resolutions of contingency). Their limited expectations about cross-case patterns mean that they draw mainly on—and can be falsified mainly by—'within-case' process-tracing evidence. This point should not be exaggerated, since most particular claims generate at least some cross-case implications at both of the logical stages that I discussed in Chapters 3 and 4. In one stage these arguments make negative claims that delineate contingency, arguing that other causes did *not* select across some range of alternatives. This involves making a general structural and possibly psychological claim of their own—about how certain given conditions do *not* shut down reasonable options—that could be evaluated across cases of similar conditions. In their other stage they invoke fairly standard causal logic to argue that once established, certain institutions or ideational elements oriented people toward certain actions. Unless they claim these institutions or ideational elements to be totally unique, this too generates cross-case expectations—that people who wind up with parliamentary institutions confront certain incentives, that people who believe in commodified labor build economies with certain dynamics, and so on—that in principle could be supported or disconfirmed in other cases. Still, most attempts to show the effects of certain institutions or ideational elements stress that their N of reasonably comparable cases is small at best.[2] In typically generating relatively weak cross-case expectations across relatively

---

[2] The most notable exceptions come in organizational sociology, where scholars tend to make institutional or ideational arguments based on large quantitative studies of many comparable organizations or arenas (like schools, town councils, firms, and so on). See Powell and DiMaggio (1991) and Brinton and Nee (1998).

small numbers of cases, particular arguments stand or fall more narrowly on within-case support.

This does not mean that particular claims must rely more on 'interpretation'. I see no reason to think that a datum in cross-case evidence is less prone to misinterpretation than one in within-case evidence. But it does mean that particular claims generate fewer (or at least narrower) observable implications. At some level this may seem an obvious and trivial point—claims of broader scope make claims over more evidence—but the generation of observable implications is not something social scientists can afford to take lightly. Most advocates of institutional and ideational explanation today spend much of their time discussing how to connect their arguments to at least some cross-case evidence alongside within-case support, wrestling with the challenges of 'small-N comparison' (among others, Collier 1991; Biernacki 1995; Mahoney and Rueschemeyer 2003). The unavoidable difficulties in so doing represent one partial sense in which general theorizing is a preferable way to proceed. General arguments stick their neck out with relatively aggressive claims about what has to happen (or is probable) across space and time. If and when general arguments do show us 'documented generality' with both cross-case and within-case support over a wide range of variation in a wide range of cases, we will have at least a little more confidence in their claims than we would for particular arguments about a similar range of variation.

Whether or not this turns out to be a crucial caveat about progress in the long run depends on what we find. My personal suspicion, as I have written more aggressively elsewhere, is that our world is a fairly particularistic one (Parsons 2003: 241). If this were right, then honest generalizers would find that their relatively more falsifiable arguments indeed tended to be falsified a great deal of the time. In this scenario, the light premium this caveat awards them for falsifiability would be outweighed by the empirical victories of particular arguments, even given a light discount to the latter for their slightly lower degree of clear falsifiability. But that is simply my own intuition. If proponents of general arguments can document reasonably specific explanatory claims across great scope in open debate with alternatives, the human sciences will certainly have made a great deal of progress.

Research Design for Open Debate

The framework's implications for research design are less radical, though they flow from these philosophical points. Just as standards for progress should not prejudge findings across abstractly plausible alternatives, so research should be designed to gather evidence equally for a variety of abstractly plausible alternatives. The latter point is much less revisionist than the former, since even strong advocates of generalizing theories have always called for careful attention to nongeneral factors (even if they reject that such factors could coalesce into alternative explanations and progress). Still, mainstream methodological advice downplays the kind of within-case, causal-mechanism-tracing evidence upon which particularistic claims disproportionately depend. My simple point, which echoes recent arguments by David Collier, Henry Brady, and their collaborators, is that we must design research to speak more evenly to the evidentiary foundations of a variety of arguments. Whatever approach we favor, we must allow a priori that several might be significantly right.

Consider first the advice of mainstream generalists. In keeping with an equation of progress with generality, King, Keohane, and Verba (fondly, 'KKV') advise us to construct research designs that help sort out general patterns. Wherever possible we should increase our number of observations, seeking the largest possible N (1994: 29). Cases should be chosen carefully to avoid selection bias, especially avoiding the mistake of choosing cases on the basis of shared outcomes (selecting on the dependent variable). Once we have constructed a universe of cases appropriate to the general patterns we seek to explore, we should use the cross-case logic of statistical regression to evaluate the strength of these patterns and their correlations with a variety of hypothetical causal conditions. Many intelligent caveats accompany this advice. They emphasize that their book is far from the last word on methods. But they leave little doubt about their view of how good social science is done.

Like any book of the stature of *Designing Social Inquiry*—though they are few and far between—it has provoked criticism. Brady and Collier led the charge (Brady and Collier 2004). Amid many quibbles about KKV's omissions or questions of emphasis, their contributors' deepest objections contest KKV's reliance on a Humean or Hempelian general-regularity definition of explanation. At the very least, they suggest, we should acknowledge that philosophers of causality advance several conceptions of what a causal inference entails, with some arguing for the logical necessity (and priority) of within-case tracing of causal mechanisms (Brady and Seawright 2004; McKeown 2004). Relatedly, they point out that insistence on increasing observations and selection bias overlooks that within-case evidence 'relies on causal-process observations that provide very different tools for inference than those of regression analysis' (Brady, Collier, and

Seawright 2004: 16). The broadest implication for research design is that cross-case regression-style studies should be supplemented by within-case research, both to support their own causal claims and to speak to alternatives. The stronger implication is that limited inferences can often be drawn from process-tracing 'case studies' (or small-N comparisons) even without broad cross-case regression.

This book's typology suggests a different route to similar advice. Brady and Collier's points are methodological in a strict sense. They portray the divide between KKV's standards and the advocates of within-case process-tracing as one between proponents of quantitative and qualitative methods. Whatever our approach and subject, they caution, we should acknowledge multiple views of causality and plausible cross-case (often quantitative) and within-case (often qualitative) leverage on it. In the broadest terms their message is one of methodological pluralism: we should craft research designs that take multiple routes to reach the best inferences. This book's typology highlights, however, that the divide between arguments that privilege cross-case versus within-case evidence is as much substantive as it is methodological. General claims suggest that there will be certain patterns to find in cross-case evidence. Particularistic claims also usually expect at least some patterns, as noted above, but they always suggest that at certain stages in the emergence of those patterns we would not have strong expectations across certain elements of cases and ranges of outcomes. Again, particularistic claims rely more heavily for support or falsification on within-case evidence. The problem with KKV-style research designs, then, is not just a methodological error of skimping on causal-mechanism, within-case support and controls on their claims. More seriously, they do not instruct us even to look for some kinds of evidence that could put them in the clearest competition with some plausible substantive alternatives. In an echo of their unscientific equation of progress with generality, they encourage research designs that only look for a subset of the coherent explanatory dynamics suggested by salient schools of thought in the human sciences.

The key implication of this book for research design is just to add a substantive underpinning to recent precautions from sophisticated methodologists. Not only is broad methodological pluralism the wise route to any causal inference, it is also necessary to organize the kind of open debate that is the basic hallmark of any remotely scientific enterprise. This is not to say that we must organize our research to look for 'all' imaginable causal dynamics, which is impossible. As I noted earlier, we are engaged in debates among scholars, not with Truth itself. In order to construct legitimate and feasible research designs, we mainly need to seek evidence for and against the handful of contending views that our colleagues have advanced (or might be expected to advance) in our chosen area of expertise. On some subjects this will mean giving special attention to several conflicting hypotheses within one of the causal categories. In some areas it may be pragmatically justifiable to set aside a whole category of logic that has no prominent defenders. Any persuasive research design, however, will set up at least some open competition across distinct logics of explanation.

Conclusion

What would be our reward for wide adoption of this framework? This book exudes a great deal of optimism about our ability to get at causal forces behind action. I repeatedly imply that if we just clarify our categories and encourage direct competition and combination, we will produce better explanations and more meaningful progress. Lest I be dismissed as naive, two words of modesty are in order.

First, I have remarked repeatedly that we will often be unable to find enough clear evidence to separate out sharp causal claims with confidence. Let me strengthen that caveat: in practically all interesting cases of human action there will always remain reasonable doubts about the specific range and strength of any causal claim we advance. Yet this makes it all the more important to try to formulate clear and distinct causal claims. Precisely because it is so hard (or impossible) to nail down strong claims in incontestable ways, getting anywhere close to that goal depends on a clear initial sense of our explanatory options.

Second, I do not expect that widespread adoption of this framework would lead to much more substantive agreement among social scientists. What little progress we have seen to date has produced a widening range of plausible explanatory approaches and more explicit methodological tools for supporting them—but not stronger agreement on which explanations are right (either generally or even in any given case that I know of). Relative to explanatory debates just a few decades ago, successful scholars now confront a wider range of sharper competitors. Yet well-trained social scientists still regularly employ slightly different ways of evaluating theorizing, methods, and empirical evidence to reach opposing conclusions about the merits of any argument. At best we agree to set aside some arguments as incoherent or unconvincing, but our negative consensus rarely narrows to anything approaching strong substantive agreement.

By no means does our inability to agree trace entirely, or even mostly, to the terminological confusion addressed in this book. We are highly fallible and subjective creatures. Even the smartest and most well-intentioned of us are beset by all manner of obstacles and odd incentives in our search for good explanations. That said, on the basis of our modest past progress in identifying a widening range of arguments and methods, I hope that this book may at least help us expand our realm of negative consensus. If its framework is clear enough, we might agree to set aside some logically or semantically confusing ways of organizing our debates and some bad reasons for excluding some explanatory options. We will likely remain unable to agree on clear substantive 'winners'. Even those who receive broad acclaim will fail to convince major groups of scholars, and will persistently face widespread doubts and challenges. But our debates could be more clearly focused around distinct logics of explanation, and that would be no small thing.

References

Achen, C. (1975). 'Mass Political Attitudes and the Survey Response', *American Political Science Review*, 69: 1218–31.

Ackerman, B. (1991). *We the People I: Foundations*. Cambridge, MA: Harvard University Press.

Adorno, T., Frenkel-Brunswick, E., Levinson, D., and Nevitt Sanford, R. (1950). *The Authoritarian Personality*. New York: Harper & Row.

Alcoff, L. (1993). 'Foucault as Epistemologist', *The Philosophical Forum*, 25: 92–124.

Alford, J. and Hibbing, J. (2004). 'The Origin of Politics: An Evolutionary Theory of Political Behavior', *Perspectives on Politics*, 2(4): 707–24.

——— Funk, C., and Hibbing, J. (2005). 'Are Political Orientations Genetically Transmitted?', *American Political Science Review*, 99(2): 153–67.

Almond, G. (1956). 'Comparative Political Systems', *Journal of Politics*, 18(3): 391–409.

——— (1960). 'Introduction: A Functional Approach to Comparative Politics', in G. Almond and J. Coleman (eds.), *The Politics of the Developing Areas*. Princeton, NJ: Princeton University Press, pp. 3–64.

——— (1983). 'Communism and Political Culture Theory', *Comparative Politics*, 15(2): 127–38.

——— (1989a). 'The Intellectual History of the Civic Culture Concept', in G. Almond and S. Verba (eds.), *The Civic Culture Revisited*. Newbury Park, CA: Sage, pp. 1–36.

——— (1989b). *A Discipline Divided: Schools and Sects in Political Science*. Newbury Park, CA: Sage.

——— and Verba, S. (1963). *The Civic Culture: Political Attitudes and Democracy in Five Nations*. Princeton, NJ: Princeton University Press.

Althusser, L. (1972). *Lenin and Philosophy, and Other Essays*, trans. B. Brewster. New York: Monthly Review Press.

Arrow, K. (1951). *Social Choice and Individual Values*. New York: Wiley.

——— (1994). 'Methodological Individualism and Social Knowledge', *American Economic Review*, 84(2): 1–9.

Arthur, W. B. (1988). 'Self-Reinforcing Mechanisms in Economics', in P. W. Anderson, K. J. Arrow and D. Pines (eds.), *The Economy as a Complex Evolving System*. Reading, MA: Addison-Wesley.

Ascher, W. and Hirschfelder-Ascher, B. (2004). 'Linking Lasswell's Political Psychology and the Policy Sciences', *Policy Sciences*, 37(1): 23–36.

Ashley, R. (1987). 'The Geopolitics of Geopolitical Space: Toward a Critical Social Theory of International Politics', *Alternatives*, 12: 403–34.

Axelrod, R. (1986). 'An Evolutionary Approach to Norms', *American Political Science Review*, 80(4): 1095–111.

Barber, J. D. (1992). *The Presidential Character: Predicting Performance in the White House*, 4th edn. Englewood Cliffs, NJ: Prentice-Hall.

Berman, S. (1998). *The Social Democratic Moment: Ideas and Politics in the Making of Interwar Europe*. Cambridge, MA: Harvard University Press.

Barry, B. (1970). *Sociologists, Economists, and Democracy*. Chicago, IL: University of Chicago Press.

Bates, R. H. (1981). *Markets and States in Tropical Africa: The Political Bases of Agricultural Policies*. Berkeley, CA: University of California Press.

—— (1989). *Beyond the Miracle of the Market: The Political Economy of Agrarian Development in Kenya*. New York: Cambridge University Press.

—— (1997). 'Area Studies and the Discipline: A Useful Controversy?' *PS: Political Science and Politics*, 30(2): 166–9.

—— (1998). 'The International Coffee Organization: An International Institution', in Bates et al. (eds.), pp. 194–229.

—— Grief, A., Levi, M., Rosenthal, J-L., and Weingast, B. (1998). *Analytic Narratives*. Princeton, NJ: Princeton University Press.

Bearman, P. (1993). *Relations into Rhetorics*. New Brunswick, NJ: Rutgers University Press.

Beauchamp, T. and Rosenberg, A. (1981). *Hume and the Problem of Causation*. Oxford: Oxford University Press.

Beck, N. (2006). 'Is Causal-Process Observation an Oxymoron?', *Political Analysis*, 14: 347–52.

Bell, D. (1973). *The Coming of Post-Industrial Society*. New York: Basic Books.

Bendix, R. (1979). *Kings or People: Power and the Mandate to Rule*. Berkeley, CA: University of California Press.

Berelson, B., Lazarsfeld, P., and McPhee, W. (1954). *Voting: A Study of Opinion Formation in a Presidential Election*. Chicago, IL: University of Chicago Press.

Berger, P. and Luckmann, T. (1967). *The Social Construction of Reality*. New York: Doubleday.

Berk, G. (1994). *Alternative Tracks: The Constitution of American Industrial Order, 1865–1917*. Baltimore, MD: Johns Hopkins University Press.

Biernacki, R. (1995). *The Fabrication of Labor: Germany and Britain, 1640–1914*. Berkeley, CA: University of California Press.

—— (1999). 'Method and Metaphor after the New Cultural History', in V. Bonnell and L. Hunt (eds.), *Beyond the Cultural Turn: New Directions in the Study of Society and Culture*. Berkeley, CA: University of California Press, pp. 62–94.

Blyth, M. (2002). *Great Transformations: Economic Ideas and Institutional Change in the Twentieth Century*. New York: Cambridge University Press.

—— (2003). 'Structures do not Come with an Instruction Sheet: Interests, Ideas and Progress in Political Science', *Perspectives on Politics*, 1(4): 695–703.

Bourdieu, P. (1977). *Outline of a Theory of Practice*, trans. R. Nice. New York: Cambridge University Press.

Brady, H. and Collier, D. (eds.) (2004). *Rethinking Social Inquiry: Diverse Tools, Shared Standards*. Lanham, MD: Rowman & Littlefield.

—— and Seawright, J. (2004). 'Framing Social Inquiry: From Models of Causation to Statistically Based Causal Inference', paper presented at conference of American Political Science Association, Chicago.

—— Collier, D., and Seawright, J. (2004). 'Refocusing the Discussion of Methodology', in Brady and Collier (eds.), pp. 3–20.

Brenner, R. (1977). 'The Origins of Capitalist Development: A Critique of Neo-Smithian Marxism', *New Left Review*, 104: 25–92.

Brinton, N. and Nee, V. (eds.) (1998). *The New Institutionalism in Sociology*. New York: Russell Sage.

Brubaker, R. (1985). 'Rethinking Classical Theory: The Sociological Vision of Pierre Bourdieu', *Theory and Society*, 14: 745–75.

Bunge, M. (1993). 'Realism and Antirealism in Social Science', *Theory and Decision*, 35(2): 207–35.

Bunzl, M. (1995). 'Pragmatism to the Rescue?', *Journal of the History of Ideas*, 56(4): 651–9.

Burt, R. (1992). *Structural Holes*. Cambridge, MA: Harvard University Press.

Campbell, A., Converse, P., Miller, W., and Stokes, D. (1960). *The American Voter*. New York: Wiley.

Campbell, J. L. (1998). 'Institutional Analysis and the Role of Ideas in Political Economy', *Theory and Society*, 27(3): 377–409.

Cartwright, N. (1983). *How the Laws of Physics Lie*. New York: Clarendon Press.

Checkel, J. (1998). 'The Constructivist Turn in International Relations Theory', *World Politics*, 50(2): 324–48.

Cohen, B. J. (1973). *The Question of Imperialism: The Political Economy of Dominance and Dependence*. New York: Basic Books.

Cohen, G. A. (1978). *Karl Marx's Theory of History: A Defense*. Princeton, NJ: Princeton University Press.

—— (1986). 'Marxism and Functional Explanation', in J. Roemer (ed.), *Analytical Marxism*. Cambridge: Cambridge University Press, pp. 221–34.

Cohen, M., March, J., and Olsen, J. (1972). 'A Garbage Can Model of Organizational Choice', *Administrative Science Quarterly*, 17(1): 1–25.

Collier, D. (1991). 'The Comparative Method: Two Decades of Change', in D. Rustow and K. Erickson (eds.), *Comparative Political Dynamics*. New York: HarperCollins, pp. 7–31.

_____ (1999). 'Building a Disciplined, Rigorous Center in Comparative Politics', *APSA-CP: APSA Comparative Politics Section*, 10(2): 1–2, 4.

_____ Brady, H., and Seawright, J. (2004). 'Sources of Leverage in Causal Inference: Toward an Alternative View of Methodology', in Brady and Collier (eds.), pp. 229–66.

Collier, R. B. and Collier, D. (1991). *Shaping the Political Agenda: Critical Junctures, the Labor Movement, and Regime Dynamics in Latin America*. Princeton, NJ: Princeton University Press.

Conover, P. and Feldman, S. (1986). 'Emotional Reactions to the Economy: I'm Mad as Hell and I'm not Going to Take it Anymore', *American Journal of Political Science*, 30: 50–78.

Converse, P. (1964). 'The Nature of Belief Systems in Mass Publics', in D. Apter (ed.), *Ideology and Discontent*. New York: Free Press, pp. 206–61.

_____ (1976). *The Dynamics of Party Support: Cohort-Analyzing Party Identification*. Beverly Hills, CA: Sage.

Cosmides, L. and Tooby, J. (1994). 'Better than Rational: Evolutionary Psychology and the Invisible Hand', *American Economic Review*, 84(2): 327–32.

Crawford, N. (2000). 'The Passion of World Politics: Propositions on Emotion and Emotional Relationships', *International Security*, 24(4): 116–56.

Crocker, J., Major, B., and Steele, C. (1998). 'Social Stigma', in Gilbert, Fiske, and Lindzey (eds.), pp. 504–53.

Dahl, R. (1986). 'On Removing Certain Impediments to Democracy in the United States', in R. Horowitz (ed.), *The Moral Foundations of the American Republic*, 3rd edn. Charlottesville, VA: University of Virginia Press, pp. 230–52.

David, P. (1985). 'Clio and the Economics of QWERTY', *American Economic Review*, 75(2): 332–37.

Davidson, D. (1963). 'Actions, Reasons, and Causes', *Journal of Philosophy*, 60(23): 685–700.

Delli Carpini, M. X. and Keeter, S. (1996). *What Americans Know About Politics and Why It Matters*. New Haven, CT: Yale University Press.

de Schweinitz, K. (1964). *Industrialization and Democracy: Economic Necessities and Political Possibilities*. New York: Free Press.

Dessler, D. (1989). 'What's at Stake in the Agency-Structure Debate?', *International Organization*, 43(3): 441–73.

Diamond, L. (ed.) (1993). *Political Culture and Democracy in Developing Countries*. Boulder, CO: Lynne Rienner.

DiMaggio, P. (1979). 'On Pierre Bourdieu', *American Journal of Sociology*, 84(6): 1460–74.

Dittmer, L. (1977). 'Political Culture and Political Symbolism: Toward a Theoretical Synthesis', *World Politics*, 29(4): 552–83.

Dobbin, F. (1994). *Forging Industrial Policy: The United States, Britain and France in the Railway Age*. New York: Cambridge University Press.

Douglas M. (1970). *Natural Symbols*. New York: Random House.

References

_____ (1986). *How Institutions Think*. Syracuse, NY: Syracuse University Press.

_____ (1992). *Risk and Blame: Essays in Cultural Theory*. New York: Routledge.

_____ and Wildavsky, A. (1982). *Risk and Culture: An Essay on the Selection of Technical and Environmental Dangers*. Berkeley, CA: University of California Press.

Downs, A. (1957). *An Economic Theory of Democracy*. New York: HarperCollins.

Duesenberry, J. (1960). 'Comment on "An Economic Analysis of Fertility"', in *Demographic and Economic Change in Developed Countries*. Princeton, NJ: National Bureau of Economic Research, pp. 231–34.

Durkheim, E. ([1897] 1951). *Suicide: A Study in Sociology*, trans. G. Simpson and J. A. Spaulding. New York: Free Press.

Eckstein, H. (1966). *Division and Cohesion in Democracy: A Study of Norway*. Princeton, NJ: Princeton University Press.

_____ (1988). 'A Culturalist Theory of Political Change', *American Political Science Review*, 82(3): 789–804.

Eggertsson, T. (1990). *Economic Behavior and Institutions*. New York: Cambridge University Press.

Elkins, D. and Simeon, R. (1979). 'A Cause in Search of Its Effect, or What Does Political Culture Explain?', *Comparative Politics*, 11(2): 127–45.

Ellis, R. J. and Thompson, M. (eds.) (1997). *Culture Matters: Essays in Honor of Aaron Wildavsky*. Boulder, CO: Westview.

_____ _____ and Wildavsky, A. (1990). *Cultural Theory*. Boulder, CO: Westview.

Elman, C. and Elman, M. F. (2002). 'How Not to Be Lakatos Intolerant: Appraising Progress in IR Research', *International Studies Quarterly*, 46(2): 231–62.

Elster, J. (1982). 'Marxism, Functionalism, and Game Theory', *Theory and Society*, 11(4): 453–82.

_____ (1983). *Explaining Technical Change*. New York: Cambridge University Press.

_____ (1986). 'Introduction', in J. Elster (ed.), *Rational Choice*. Oxford: Basil Blackwell Press, pp. 1–33.

_____ (1998). 'A Plea for Mechanisms', in P. Hedstrom and R. Swedberg (eds.), *Social Mechanisms*. New York: Cambridge University Press, pp. 45–73.

_____ (2000). 'Rational Choice History: A Case of Excessive Ambition', *American Political Science Review*, 94(3): 685–95.

Emirbayer, M. (1997). 'Manifesto for a Relational Sociology', *American Journal of Sociology*, 103(2): 281–317.

Erikson, E. (1958). *Young Man Luther*. New York: W.W. Norton.

Erikson, R. (1979). 'The SRC Panel Data and Mass Political Attitudes', *British Journal of Political Science*, 9: 89–114.

_____ Makuen, M., and Stimson, J. (2002). *The Macro Polity*. New York: Cambridge University Press.

Ertman, T. (1997). *Birth of the Leviathan: Building States and Regimes in Medieval and Early Modern Europe*. New York: Cambridge University Press.

Eulau, H. and Zlomke, S. (1999). 'Harold Lasswell's Legacy to Mainstream Political Science: A Neglected Agenda', *Annual Review of Political Science*, 2: 75–89.

Evans, P. (1997). Review of S. Huntington, *The Clash of Civilizations and the Remaking of the World Order*, in *Contemporary Sociology* 26(6): 691–3.

Farr, J. (1995). 'Remembering the Revolution: Behavioralism in American Political Science', in J. Farr et al. (eds.), *Political Science in History*. New York: Cambridge University Press, pp. 198–224.

Ferejohn, J. (2002). 'Rational Choice Theory and Social Explanation', *Economics and Philosophy*, 18(2): 211–34.

―――― (2004). 'External and Internal Explanation', in I. Shapiro, R. Smith, and T. Masoud (eds.), *Problems and Methods in Political Science*. New York: Cambridge University Press, pp. 144–66.

Festinger, L. (1957). *A Theory of Cognitive Dissonance*. Evanston, IL: Row, Peterson.

Finnemore, M. (1996). *National Interests in International Society*. Ithaca, NY: Cornell University Press.

―――― and Sikkink, K. (2001). 'Taking Stock: The Constructivist Research Program in International Relations and Comparative Politics', *Annual Review of Political Science*, 4: 391–416.

Fiorina, M. P. (1995). 'Rational Choice, Empirical Contributions, and the Scientific Enterprise', *Critical Review*, 9(1–2): 85–94.

Fischoff, B. (1983). 'Predicting Frames', *Journal of Experimental Psychology: Learning, Memory, and Cognition*, 9: 103–16.

Fiske, A. P., Kitayama, S., Markus, H. R., and Nisbett, R. (1998). 'The Cultural Matrix of Social Psychology', in Gilbert, Fiske, and Lindzey (eds.), pp. 915–81.

Fiske, S. and Taylor, S. (1984). *Social Cognition*. New York: Random House.

Fligstein, N. (1990). *The Transformation of Corporate Control*. Cambridge, MA: Harvard University Press.

―――― and Mara-Drita, I. (1996). 'How to Make a Market: Reflections on the Attempt to Create a Single Market in the European Union', *American Journal of Sociology*, 102(1): 1–33.

Formisano, R. (2001). 'The Concept of Political Culture', *The Journal of Interdisciplinary History*, 31(3): 393–426.

Foucault, M. (1972). *The Archaeology of Knowledge*, trans. A. M. Sheridan Smith. New York: Pantheon Books.

Friedman, J. (ed.) (1996). *The Rational Choice Controversy: Economic Models of Politics Reconsidered*. New Haven, CT: Yale University Press.

Friedman, M. (1953). *Essays in Positive Economics*. Chicago, IL: University of Chicago Press.

Garfinkel, H. (1967). *Studies in Ethnomethodology*. Englewood Cliffs, NJ: Prentice-Hall.

Garrett, G. and Tsebelis, G. (1996). 'An Institutionalist Critique of Intergovernmentalism', *International Organization*, 50(2): 269–99.

Geertz, C. (1973). 'Thick Description: Toward an Interpretive Theory of Culture', in C. Geertz, *The Interpretation of Cultures*. New York: Basic Books, pp. 3–32.

References

Gendzel, G. (1997). 'Political Culture: Genealogy of a Concept', *Journal of Interdisciplinary History*, 28(2): 225–50.

George, A. (1969). 'The Operational Code: A Neglected Approach to the Study of Political Leaders and Decision-Making', *International Studies Quarterly*, 13: 190–222.

—— (1979). 'Case Studies and Theory Development: The Method of Structured Focused Comparison', in P. Laren (ed.), *Diplomacy: New Approaches in History, Theory and Policy*. New York: Free Press, pp. 43–68.

—— and George, J. (1956). *Woodrow Wilson and Colonel House: A Personality Study*. New York: Dover.

Giddens, A. (1979). *Central Problems in Social Theory*. Berkeley, CA: University of California Press.

Gilbert, D., Fiske S., and Lindzey G. (eds.) (1998). *Handbook of Social Psychology*, 4th edn. New York: Oxford University Press.

Gilbert, M. (1989). *On Social Facts*. Princeton, NJ: Princeton University Press.

Goethals, G. (2005). 'Presidential Leadership', *Annual Review of Psychology*, 56: 545–70.

Gollwitzer, P. and Brandstätter, V. (1995). 'Motivation', in A. Manstead and M. Hewstone (eds.), *Blackwell Encyclopedia of Social Psychology*. Cambridge, MA: Basil Blackwell.

Goodin, R. and Tilly, C. (eds.) (2006). *Oxford Handbook of Contextual Political Analysis*. New York: Oxford University Press.

Goodwin, B. (1994). *How the Leopard Changed His Spots: The Evolution of Complexity*. New York: Scribner.

Gottfried, R. (1983). *The Black Death*. New York: Free Press.

Granovetter, M. (1985). 'Economic Action and Social Structure: The Problem of Embeddedness', *American Journal of Sociology*, 91(3): 481–510.

Green, D. and Shapiro, I. (1994). *Pathologies of Rational Choice Theory*. New Haven, CT: Yale University Press.

Gurr, T. (1970). *Why Men Rebel*. Princeton, NJ: Princeton University Press.

Hall, P. A. (1986). *Governing the Economy*. New York: Oxford University Press.

—— (1994). 'Central Bank Independence and Coordinated Wage Bargaining: Their Interdependence in Germany and Europe', *German Politics and Society*, 31(1): 1–23.

—— (ed.) (1989). *The Political Power of Economic Ideas: Keynesianism Across Nations*. Princeton, NJ: Princeton University Press.

—— and Soskice, D. (eds.) (2001). *Varieties of Capitalism: The Institutional Foundations of Comparative Advantage*. New York: Oxford University Press.

—— and Taylor, R. (1996). 'Political Science and the Three New Institutionalisms', *Political Studies*, 44: 936–57.

—— —— (1998). 'The Potential of Historical Institutionalism: A Response to Hay and Wincott', *Political Studies*, 48: 958–62.

Hannan, M. and Freeman, J. (1989). *Organizational Ecology*. Cambridge, MA: Harvard University Press.

Hardin, R. (1982). *Collective Action*. Baltimore, MD: Johns Hopkins University Press.

Harre, R. and Madden, E. (1975). *Causal Powers*. Oxford: Blackwell.

Harris, M. (2001). *The Rise of Anthropological Theory*, 2nd edn. New York: Rowman & Littlefield.

Hattam, V. (1992). 'Institutions and Political Change: Working-Class Formation in England and the United States', in Steinmo, Thelen, and Longstreth (eds.), pp. 155–87.

____ (1993). *Labor Visions and State Power: The Origins of Business Unionism in the United States*. Princeton, NJ: Princeton University Press.

Hay, C. (2002). *Political Analysis: A Critical Introduction*. Houndmills, UK: Palgrave.

Hedstrom, P. and Swedberg, R. (eds.) (1998). *Social Mechanisms*. New York: Cambridge University Press.

Hempel, C. (1942). 'The Function of General Laws in History', *Journal of Philosophy*, 39: 35–48.

Herlihy, D. (1997). *The Black Death and the Transformation of the West*. Cambridge, MA: Harvard University Press.

Hermann, M. (1986.) 'What is political psychology?', in M. Hermann (ed.), *Political Psychology*. San Francisco, CA: Jossey-Bass, pp. 1–10.

____ (2002). 'Political Psychology as a Perspective in the Study of Politics', in K. Monroe (ed.), *Political Psychology*. Mahwah, NJ: Lawrence Erlbaum, pp. 43–60.

____ (2003). 'Assessing Leadership Style: Trait Analysis', in Post (ed.), pp. 178–213.

Hirschman, A. (1977). *The Passions and the Interests: Political Arguments for Capitalism before Its Triumph*. Princeton, NJ: Princeton University Press.

Hobbes, T. ([1660] 1968). *Leviathan*. New York: Penguin.

Hofstede, G. (1984). *Culture's Consequences: International Differences in Work-Related Values*. Beverly Hills, CA: Sage.

Holland, P. (1986). 'Statistics and Causal Inference', *Journal of the American Statistical Association*, 81(396): 945–60.

Hollis, M. and Smith, S. (1990). *Explaining and Understanding International Relations*. Oxford: Clarendon Press.

Holsti, O. and Rosenau, J. (1979). 'Vietnam, Consensus, and the Belief Systems of American Leaders', *World Politics*, 32(1): 1–56.

Horowitz, D. (1985). *Ethnic Groups in Conflict*. Berkeley, CA: University of California Press.

Hume, D. ([1738] 1978). *Enquiry Concerning Human Understanding*, 3rd edn. Oxford: Clarendon Press.

Huntington, S. (1993). 'The Clash of Civilizations', *Foreign Affairs*, 72(3): 22–8.

____ (1996). *The Clash of Civilizations and the Remaking of the World Order*. New York: Simon & Schuster.

Huppert, G. (1998). *After the Black Death*. Bloomington, IN: Indiana University Press.

Hyman, H. (1959). *Political Socialization: A Study in the Psychology of Political Behavior*. Glencoe, IL: Free Press.

Immergut, E. (1992). *Health Politics: Interests and Institutions in Western Europe*. New York: Cambridge University Press.

—— (1998). 'The Theoretical Core of the New Institutionalism', *Politics and Society*, 26(1): 5–34.

Inglehart, R. (1977). *The Silent Revolution*. Princeton, NJ: Princeton University Press.

—— (1988). 'The Renaissance of Political Culture', *American Political Science Review*, 82(4): 1203–30.

—— (1989). *Culture Shift in Advanced Industrial Society*. Princeton, NJ: Princeton University Press.

—— (1997). *Modernization and Postmodernization*. Princeton, NJ: Princeton University Press.

Jackman, R. W. and Miller, R. A. (1996). 'A Renaissance of Political Culture?' *American Journal of Political Science*, 40(3): 632–59.

Janis, I. (1972). *Victims of Groupthink: A Psychological Study of Foreign-Policy Decisions and Fiascoes*. Boston, MA: Houghton Mifflin.

Janos, A. (1986). *Politics and Paradigms: Changing Theories of Change in Social Science*. Stanford, CA: Stanford University Press.

—— (1989). 'The Politics of Backwardness in Continental Europe, 1780–1945', *World Politics*, 41(3): 325–58.

Jennings, M. K. and Niemi, R. (1974). *The Political Character of Adolescence: The Influence of Families and Schools*. Princeton, NJ: Princeton University Press.

—— —— (1981). *Generations and Politics*. Princeton, NJ: Princeton University Press.

Jervis, R. (1976). *Perception and Misperception in International Politics*. Princeton, NJ: Princeton University Press.

—— (1997). Review of S. Huntington, *The Clash of Civilizations and the Remaking of the World Order*, in *Political Science Quarterly*, 112(2): 307–8.

Jones, R. A. (1986). *Emile Durkheim: An Introduction to Four Major Works*. Beverly Hills, CA: Sage.

Kahler, M. (1998). 'Rationality in International Relations', *International Organization*, 52(4): 919–41.

Kahneman, D. and Tversky, A. (1972). 'Subjective Probability: A Judgement of Representativeness', *Cognitive Psychology*, 3: 430–54.

—— —— (1973). 'On the Psychology of Prediction', *Psychological Review*, 80: 237–51.

—— Slovic, P., and Tversky, A. (eds.) (1982). *Judgment under Uncertainty: Heuristics and Biases*. New York: Cambridge University Press.

Katzenstein, P. J. (ed.)(1996). *The Culture of National Security*. New York: Columbia University Press.

Katznelson, I. (1997). 'Structure and Configuration in Comparative Politics', in Lichbach and Zuckerman (eds.), pp. 81–112.

____ and Milner, H. (eds.) (2002). *Political Science: The State of the Discipline*. New York: W.W. Norton.

Keat, R. and Urry, J. (1983). *Social Theory as Science*, 2nd edn. London: Routledge.

Keohane, R. (1986). 'Theory of World Politics: Structural Realism and Beyond', in R. Keohane (ed.), *Neorealism and Its Critics*. New York: Columbia University Press, pp. 158–203.

Khong, Y. F. (1991). *Analogies at War*. Princeton, NJ: Princeton University Press.

Kincaid, H. (1996). *Philosophical Foundations of the Social Sciences*. New York: Cambridge University Press.

Kinder, D. (1998). 'Opinion and Action in the Realm of Politics', in Gilbert, Fiske, and Lindzey (eds.), pp. 778–867.

King, G., Keohane, R., and Verba, S. (1994). *Designing Social Inquiry*. Princeton, NJ: Princeton University Press.

Kiser, E. and Hechter, M. (1991). 'The Role of General Theory in Comparative Historical Sociology', *American Journal of Sociology*, 97(1): 1–30.

Kohli, A. et al. (1995). 'The Role of Theory in Comparative Politics: A Symposium', *World Politics*, 48(1): 1–49.

Krasner, S. (1984). 'Approaches to the State: Alternative Conceptions and Historical Dynamics', *Comparative Politics*, 16: 223–46.

____ (ed.) (1983). *International Regimes*. Ithaca, NY: Cornell University Press.

Kratochwil, F. (1989). *Rules, Norms, and Decisions*. Cambridge: Cambridge University Press.

Kuklinski, J. (2002). 'Political Psychology and the Study of Politics', in J. Kuklinski (ed.), *Thinking about Political Psychology*. New York: Cambridge University Press, pp. 1–22.

Laitin, D. (1995). 'The Civic Culture at 30', *American Political Science Review*, 89(1): 168–73.

____ (2002). 'Comparative Politics: The State of the Subdiscipline', in Katznelson and Milner (eds.), pp. 630–59.

Lakatos, I. (1970). 'Falsification and the Methodology of Scientific Research Programmes', in I. Lakatos and A. Musgrave (eds.), *Criticism and the Growth of Knowledge*. New York: Cambridge University Press, pp. 91–196.

____ (1971). 'History of Science and its Rational Reconstructions', *Boston Studies in the Philosophy of Science*, 8.

Lane, R. (1962). *Political Ideology: Why the American Common Man Believes What He Does*. Glencoe, IL: Free Press.

Larson, D. (1985). *Origins of Containment: A Psychological Explanation*. Princeton, NJ: Princeton University Press.

Lasswell, H. (1930). *Psychopathology and Politics*. Chicago: University of Chicago Press.

_____ (1935). *World Politics and Personality*. New York: McGraw-Hill.

_____ (1936). *Politics: Who Gets What, When, and How*. New York: McGraw-Hill.

_____ (1948). *Power and Personality*. New York: W.W. Norton.

_____ (1977). 'The Psychology of Hitlerism', in D. Marvick (ed.), *Harold Lasswell on Political Sociology*. Chicago, IL: University of Chicago Press, pp. 294–304.

Lebow, R. N. (1981). *Between Peace and War: The Nature of International Crisis*. Baltimore, MD: Johns Hopkins University Press.

_____ (2000). 'What's So Different about a Counterfactual?', *World Politics*, 52(4): 550–85.

Legro, J. (1995). *Cooperation under Fire*. Ithaca, NY: Cornell University Press.

Lerner, D. (1958). *The Passing of Traditional Society*. New York: Free Press.

Levi, M. (1988). *Of Rule and Revenue*. Berkeley, CA: University of California Press.

_____ (1997). 'A Model, a Method, and a Map: Rational Choice in Comparative and Historical Analysis', in Lichbach and Zuckerman (eds.), pp. 19–41.

_____ (1998). 'Conscription: The Price of Citizenship', in Bates et al. (eds.), pp. 109–47.

Lévi-Strauss, C. (1966). *The Savage Mind*. Chicago, IL: University of Chicago Press.

Levy, J. (1994). 'An Introduction to Prospect Theory', in B. Farnham (ed.), *Avoiding Losses/Taking Risks: Prospect Theory and International Conflict*. Ann Arbor, MI: University of Michigan Press, pp. 7–22.

_____ (2003). 'Political Psychology and Foreign Policy', in Sears, Huddy, and Jervis (eds.), pp. 253–84.

Lichbach, M. and Zuckerman, A. (eds.) (1997). *Comparative Politics: Rationality, Culture, and Structure*. New York: Cambridge University Press.

Lieberman, E. (2001). 'Causal Inference in Historical Institutional Analysis: A Specification of Periodization Strategies', *Comparative Political Studies*, 34(9): 1011–35.

Lijphart, A. (1989). 'The Structure of Inference', in G. Almond and S. Verba (eds.), *The Civic Culture Revisited*. Newbury Park, CA: Sage, pp. 57–102.

Lipset, S. M. (1959). *Political Man*. New York: Doubleday.

Little, D. (1991). *Varieties of Social Explanation*. Boulder, CO: Westview.

Lodge, M. (1995). 'Toward a Procedural Model of Candidate Evaluation', in M. Lodge and K. McGraw (eds.), *Political Judgment*. Ann Arbor, MI: University of Michigan Press, pp. 11–140.

Lukes, S. (1968). 'Methodological Individualism Reconsidered', *British Journal of Sociology*, 19: 119–29.

_____ (1973). *Emile Durkheim: His Life and Work*. New York: Harper & Row.

_____ and Hollis, M. (eds.) (1982). *Rationality and Relativism*. Oxford: Blackwell.

Mahoney, J. (2000). 'Path Dependence in Historical Sociology', *Theory and Society*, 29: 507–48.

_____ and Rueschemeyer, D. (eds.) (2003). *Comparative Historical Analysis in the Social Sciences*. New York: Cambridge University Press.

____ and Schensul, D. (2006). 'Historical Context and Path Dependence', in Goodin and Tilly (eds.), pp. 454–71.

March, J. and Olsen, J. P. (1989). *Rediscovering Institutions: The Organizational Basis of Politics*. New York: Free Press.

Marcus, G. (2000). 'Emotions in Politics', *Annual Review of Political Science*, 3: 221–50.

____ and MacKuen, M. (1993). 'Anxiety, Enthusiasm and the Vote: The Emotional Underpinnings of Learning and Involvement during Presidential Campaigns', *American Political Science Review*, 87: 688–701.

____ ____ (2001). 'Emotions and Politics: The Dynamic Functions of Emotionality', in J. Kuklinski (ed.) *Citizens and Politics*. New York: Cambridge University Press, pp. 41–67.

Marsh, D. and Stoker, G. (eds.) (2002). *Theory and Methods in Political Science*. New York: Palgrave/Macmillan.

Martin, L. (1992). 'Interests, Power and Multilateralism', *International Organization*, 46(4): 765–92.

Marx, K. ([1849] 1978). 'Wage Labour and Capital', reprinted in R. Tucker (ed.), *The Marx-Engels Reader*, 2nd edn. New York: W.W. Norton, pp. 203–17.

____ ([1852] 1978). *The Eighteenth Brumaire of Louis Bonaparte*, reprinted in R. Tucker (ed.), *The Marx-Engels Reader*, 2nd edn. New York: W.W. Norton, pp. 594–617.

____ ([1859] 1978). Preface to *A Contribution to the Critique of Political Economy*, reprinted in R. Tucker (ed.), *The Marx-Engels Reader*, 2nd edn. New York: W.W. Norton, pp. 3–6.

Mazlish, B. (1972). *In Search of Nixon: A Psychohistorical Inquiry*. New York: Basic Books.

McDermott, R. (1998). *Risk-Taking in International Politics: Prospect Theory in American Foreign Policy*. Ann Arbor, MI: University of Michigan Press.

____ (2004a). *Political Psychology in International Relations*. Ann Arbor, MI: University of Michigan Press.

____ (2004b). 'The Feeling of Rationality: The Meaning of Neuroscientific Advances for Political Science', *Perspectives on Politics*, 2(4): 691–706.

____ (2004c). 'Prospect Theory in Political Science: Gains and Losses from the First Decade', *Political Psychology*, 25(2): 289–312.

McGraw, K. (2006). 'Why and How Psychology Matters', in Goodin and Tilly, pp. 131–56.

McKeown, T. (2004). 'Case Studies and the Limits of the Quantitative Worldview', in Brady and Collier (eds.), pp. 139–68.

McMullin, E. (1984). 'Two Ideals of Explanation in Natural Science', *Midwest Studies in Philosophy*, 9: 205–20.

McNamara, K. (1998). *The Currency of Ideas: Monetary Politics in the European Union*. Ithaca, NY: Cornell University Press.

References

Mearsheimer, J. (1990). 'Back to the Future: Instability in Europe After the Cold War', *International Security*, 15(4): 5–56.

Mercer, J. (1995). 'Anarchy and Identity', *International Organization*, 49(2): 229–52.

—— (2005). 'Rationality and Psychology in International Politics', *International Organization*, 59(1): 77–106.

—— (2006). 'Human Nature and the First Image: Emotion in International Politics', *Journal of International Relations and Development*, 9(3): 288–303.

Merton, R. (1957). *Social Theory and Social Structure*. Glencoe, IL: Free Press.

Meyer, J. and Hannan, M. (eds.) (1979). *National Development and the World System*. Chicago, IL: University of Chicago Press.

—— Boli, J., Thomas, G., and Ramirez, F. (1997). 'World Society and the Nation-State', *American Journal of Sociology*, 103: 144–81.

Miller, R. W. (1978). 'Methodological Individualism and Social Explanation', *Philosophy of Science*, 45(3): 387–414.

Miller, W. and Shanks, J. (1996). *The New American Voter*. Cambridge, MA: Harvard University Press.

Moe, T. (1984). 'The New Economics of Organization', *American Journal of Political Science*, 28: 739–77.

Monroe, K. (ed.) (2002). *Political Psychology*. Mahwah, NJ: Lawrence Erlbaum.

Moore, B., Jr. (1966). *Social Origins of Dictatorship and Democracy*. Boston, MA: Beacon.

Morgenthau, H. (1954). *Politics among Nations*. New York: Knopf.

Morrison, K. (1995). *Marx, Durkheim, Weber: Formations of Modern Social Thought*. Beverly Hills, CA: Sage.

Morrow, J. (1994). *Game Theory for Political Scientists*. Princeton, NJ: Princeton University Press.

Nadeau, R., Niemi, R., and Amato, T. (1995). 'Emotions, Issue Importance, and Political Learning', *American Journal of Political Science*, 39: 558–74.

Nicolis, G. and Prigogine, I. (1989). *Exploring Complexity: An Introduction*. New York: W. H. Freeman.

Nie, N., Verba, S., and Petrovik, J. (1976). *The Changing American Voter*. Cambridge, MA: Harvard University Press.

Nisbett, R. (2003). *The Geography of Thought: How Asians and Westerners Think Differently . . . and Why*. New York: Free Press.

—— and Ross, L. (1980). *Human Inference: Strategies and Shortcomings of Social Judgment*. Englewood Cliffs, NJ: Prentice-Hall.

North, D. C. (1986). 'The New Institutional Economics', *Journal of Institutional and Theoretical Economics*, 142: 230–37.

—— (1990). *Institutions, Institutional Change and Economic Performance*. New York: Cambridge University Press.

Nurmi, H. (1999). *Voting Paradoxes and How to Deal With Them*. Berlin: Springer.

Olson, M. (1965). *Logic of Collective Action*. Cambridge, MA: Harvard University Press.

Onuf, N. (1989). *World of Our Making*. Columbia, SC: University of South Carolina Press.

Orren, K. and Skowronek, S. (2004). *The Search for American Political Development*. New York: Cambridge University Press.

Oye, K. (ed.) (1993). *Cooperation Under Anarchy*. Princeton, NJ: Princeton University Press.

Padgett, J. and Ansell, C. (1993). 'Robust Action and the Rise of the Medici, 1400–1434', *American Journal of Sociology*, 98: 1259–319.

Page, B. and Shapiro, R. (1992). *The Rational Public*. Chicago, IL: University of Chicago Press.

Parson, C. (2003). *A Certain Idea of Europe*. Ithaca, NY: Cornell University Press.

Pateman, C. (1989). 'The Civic Culture: A Philosophical Critique', in G. Almond and S. Verba (eds.), *The Civic Culture Revisited*. Newbury Park, CA: Sage, pp. 57–102.

Pettit, P. (1993). *The Common Mind*. New York: Oxford University Press.

Pierson, P. (2004). *Politics in Time: History, Institutions and Social Analysis*. Princeton, NJ: Princeton University Press.

_____ and Skocpol, T. (2002). 'Historical Institutionalism in Contemporary Political Science', in Katznelson and Milner (eds.), pp. 693–721.

Pittman, T. (1998). 'Motivation', in Gilbert, Fiske, and Lindzey (eds.), pp. 549–90.

Polanyi, K. (1944). *The Great Transformation*. Boston, MA: Beacon.

Popkin, S. (1979). *The Rational Peasant: The Political Economy of Rural Society in Vietnam*. Berkeley, CA: University of California Press.

_____ (1991). *The Reasoning Voter*. Chicago, IL: University of Chicago Press.

Popper, K. (1945). *The Open Society and Its Enemies*. London: Routledge & Kegan Paul.

Post, J. (ed.) (2003). *The Psychological Assessment of Political Leaders*. Ann Arbor, MI: University of Michigan Press.

Poulantzas, N. (1973). *Political Power and Social Classes*, trans. T. O'Hagan. London: NLB.

Powell, R. (1991). 'Absolute and Relative Gains in International Relations Theory', *American Political Science Review*, 85(4): 1303–20.

Powell, W. and DiMaggio, P. (1991). 'Introduction' in W. Powell and P. DiMaggio (eds.), *The New Institutionalism in Organizational Analysis*. Chicago, IL: University of Chicago Press, pp. 1–40.

Przeworski, A. (1985). *Capitalism and Social Democracy*. Cambridge: Cambridge University Press.

_____ and Teune, H. (1970). *Logic of Comparative Social Inquiry*. New York: John Wiley & Sons.

Putnam, R. (1993). *Making Democracy Work: Civic Traditions in Modern Italy*. Princeton, NJ: Princeton University Press.

Pye, L. (1968). *The Spirit of Chinese Politics: A Psychocultural Study of the Authority Crisis in Political Development*. Cambridge, MA: MIT Press.

References

___ (1972). 'Culture and Political Science: Problems in the Evaluation of the Concept of Political Culture', *Social Science Quarterly*, 53(2): 285–96.

___ (1981). *The Mandarin and the Cadre: China's Political Cultures*. Ann Arbor, MI: University of Michigan Press.

___ and Verba, S. (eds.) (1965). *Political Culture and Political Development*. Princeton, NJ: Princeton University Press.

Rabin, M. (2000). 'Risk Aversion and Expected-Utility Theory: A Calibration Theorem', *Econometrica*, 68(5): 1281–92.

Reddy, W. (1984). *The Rise of Market Culture: The Textile Trade & French Society, 1750–1900*. New York: Cambridge University Press.

Renshon, S. (1996). *The Psychological Assessment of Presidential Candidates*. New York: New York University Press.

___ (2002). 'Lost in Plain Sight: The Cultural Foundations of Political Psychology', in K. Monroe (ed.), *Political Psychology*. Mahwah, NJ: Lawrence Erlbaum, pp. 121–40.

___ (2003). 'Psychoanalytic Assessments of Character and Performance in Presidents and Candidates: Some Observations on Theory and Method', in Post (ed.), 105–36.

Ridley, M. (2003). *Nature via Nurture: Genes, Experience, and What Makes Us Human*. New York: HarperCollins.

Riker, W. (1980). 'Implications from the Disequilibrium of Majority Rule for the Study of Institutions', *American Political Science Review*, 74: 432–46.

Roemer, J. (1982). *A General Theory of Exploitation and Class*. Cambridge, MA: Harvard University Press.

Rogow, A. (ed.) (1977). *Politics, Personality, and Social Science in the Twentieth Century: Essays in Honor of Harold Lasswell*. Chicago, IL: University of Chicago Press.

Rogowski, R. (1989). *Commerce and Coalitions: How Trade Affects Domestic Political Alignments*. Princeton, NJ: Princeton University Press.

Rosecrance, R. (1998). Review of S. Huntington, *The Clash of Civilizations and the Remaking of the World Order*, in *The American Political Science Review*, 92(4): 978–80.

Rosen, S. (2005). *War and Human Nature*. Princeton, NJ: Princeton University Press.

Ross, M. and Sicoly, F. (1979). 'Egocentric Biases in Availability and Attribution', *Journal of Personality and Social Psychology*, 37: 322–36.

Rostow, W. W. (1960). *The Stages of Economic Growth: A Non-Communist Manifesto*. New York: Cambridge University Press.

Rubin, D. (1974). 'Estimating Causal Effects of Treatments in Randomized and Non-randomized Studies', *Journal of Education Psychology*, 66, pp. 688–701.

Ruggie, J. (1998). 'What Makes the World Hang Together? Neo-Utilitarianism and the Social Constructivist Challenge', *International Organization*, 52: 855–85.

Salmon, W. (1998). *Causality and Explanation*. Oxford: Oxford University Press.

Sawyer, R. K. (2001). 'Emergence in Sociology: Contemporary Philosophy of Mind and Some Implications for Sociological Theory', *American Journal of Sociology*, 107: 51–85.

Schwartz, S. (1999). 'A Theory of Cultural Values and Some Expectations for Work', *Applied Psychology*, 48(1): 23–47.

Scott, W. R. and Meyer, J. W. (1994). *Institutional Environments and Organizations*. Thousand Oaks, CA: Sage.

Scriven, M. (1975). 'Causation as Explanation', *Nous*, 9: 3–16.

Searle, J. (1990). 'Collective Intentions and Actions', in P. Cohen, J. Morgan, and M. Pollack (eds.), *Intentions in Communication*. Cambridge, MA: MIT Press, 401–15.

—— (1995). *Construction of Social Reality*. New York: Free Press.

Sears, D. (1987). 'Political Psychology', *Annual Review of Psychology*, 38: 229–55.

—— (2001). 'The Role of Affect in Symbolic Politics', in J. Kuklinski (ed.), *Citizens and Politics*. New York: Cambridge University Press, pp. 14–40.

—— and Levy, S. (2003). 'Childhood and Adult Political Development', in Sears, Huddy, and Jervis (eds.), pp. 60–109.

—— Huddy, L., and Jervis, R. (eds.) (2003). *Oxford Handbook of Political Psychology*. New York: Oxford University Press, esp. pp. 3–18.

Sewell, W. H. Jr. (1996). 'Three Temporalities: Toward an Eventful Sociology', in T. McDonald (ed.), *The Historic Turn in the Human Sciences*. Ann Arbor, MI: University of Michigan Press, pp. 245–80.

—— (1999). 'The Concept(s) of Culture', in V. Bonnell and L. Hunt (eds.), *Beyond the Cultural Turn: New Directions in the Study of Society and Culture*. Berkeley, CA: University of California Press, pp. 35–61.

Shapiro, I. (1998). 'Can the Rational Choice Framework Cope with Culture?' *PS*, 31(1): 40–42.

Shepsle, K. (1979). 'Institutional Arrangements and Equilibrium in Multidimensional Voting Models', *American Journal of Political Science*, 23(1): 27–59.

—— (1986). 'Institutional Equilibrium and Equilibrium Institutions', in H. F. Weisberg (ed.), *Political Science: The Science of Politics*. New York: Agathon, pp. 51–81.

—— (1989). 'Studying Institutions: Some Lessons from the Rational Choice Approach', *Journal of Theoretical Politics*, 1(2): 131–47.

—— and Bonchek, M. (1997). *Analyzing Politics: Rationality, Behavior, and Institutions*. New York: W.W. Norton.

—— and Weingast, B. (eds.) (1995). *Positive Theories of Congressional Institutions*. Ann Arbor, MI: University of Michigan Press.

Sidanius, J. and Kurzban, R. (2003). 'Evolutionary Approaches to Political Psychology', in Sears, Huddy, and Jervis (eds.), pp. 146–81.

Sikkink, K. (1991). *Ideas and Institutions: Developmentalism in Argentina and Brazil*. Ithaca, NY: Cornell University Press.

References

Simonton, D. (1987). *Why Presidents Succeed: A Political Psychology of Leadership*. New Haven, CT: Yale University Press.

Singer, D. (1961). 'The Level of Analysis Problem in International Relations', in K. Knorr and S. Verba (eds.), *The International System: Theoretical Essays*. Princeton, NJ: Princeton University Press, pp. 77–92.

Skocpol, T. (1979). *States and Social Revolutions: A Comparative Analysis of France, Russia, and China*. New York: Cambridge University Press.

Skowronek, S. (1982). *Building a New American State: The Expansion of National Administrative Capacities, 1877–1920*. New York: Cambridge University Press.

Sniderman, P., Brody, R., and Tetlock, P. (1993). *Reasoning and Choice: Explorations in Political Psychology*. New York: Cambridge University Press.

Sober, E. and Wilson, D. S. (1998). *Unto Others: The Evolution and Psychology of Unselfish Behavior*. New York: Cambridge University Press.

Somers, M. (1995). 'What's Political or Cultural about Political Culture and the Public Sphere? Toward an Historical Sociology of Concept Formation', *Sociological Theory*, 13(2): 113–44.

Stein, J. Gross. (2002). 'Psychological Explanations of International Conflict', in W.Carlsnaes, T. Risse, and B. Simmons (eds.), *Handbook of International Relations*. Thousand Oaks, CA: Sage, 292–308.

Stein, R. (1991). *Psychoanalytic Theories of Affect*. New York: Praeger.

Steinmo, S. (1993). *Taxation and Democracy*. New Haven, CT: Yale University Press.

——— Thelen, K., and Longstreth, F. (eds.) (1992). *Structuring Politics: Historical Institutionalism in Comparative Analysis*. New York: Cambridge University Press.

——— (1994). 'American Exceptionalism Reconsidered: Culture or Institutions?', in L. Dodd and C. Jillson (eds.), *The Dynamics of American Politics*. Boulder, CO: Westview, pp. 106–31.

Stimson, J. (1991). *Public Opinion in America: Moods, Cycles and Swings*. Boulder, CO: Westview.

Stinchcombe, A. (1968). *Constructing Social Theories*. Chicago, IL: University of Chicago Press.

——— (1978). *Theoretical Methods in Social History*. New York: Academic Press.

Stouffer, S., Suchman, E., DeVinney, L., Star, S., and Williams, R. Jr. (1949). *The American Soldier*, Vol. 1: *Adjustment During Army Life*. Princeton, NJ: Princeton University Press.

Strang, D. (1991). 'Anomaly and Commonplace in European Political Expansion: Realist and Institutional Accounts', *International Organization*, 45: 143–62.

Streeck, W. and Thelen, K. (eds.) (2005). *Beyond Continuity: Institutional Change in Advanced Political Economies*. New York: Oxford University Press.

Sullivan, D. and Masters, R. (1988). ' "Happy Warriors": Leaders' Facial Displays, Viewers' Emotions, and Political Support', *American Journal of Political Science*, 32: 345–68.

Sullivan, J., Rahn, W., and Rudolph, T. (2002). 'The Contours of Political Psychology: Situating Research on Political Information Processing', in J. Kuklinski (ed.),

Thinking about Political Psychology. New York: Cambridge University Press, pp. 23–47.

Swidler, A. (1986). 'Culture in Action: Symbols and Strategies', *American Sociological Review*, 51(2): 273–86.

Tajfel, H. and Turner, J. (1986). 'The Social Identity Theory of Intergroup Behavior', in S. Worchel and W. Austin (eds.), *Psychology of Intergroup Relations*, 2nd edn. Chicago, IL: Nelson-Hall, pp. 2–24.

Taylor, C. (1985). *Philosophy and the Human Sciences*. Cambridge: Cambridge University Press.

Taylor, S. (1982). 'The Availability Bias in Social Perception and Interaction', in Kahneman, Slovic, and Tversky (eds.), pp. 190–200.

Tedeschi, J. (1988). 'How Does One Describe a Platypus? An Outsider's Questions for Cross-Cultural Psychology', in M. Bond (ed.), *The Cross-Cultural Challenge to Social Psychology*. Thousand Oaks, CA: Sage, pp. 14–28.

Tetlock, P. (1998). 'Social Psychology and World Politics', in Gilbert, Fiske, and Lindzey (eds.), pp. 868–912.

—— and Belkin, A. (eds.) (1996). *Counterfactual Thought Experiments in World Politics*. Princeton, NJ: Princeton University Press.

—— and McGuire, C. (1986). 'Cognitive Perspectives on Foreign Policy', in R. White (ed.), *Psychology and the Prevention of Nuclear War*. New York: NYU Press.

Thelen, K. (2004). *How Institutions Evolve: The Political Economy of Skills in Germany, Britain, the United States, and Japan*. New York: Cambridge University Press.

—— and Steinmo, S. (1992). 'Historical Institutionalism in Comparative Politics', in Steinmo, Thelen, and Longstreth (eds.), pp. 1–32.

Thompson, M., Verweij, M., and Ellis, R. (2006). 'Why and How Culture Matters', in Goodin and Tilly (eds.), pp. 319–40.

Tilly, C. (1990). *Coercion, Capital, and European States*. Cambridge, MA: Blackwell.

—— and Goodin, R. (2006). 'It Depends', in Goodin and Tilly (eds.), 3–32.

Tiryakian, E. (1997). Review of S. Huntington, *The Clash of Civilizations and the Remaking of World Order*, in *American Journal of Sociology*, 103(2): 475–77.

Tollefsen, D. (2002). 'Collective Intentionality in the Social Sciences', *Philosophy of the Social Sciences*, 32: 25–50.

Tooby, J. and Cosmides, L. (1990). 'The Past Explains the Present: Emotional Adaptations and the Structure of Ancestral Environments', *Ethology and Sociobiology*, 11: 375–424.

Tsebelis, G. (1990). *Nested Games*. Berkeley, CA: University of California Press.

Turner, J. (1987). *Rediscovering the Social Group*. New York: Basil Blackwell.

Turner, S. (2000). 'Introduction', in S. Turner (ed.), *The Cambridge Companion to Weber*. New York: Cambridge University Press, pp. 1–20.

Tversky, A. and Kahneman, D. (1973). *Availability: A Heuristic for Judging Frequency and Probability*. New York: Academic Press.

—— —— (1982), 'Judgment under Uncertainty: Heuristics and Biases', in Kahneman, Slovic, and Tversky (eds.), pp. 3–20.

References

Unger, R. (1987). *Politics: A Work in Constructive Social Theory*, 3 vols. Cambridge: Cambridge University Press.

van Pirijs, P. (1981). *Evolutionary Explanation in the Social Sciences*. Totawa, NJ: Rowman & Littlefield.

Veblen, T. (1915). *Imperial Germany and the Industrial Revolution*. New York: Macmillan.

von Hintze, O. (1970). 'Machtpolitik und Regierungsverfassung', in G. Oestreich (ed.), *Staat und Verfassung*. Göttingen: Vandenhoeck & Ruprecht, pp. 424–56.

Walker, I. and Smith, H. (eds.) (2002). *Relative Deprivation: Specification, Development, and Integration*. New York: Cambridge University Press.

Walker, R. B. J. (1993). *Inside/Outside: International Relations as Political Theory*. Cambridge: Cambridge University Press.

Wallerstein, I. (1974). 'The Rise and Future Demise of the World Capitalist System: Concepts for Comparative Analysis', *Comparative Studies in Society & History*, 16(4): 387–415.

Waltz, K. (1954). *Man, the State, and War*. New York: Columbia University Press.

—— (1979). *Theory of International Politics*. Reading, MA: Addison-Wesley.

—— (1986). 'Reflections on *Theory of International Politics*: A Response to My Critics', in R. Keohane (ed.), *Neorealism and Its Critics*. New York: Columbia University Press, pp. 322–46.

Watkins, J. (1957). 'Historical Explanation in the Social Sciences', *British Journal for the Philosophy of Science*, 8(30): 104–17.

Weber, M. ([1930] 1958). *The Protestant Ethic and the Spirit of Capitalism*, trans. T. Parsons. New York: Scribner.

—— ([1922] 1958). 'Social Psychology of the World's Religions', in H. H. Gerth and C. Wright Mills (eds.), *From Max Weber: Essays in Sociology*. New York: Oxford University Press.

Weiner, B. (1992). *Human Motivation*. Newbury Park, CA: Sage.

Weingast, B. (1997). 'The Political Foundations of Democracy and the Rule of Law', *American Political Science Review*, 91(2): 245–63.

—— (2002). 'Rational-Choice Institutionalism', in Katznelson and Milner (eds.), pp. 660–92.

—— and Marshall, W. (1988). 'The Industrial Organization of Congress', *Journal of Political Economy*, 96(1): 132–63.

Wendt, A. (1987). 'The Agent-Structure Problem in International Relations Theory', *International Organization*, 41(3): 335–70.

—— (1998). 'On Constitution and Causation in International Relations', *Review of International Studies*, 24: 101–18.

—— (1999). *Social Theory of International Politics*. New York: Cambridge University Press.

—— (2004)."The State as Person in International Theory", *Review of International Studies*, 30, pp. 289–316.

White, H. (1992). *Identity and Control: A Structural Theory of Social Action*. Princeton, NJ: Princeton University Press.

Wight, C. (2004). 'State Agency: Social Action without Human Activity?' *Review of International Studies*, 30, pp. 269–280.

Wildavsky, A. (1987). 'Choosing Preferences by Constructing Institutions: A Cultural Theory of Preference Formation', *American Political Science Review*, 81(1): 3–21.

Williamson, O. (1975). *Markets and Hierarchies*. New York: Free Press.

Wilson, R. W. (1992). *Compliance Ideologies: Rethinking Political Culture*. New York: Cambridge University Press.

Winter, D. (1987). 'Leader Appeal, Leader Performance and the Motive Profiles of Leaders and Followers: A Study of American Presidents and Elections', *Journal of Personality and Social Psychology*, 52: 196–202.

—— (2003). 'Assessing Leaders' Personalities: A Historical Survey of Academic Research Studies', in Post (ed.), pp. 11–38.

Young, O. R. (1986). 'International Regimes: Toward a New Theory of Institutions', *World Politics*, 39: 104–22.

Zajonc, R. (1998). 'Emotion', in Gilbert, Fiske, and Lindzey (eds.), pp. 591–632.

Zaller, J. (1992). *The Nature and Origins of Mass Opinion*. New York: Cambridge University Press.

—— and Feldman, S. (1992). 'A Simple Theory of the Survey Response: Answering Questions versus Revealing Preferences', *American Journal of Political Science*, 36: 579–616.

Zysman, J. (1983). *Governments, Markets, and Growth: Financial Systems and the Politics of Industrial Change*. Ithaca, NY: Cornell University Press.

Index

Administrative state, 17–18, 86
Affective arguments, in ideational
explanation, 121–129; in psychological
explanation, 13, 40, 137–138, 148–160
Agency, 49, 53, 56, 78, 130
Agriculture, commercialization of, 16–17
Alford, John, 27, 135, 139–140, 159
Almond, Gabriel, 25, 117–121, 125
Althusser, Louis, 50
American politics, 17–18, 77, 86, 89, 106,
140, 153, 156–160
Anarchy, 26–27, 60
A-rationality, 64n. 6, 98–101, 104, 134, 152

Barber, James David, 153–154
Barnett, Michael, 127
Bates, Robert, 42, 54, 76, 80–83
Behavioralism, behavioral revolution,
37n. 8, 59; in psychology, 143–144
Bell, Daniel, 145
Benedict, Ruth, 153
Berger, Peter, 126, 132
Berk, Gerald, 127
Berman, Sheri, 128
Biernacki, Richard, 104, 119, 127, 129, 169
Boundaries of explanation, 21–36
Bourdieu, Pierre, 96, 126–127, 132
Bourgeois, 17, 66
Bracketing (of endogenous relationships),
43, 118
Brady, Henry, 22–23, 168, 170–171
Britain, 17–18, 60, 89, 118

Campbell, Angus, 144, 157–158
Campbell, John L., 127
Carter, Jimmy, 19, 142
Causal explanation, 7, 22–23, 28–36; and
institutionalism, 91–92; and culture or
ideas, 105–113; standing conditions
versus instigating conditions, 109n. 8
Causal segments, 14–16, 31–32, 37–38, 45
Civic behavior, 16, 99–100

The Civic Culture, 116–121
Civil War (US), 17, 86
Class, class actors, 17–18, 58–59, 86, 89–90
Cognitive arguments, in ideational
explanation, 121–129; in psychological
explanation, 13, 40, 148–160
Cognitive dissonance, 150
Collective action, 24, 58–61, 75, 77, 86
Collective intentions, 24
Collier, David, 22–23, 73, 168, 170–171
Combination of causal logics, 42–45, 89–91,
100–101, 128–129
Comparative politics, 8–9, 16, 42, 60, 128;
comparison in small-N studies, 168–169
Compatibility of causal logics see
combination
Competition between causal logics, 42–45,
164–171
Complexity theory, 33
Constitution (US), 17
Constitutiveness, 28–31, 43, 105–108
Contingency, 5, 13–14, 31–36; and
institutionalism, 71–74; empirical
demonstration of, 91–92; and Humean
explanation, 110–111
Conventions, 17, 66, 69–71, 75, 92,
100–101, 114
Converse, Philip, 144, 157–158
Correlation, 7, 22–23, 112, 168
Counterfactuals, 14, 161, 166
Critical junctures, 35, 74, 100
Culture, 9, 14, 18–19, 28–31, 94–132; and
structuralism, 41, 50; and institutions,
99–101; in sociological institutionalism,
74–76; in historical institutionalism,
87–91; political culture, 94, 117–121;
cultural psychology, 102, 139, 161

Darwinian evolutionary theory, 26
Democracy, 16, 58, 99, 117–118
Democratization, 16–17
Descartes, René, 97

Designing Social Inquiry, 7, 22, 106, 165, 170–171
Determinism, 35; and rational choice theory, 56; structural, 57; cultural, 97–98; psychological or genetic, 139, 159
Dewey, John, 44n. 11
Dialectics, 43, 58–59, 118
Dichotomies, 12–15, 36–38
Dictatorship, 16–17
Dimaggio, Paul, 69–70, 74–76, 122, 125–127, 168n. 2
Dobbin, Frank, 18–19, 90, 127
Douglas, Mary, 146
Downs, Anthony, 157
Durkheim, Émile, 75, 115, 124–125, 132, 136, 144–146, 153, 162

Eckstein, Harry, 117
Elkins, David, 113
Elster, Jon, 7, 22–23, 25, 56, 62–63, 82, 84
Emirbayer, Mustafa, 44
Endogenous relationships, 43
Environmental selection, 25–28
Equilibria, 53, 76–80; structure-induced equilibrium, 78–80, 82–83, 93
Ertman, Thomas, 60–61
Evans, Peter, 42, 119
Evolutionary argument, 25–28
Evolutionary psychology, 27, 139–140
Exogenous causes, 13–14, 16–17, 19, 31–36, 44n. 11, 51; and institutionalism, 68, 71–73, 76–85
Exploitation, 58–59, 141

Falsifiability, 167–169
Feldman, Stanley, 158–159
Ferejohn, John, 29
Feudalism, 17
Finnemore, Martha, 127
Fligstein, Neil, 67, 74, 127
Foreign policy, 26, 154–156
Foucault, Michel, 50, 97
Framing, 44n. 11, 141, 144, 150
France, 18; French Revolution, 31
Freud, Sigmund, Freudian psychoanalysis, 135, 152–154
Functionalism, 7, 25, 143, 145, 153
Funk, Carolyn, 27, 135, 139–140, 159

Game theory, 53, 55, 62–63, 76, 80, 84
Garbage-can model, 156n. 10
Garfinkel, Harold, 126, 132
Garrett, Geoffrey, 81
Geography, 12n. 3

George, Alexander, 144
Generalization, 5, 13–15, 31–36, 164–169
Genetics, 27, 139–140
Germany, 17, 118, 152
Goodin, Robert, 10–11
Goodwin, Brian, 26
Gross Stein, Janice, 154–155
Gurr, Ted, 141

Hall, Peter A., 67, 69, 85, 87–88, 128
Hard-wiredness, 12–14, 19, 27, 33, 45, 97, 103, 133–147
Hattam, Victoria, 89–90, 127
Hay, Colin, 11n. 2
Hermann, Margaret, 147, 154
Hermeneutics, 28
Hibbing, John, 27, 135, 139–140, 159
Hirschman, Albert, 16
Historical causes, 73
Hobbes, Thomas, 60–61
Holism, 8–10, 23–25
Hollis, Martin, 13, 28, 106, 111
Holsti, Ole, 144
Horowitz, Donald, 156
Hume, Humean view of explanation, 7, 22–23, 31, 105–113; and contingency, 110–111
Huntington, Samuel, 117–121

Ideas, definition of, 95–96
Ideational explanation, 12–14, 28–36, 94–132; and rationality, 98–101; and irrationality, 101–104; boundaries with structural or institutional explanation, 98–101; boundaries with psychological explanation, 101–104; variants of, 121–129; demonstration of ideational claims, 113–116, 129–130
Immergut, Ellen, 88, 91
Individualism, methodological, 7–8, 10–11, 23–25, 37n. 9, 41, 44n. 11, 53–56; in liberal theory, 58–59; in Marxism, 24n. 1, 58–60; in realism, 61; in institutionalism, 67, 69–70, 81, 87; in ideational explanation, 121–124; in psychological explanation, 150
Industrialization, 17–18, 86, 89–90
Inglehart, Ronald, 117–118, 145–146, 162
Instinctual arguments, 13, 40, 148–154
Institutions, definition of, 66–67, 69–70
Institutional explanation, 12–15, 17–18, 31–36, 66–93; and rationality, 70; demonstration of institutional claims, 91–92; historical institutionalism, 85–91;

Institutional explanation (*Cont.*)
rationalist institutionalism, 76–85;
sociological institutionalism, 41, 74–76,
88, 93, 100, 127; boundary with structural
explanation, 69–74; boundary with
ideational explanation, 98–101
International relations, 8–9, 60–61, 95n. 1
Interpretation, methodological difficulty of,
113–116, 129–130, 135
Interpretive logic, 18–19, 37, 115; and
explanation, 28–35, 105–108
Interests, 9–10, 16–17, 44
Irrationality, 13, 19, 40, 42, 98; and
ideational explanation, 101–104, 110,
126; and psychological explanation,
133–138
Isomorphism, 26–27, 127

Janos, Andrew, 57, 125, 142
Jervis, Robert, 155

Kahneman, Daniel, 140, 155
Katzenstein, Peter, 15, 42, 67, 87, 127
Keohane, Robert, 106, 165, 170–171
Khong, Yuen Foong, 144
Kinder, Donald, 156–158
King, Gary, 7, 22, 106, 165, 170–171
Krasner, Stephen, 69
Kratochwil, Friedrich, 128

Laitin, David, 8, 99, 119, 123
Lakatos, Imre, 164–165
Lamarckian evolutionary theory, 26
Lasswell, Harold, 152–154
Laws, 5, 10, 22, 106, 112
Leadership studies, 152–154
Legro, Jeffrey, 127
Lerner, Daniel, 145
Levels of analysis, 8, 12
Levi, Margaret, 53–54, 80–84
Liberalism, 57–58
Lichbach, Mark Irving, 9, 52–53
Little, Daniel, 7, 22, 24–25
Lodge, Milton, 158
Logic of Comparative Social Inquiry, 165
Luckmann, Thomas, 126

Mahoney, James, 14, 68, 92, 169
Man-made causes, 5, 13–15, 31–36, 164–167
Marx, Karl, 15, 50–51, 61, 82, 86; Marxism,
4, 50–51, 56–59, 66; and rationality, 55;
and individualism, 24n. 1, 58–60;
neo-Marxism, 8; and functionalism, 25;
and relative deprivation, 141

Materialism, 7–8, 12–14, 17–18, 39, 50–52
McDermott, Rose, 18, 137–138, 142
McNamara, Kathleen, 128
Mearsheimer, John, 54–55, 61–62
Mechanisms, 22–23; and methodological
individualism, 23–25
Mercer, Jon, 137–138, 156
Merton, Robert, 15
Methods, breakdowns by, 8, 12, 84, 88n. 8
Methodological individualism *see*
individualism
Meyer, John, 33, 67, 127
Micro-foundations, 13, 70, 128, 138
Middle-range theory, 15
Misperception, 40, 134, 155
Modernization theory, 58n. 4, 145
Modes of production, 12n. 3, 58–59, 114
Moore, Barrington, Jr., 16–17, 116–117
Motives (in psychology), 148

Neo-liberalism, 9
Neo-Marxism, 8
Neo-realism, 9, 25–27
Norms, 28–31, 41, 50, 88, 106–107; in
institutional explanation, 66–70,
99–101
Normative argument, 23
North, Douglass, 67, 69, 73, 77, 79,
82

Objectivity, objective rationality, 13, 29, 37;
and structural explanation, 51–54; and
institutional explanation, 67–71; and
ideational explanation, 98–101; and
psychological explanation, 137–138; *see
also* rationality
Onuf, Nicolas, 128
Operational codes, 144
Organizational sociology, 27, 168n. 2
Out-groups, 14, 136

Parsimony, 14–15
Parsons, Talcott, 125, 145
Particular explanation, 5, 13–15, 31–36; and
scientific progress, 164–169
Path dependence, 12, 39, 68–74; and
rationalist institutionalism, 76–85; and
historical institutionalism, 85–88
Pavlov, Ivan, 143
Personality studies, 152–155
Philosophy of science, 5, 164–169
Polanyi, Karl, 102–103
Political economy, 18, 50–60, 103–104
Popkin, Samuel, 54

Positional logic, 12–15, 19–20, 37–39, 44–45

Postmodern theory, 42; postmodern culture, 145–146

Poulantzas, Nicos, 49

Powell, Walter, 69–70, 74–76, 122, 125–127, 168n. 2

Practices, in ideational explanation, 96, 99–100, 126–127; and institutional explanation, 99–100

Prediction, 23

Preferences, 9–10

Problem-driven research, 15

Progress, standards for, 5, 164–169

Prospect theory, 19, 140–142

Prussia, 17

Przeworski, Adam, 61, 165

Psychobiography, 152

Psychological explanation, 12–15, 19, 40, 133–162; and rationality, 137–138, 143; boundary with ideational explanation, 101–104; variants of, 147–160; demonstration of psychological claims, 160–161; cultural psychology, 102, 139, 161; and evolutionary psychology, 27

Public opinion, 156–160

Putnam, Robert, 16, 99–100

Pye, Lucien, 117–120, 125

Rational choice, 42, 56

Rationalist institutionalism see institutionalism

Rationality, rationalism, 9, 29, 37; multiple rationalities, 13; empirical demonstrability of, 63–64; and rhetorical evidence, 63, 112; and structural explanation, 51–54; and institutional explanation, 67–71; and ideational explanation, 98–101; and psychological explanation, 137–138

Realism, 59–60

Reddy, William, 103–104

Regime theory, 69

Relational approaches, 44n. 11

Relative deprivation, 140–142

Renshon, Stanley, 153

Research design, 169–171

Revolution, 86, 141; French Revolution, 31; Chinese Cultural Revolution, 97

Rhetoric, and argument, 5

Riker, William, 77

Risk, 19

Rogowski, Ronald, 54–55, 61

Scott, James, 42

Sequencing of causal segments see combination

Shepsle, Kenneth, 11n. 2, 62, 77–78, 82

Skinner, B.F., 143

Skocpol, Theda, 42, 61, 85–90

Skowronek, Stephen, 17–18, 85–90

Sikkink, Kathryn, 128

Smith, Adam, 57, 61

Smith, Steve, 7, 28, 106–107, 111

Social construction, 28–31, 43, 105–108

Social identity theory (SIT), 155

Social kinds, 107, 111

Somers, Margaret, 94

Sovereignty, 28, 30, 106

State, as unitary actor, 61

Steinmo, Sven, 67, 85–90

Stinchcombe, Arthur, 15, 73

Stouffer, Samuel, 140

Strang, David, 127

Structural functionalism, 25

Structure, structuralism, definitions of, 50–56

Structural explanation, 9, 12–17, 49–65; and rationality, 51–54; demonstration of structural claims, 62–64; and rhetorical evidence, 63, 112; variants of, 56–62; boundary with institutionalist explanation, 69–74; boundary with ideational explanation, 98–101

Supervenience, 24n. 1

Substantialist approaches, 44n. 11

Sunk costs, 72n. 5, 79

Swidler, Ann, 96, 121–122, 127

Systems, system-level, 8–9, 24, 35, 128, 145

Tajfel, Henry, 155

Taken for grantedness, 121

Tautology, and ideational explanation, 104, 116–120

Teune, Henry, 165

Tilly, Charles, 10–11, 61

Time, 12, 74

Transaction costs, 77–79, 87, 100

Tsebelis, George, 54–55, 62–63, 80–83

Turner, John, 155

Tversky, Amos, 140, 155

Understanding see Verstehen

Unintended or unforeseen consequences and institutionalism, 73, 78–79;

Veblen, Thorstein, 141
Verba, Sidney, 106, 117–119, 165, 170–171
Verstehen, 28–31, 43, 105–108, 111–112
Von Hintze, Otto, 60

Wallerstein, Immanuel, 8
Waltz, Kenneth, 8, 26–27, 49, 112
Watson, John, 143
Weber, Max, 7, 28–29, 42, 45, 94, 105, 111–112; and *Protestant Ethic*, 16, 122, 125
Weingast, Barry, 62, 67, 80–82

Welfare state, 66, 73n. 6
Wendt, Alexander, 7–9, 24, 28–30, 36, 43, 106–108, 128
Wight, Colin, 24
Wildavsky, Aaron, 117, 146
Within-case inference, 21, 168–171
World systems theory, 33, 35, 67, 127

Young, Oran, 69

Zaller, John, 158
Zuckerman, Alan, 9, 52–53